STATISTICS FOR SOCIAL WORKERS

STATISTICS FOR SOCIAL WORKERS

Robert W. Weinbach
University of South Carolina

Richard M. Grinnell, Jr.
University of Calgary

Longman
New York & London

Senior Editor: David J. Estrin
Production Editor: Pamela Nelson
Cover Design: Stephan Zander
Text Art: J & R Art Services
Production Supervisor: Judith Stern
Compositor: Intergraphic Technology
Printer and Binder: Alpine Press Inc.

Statistics for Social Workers

Longman Inc., 95 Church Street, White Plains, N.Y. 10601

Associated companies: Longman Group Ltd., London; Longman Cheshire Pty., Melbourne; Longman Paul Pty., Auckland; Copp Clark Pitman, Toronto; Pitman Publishing Inc., New York

Library of Congress Cataloging-in-Publication Data

Weinbach, Robert W.
Statistics for social workers.

Bibliography: p.
Includes index.
1. Social sciences—Statistical methods. 2. Social service—Statistical methods. 3. Statistics.
I. Grinnell, Richard M. II. title.
HA29.W42 1987 519.5′024′362 86-2896
ISBN 0-582-29034-1

89 9 8 7 6 5

CONTENTS

PREFACE

The only topic that arouses more apprehension among social workers than research methods is statistics. The reason for this is easy to understand. Social workers often view statistics as an abstract topic with little to offer those who are not mathematically oriented. It is especially not for those who are "people-oriented." Some of us even believe that the field of statistics is unrelated to social work practice. We feel we will not need to know statistics; rather than work with numbers and formulas, we want to develop and refine the helping skills (usually therapeutic) that we will use with clients. Ironically, the use of statistics is very relevant to developing and refining those helping skills we feel we so desperately need. Statistical procedures are powerful tools that, when properly applied, allow us to answer some of the most important questions about practice.

Statistical procedures are based on rules for decision making that are applicable to effective social work practice. They are extensions and refinements of ideas that we already understand. Everyday expressions such as *on the average*, *it looks like rain*, and *fat chance*, are based on statistical concepts. For many of us, however, these same expressions take on an air of mystery when stated in statistical terms such as *expected value*, *probability*, and *confidence level*.

The study of statistics provides us with an understanding of the concepts underlying sound social work practice. It lends power and precision to professional social work decision making while at the same time giving us a better understanding of how knowledge for practice is generated and evaluated.

Statistical thinking is something all social workers engage in naturally when they organize and evaluate the large amount of client and agency data that they handle every day. By this, we don't mean that the use of statistics by social workers is a simple or casual affair. Nor, on the other hand, is the use of statistics an esoteric activity intended only for an enlightened few. Most applied statistics can be interpreted by anyone with a sound understanding of a few basic concepts including conceptualization, operationalization, independent and dependent variables, hypotheses, central tendency, variation, randomness, sampling distributions, probability, and a few others. A sound grasp of the basics is essential, in fact, if one wishes to go beyond statistics as covered in this book.

One stumbling block to the mastery of statistics for many social workers is that a majority of people who write statistics books are often most comfortable illustrating the elegance of mathematical proofs and describing the procedures they use in the special language of mathematical notation. We feel that this approach presents difficulties for those who do not have strong mathematical backgrounds and who are more comfortable expressing themselves in English. As a result, reader interest in a potentially useful research topic may be quickly lost or never acquired in the first place.

In this book, we have tried to explain statistics in words rather than symbols and through practical examples of basic research and statistical concepts. Social work practice problems and examples are interspersed throughout the entire book to facilitate understanding of the application of statistics. We demonstrate that statistics can be used to answer social work research questions and to resolve practical issues that arise in everyday practice situations.

The book begins by reviewing a number of methodological concepts central to the quality of data that can be accumulated. We focus on the ways to summarize and describe data and then move to fundamental concepts of statistical testing—probability, sampling distributions, and statistical inference. Finally, we illustrate the use of specific statistical tests that are commonly used to address social work research and practice problems.

After teaching statistics courses for several years, we have become acutely aware of a need for a book that emphasizes the fundamental statistical concepts, such as the testing of hypotheses and the role that chance plays in their acceptance or rejection. There is, we think, a danger in teaching practices that present a concept only once and then assume student mastery of it. We feel that the only way to understand statistical concepts is through repetition; our discussions with other statistics instructors confirm this impression. Readers will, therefore, observe a tendency in this book to explain a single idea in two or more different ways.

The fact that many of us learned statistical procedures by rote rather than by gaining a real conceptual understanding of them is well known to instructors who watch students actually attempting to apply statistics two or three semesters after they have completed the basic stat course. That is why we have chosen a different approach. Not wanting the readers to lose track of ideas in the tedium of numerical computations, we have relied upon data involving only comprehensible numbers. Some concepts are examined both verbally and graphically.

Formulas are kept to a minimum and always introduced with complete verbal translations. Our intent is to impart to the readers a clear understanding of various topics usually covered in a first statistics course without forcing them to grapple with elaborate mathematical symbols or notation.

This book is designed for people who are studying statistics for the first time. It would also be a valuable tool for those who have previously taken statistics but who may have never really understood what they studied. We endeavored to write a statistics book that is readable, relevant, and suitable for social workers—one that is "reader-friendly."

The primary emphasis of this book is on the proper *insight* into concepts; only after each new concept is thoroughly presented are illustrations in the use of the statistic discussed. Our hope is that readers will be able not only to make *use* of the basic statistical concepts but to *think* using the logic of statistics. Readers will learn the subject more thoroughly and pleasurably through this approach, we feel, than if they had merely gone the mathematical route.

This book is suitable for research methods and statistics courses of various lengths and different emphases. Instructors can tailor their own course to suit the backgrounds and needs of their students.

Enough statistics are included so that the book can serve as the primary text for a basic statistics course. The social worker of today often finds it difficult to read articles in the professional journals because of an increased emphasis on statistical terminology and application. This book is intended to increase the reader's understanding of what statistical methods are and how they should be used. It will help students become more critical consumers of research reports in the professional literature and use discretion in applying new knowledge to practice and research situations.

References have generally been omitted from the text of this book to avoid loading the reader with what may seem to be unnecessary detail. We have no intention of giving the impression that we have proceeded in a vacuum or that all the book's content is original. It has been written by integrating the efforts of many people, and the concepts expressed in this book have been gleaned from many sources. While a few of the main contributors of ideas have been specifically acknowledged by references within the text of the chapters, others are included in the list of advanced statistical and/or methodological texts that can be found in the "Further Reading" section at the end of each chapter.

This book will *not* provide the readers with all they will ever need to know about statistics. Only three of the statistics commonly used for hypothesis testing in social work research are presented in any detail (χ^2, r, t). They have been selected partly because the reader of social work literature encounters them frequently and needs to understand them to assess many of the research-oriented articles presented within social work journals. Moreover, these concepts illustrate both the commonalities and the variations of statistics; readers who can comprehend the basic ideas behind them will have gone a long way toward understanding *any* statistic.

Many people contributed to the completion of this book. Hundreds of students, through questions and challenges posed during class sessions over the past fifteen years, have served to shape the authors' thinking about statistics and its relationship to social work practice. A number of faculty colleagues have kindly shared their expertise in critiquing earlier drafts of the text. They are Floyd Bolitho, Joe Hornick, Larry Icard, Lynn McDonald, and Isabel Wolock. The painstaking task of manuscript preparation was greatly facilitated by the work of Jo Coleman, Kim Moore, Nan Neel, Joanne Paetsch, and Sheila Hoffman. Irving Rockwood provided many valuable insights through his careful review of the manuscript and through assuming the perspective of a student of statistics. Finally, we owe a special debt to our colleague Allen Rubin of the University of Texas at Austin. Allen, who is not known for avoiding the unpopular position, provided exactly what was needed: a candid, sometimes biting, but always knowledgeable and thorough review of the text. All of the above people may take partial credit for whatever achievements the book represents; we alone must share responsibility for its shortcomings.

Robert W. Weinbach
Richard M. Grinnell, Jr.

1

FOUNDATION CONCEPTS FOR UNDERSTANDING STATISTICS

Social workers need statistical knowledge. This need is precipitated, in part, by the increasingly research-related content of articles published in major social work journals and in the current tendency toward empirically oriented social work practice textbooks.

Professional social work literature frequently contains the results of quantitatively oriented research studies. Published articles often use statistics in such a way that statistical literacy is required by readers. A knowledge of statistics is crucial to many decisions—for example, whether a newly tested treatment method should, or could, be used by readers within their individual practice situations. Social workers are confronted with journal articles and books containing statistical arguments. This book will help us to understand and assess the merit of these arguments.

As responsible professionals, we must regularly evaluate our own effectiveness as social workers. In order to do this, we must rely on more than personal insight or intuition; our evaluations must be empirically based.

To become a part of our profession's knowledge base, we must communicate our findings to others. If we are to be credible, we must demonstrate that our data were generated according to specific rules. These rules are not hard to understand; they are based on logic and scientific methods that we regularly apply to social work situations. We apply them in a similar manner whether we collect and analyze data for practice or for a research study.

When social workers make practice decisions, they frequently rely on common sense and past experiences. However, we must remember "common sense" told us that welfare recipients prefer not to work, that women don't make good supervisors, and that punishment (not reward) makes students learn faster. Greater awareness through sound research methods *and* statistical procedures has led us to dismiss all three beliefs.

Understanding and using statistical procedures appropriately allows the social worker to move toward the objective of empirically based practice. The chapters that follow should provide invaluable insights into statistics for evaluating the reader's own practice or the published research findings of others. Before we study the statistical tests, it is useful to review a few basic concepts and to become familiar with the measurement process that is used in statistics to generate and analyze data. Statistical tests produce meaningful results *only* when sound principles of measurement are employed. Even the best statistical tests are useless if the data being examined are questionable.

DATA, VARIABLES, AND STATISTICS

Many of our activities as social work practitioners involve collecting and organizing information (data) about various aspects of our profession and about our clients. Researchers from all disciplines engage in some form of structured data gathering. The social work profession uses a wide variety of research methods to collect data, including questionnaire surveys, telephone surveys, content analyses, planned experiments, and direct observation of behavior in natural settings. In addition, we use data already observed and recorded for other purposes, such as police records, census materials, and agency and hospital records. The information gathered by these and other methods is collectively called *data*.

Data are the starting points for scientific conclusions; therefore we must be highly accurate when collecting information. No conclusion based on a research study's findings can be better than the data contributing to the conclusion.

There is always a limit to how much data can be realistically collected and used. In research studies, we limit our data to information about certain variables. A variable is more than just a characteristic or attribute. It is anything we can measure that can assume more than one form, state, or type; it must vary among cases in a population. Mortality, although it is a characteristic of human beings, does not meet this criterion. A variable must also be measurable. Without being too philosophical, we can say that all variables that social workers (in research *and* practice) deal with are potentially measurable. We can, for example, measure the variable "gender" by classifying our clients as male or female; we can measure the variable "age" by classifying them according to their age at their last birthday; and we can measure the variable "number of active clients" in a specific social work agency in a given month by obtaining a simple census count. The variations for a given variable are referred to as the variable's *values*. For example, "male" and "female" are values for the variable "gender."

Selecting specific variables to study and finding meaningful ways to identify their different values are important phases in the social work research process. If, for example, we want to learn something about the relative effectiveness of two different methods for treating depressed clients, we must provide operational definitions of both effectiveness and different treatment methods in terms of characteristics that can be objectively measured. One indicator of clients' level of depression might be the score each client obtains on a depression scale. All client scores viewed together may suggest a pattern. It might appear, for example, that clients who were treated individually score lower than clients treated in a group. But we would be premature if we concluded, on the basis of the apparent pattern of scores, that treatment effectiveness and treatment methods are related. Statistics can take some of the guesswork out of any conclusions we wish to make regarding the relationship between variables. The results of statistical testing help us make more informed statements about the variable "treatment effectiveness" and how it may or may not relate to other variables.

Whether or not the results of statistical testing ultimately suggest to us that individual treatment is more effective than group treatment will depend, in part, upon our personal values or opinions, as well as others' impressions of how well the depression scale really measures depression. Statistical tests only perform mathematical operations—nothing more, nothing less.

Much, if not most, of social work practice and research requires measuring variables that are not easily observed or quantified. Often we must measure variables that we cannot directly see. Various methods have been developed for use in these situations. One method is to record the verbal, written, and/or physical responses of clients to specific stimuli. For example, we may wish to find out the extent to which computerization in a particular social work agency has affected the level of job satisfaction of the social workers within the agency. We would probably need to measure job satisfaction both before *and* after computerization. One way to measure current job satisfaction of the workers is to ask them directly. Another way is to have the workers complete a job satisfaction scale. Or we might measure a physical response such as job absenteeism, which research indicates is directly related to job satisfaction. If at all possible, we would want to use all of these indicators to contribute to our overall measurement of the job satisfaction level of the social workers.

We may also wish to ask questions such as, "What difference does it make if some workers are less satisfied with their jobs now than before?" In this instance, we would be treating the variable, job satisfaction, somewhat differently. In the first example, our primary aim is to identify and measure a variable, current job satisfaction. In the second instance, our chief goal is to identify and understand a variable or variables that may result from the workers' job satisfaction. The following section will elaborate on why this distinction is important to our study of statistics.

Dependent and Independent Variables

In social work research, as in social work practice, we are often interested in seeking a relationship between two or more variables. Usually there is one variable, called the *dependent variable*, that we particularly wish to examine in our research study. We want to know as much as possible about why values of the dependent variable vary in order to be in a better position to affect their variation. Frequently the different values of the dependent variable may be related to the effects of some other factors. These factors are referred to as *independent variables*.

Job satisfaction among social workers may *depend*, among other things, on the kind of supervision they receive (satisfaction = *depend*ent variable). Variations in students' grades in a research course may *depend* on students' motivation, on the amount of time they study, and on their basic intellectual capacity (grades = *depend*ent variable). Whether or not a student obtains a fellowship from a university may *depend* on the student's academic record and the availability of fellowships, as well as on competition from other students (obtaining a fellowship = *depend*ent variable). In each of these examples, different values of the dependent variable are all logically dependent upon the other (independent) variables, or at least we would like to know if they are. In each example, it would be illogical, if not absurd, to believe that the direction of the relationship could be the reverse.

We as social workers are most interested in explaining differences in variables such as job satisfaction, grades, or success in obtaining a fellowship. Therefore, they will be dependent variables in our research study. Of course, researchers doing other studies, perhaps in other disciplines, might explore the reasons for the variations in kinds of supervision, student motivation, or methods employed to seek a fellowship. If so, such variables would become the dependent variables in those studies, and the researchers would use other factors as independent variables. Thus a given variable is referred to as dependent or independent based on logic and on the focus of investigation in a given research study. Identification of dependent and independent variables in a study is critical both to hypothesis formulation and to interpretation of the statistical testing results.

CONCEPTUALIZATION AND OPERATIONALIZATION

Before we begin a research study, a problem may appear extremely complex. It may seem to take many forms and to be related, or possibly related, to many other phenomena that, in themselves, may be difficult to understand. In social work practice and research we seek to make this tangle manageable by identifying what we feel to be the most important variables and stating the variations, or values, they may assume, by identifying possible interconnections between them, and by deciding how best to measure them.

Conceptualization

To begin our study of a problem, we should select the most potentially fruitful independent and dependent variables to examine—a process called conceptualization. Then we need to specify as precisely as possible what we have in mind when we refer to those variables. For example, the hypothesis "Among children age 3 to 10, Treatment A will be associated with less severe autistic behavior than will Treatment B" suggests a belief that different treatment techniques affect autistic behavior differently. In order to examine the relationship between type of treatment and the autistic behavior, we must clearly state the meaning of both variables and the proposed relationships. For instance, the conceptualization of exactly what constitutes Treatment A (behavioral therapy) might include the introduction of shaping techniques once a week, the application of positive reinforcement during school hours, or both. Autistic behavior may be conceptualized to include self-destructive behaviors during school hours, responses on an autistic scale completed by school personnel, social isolation, or all three. Without first delineating the *meaning* of independent and dependent variables, it would be virtually impossible to attempt to establish a relationship between them. This is why conceptualization is so important.

Operationalization

The process of selecting and specifying the devices that will be used to measure the dependent variables and independent variables that we have described under "Conceptualization" is referred to as *operationalization*. It further clarifies the meaning of our variables by reducing them to observable and measurable dimensions. Operationalization attaches quantitative meanings to the different values of the variables.

The specific methods used to measure variables may differ from place to place, time to time, person to person, or study to study. For example, in different research situations, indicants for the variable self-esteem might include observations of client behaviors, subjective diagnosis of clients by social workers, self-reports of clients, or responses on standardized scales.

The conceptualization and operationalization processes provide a necessary and orderly method for observing and standardizing the measurement of variables. Good measurement makes it possible for statistics to accurately summarize or describe research findings and to analyze the relationships that appear to exist between variables.

LEVELS OF MEASUREMENT

The four labels commonly applied to measurement levels reflect increasing precision: (1) nominal, (2) ordinal, (3) interval, and (4) ratio. One of the best explanations of the four levels of measurement has been published by Bostwick and Kyte (1985). We have relied heavily on their work in the discussion that follows.

Nominal Measurement

The least precise (crudest) level of measurement is referred to as nominal. The word *nominal* suggests the assignment of names to categories (values) that are discrete, or distinct, from each other. Nominal measurement is essentially a classification system that involves the categorization of variables into subclasses. Different values reflect only a difference in kind—nothing more. Because no implication of a quantifiable difference is made, no rank ordering of values is possible. Variables such as gender, race, and political party affiliation are usually regarded as nominal-level variables. Other examples are marital status, referral source, diagnosis, occupation, and type of treatment.

The requirements of nominal-level measurement are minimal. A nominally measured variable may have two or more categories, and the categories must be distinct, mutually exclusive, and exhaustive. The terms *distinct* and *mutually exclusive* mean that each case must appropriately fit into only one of the categories; *exhaustive* indicates that there must be an appropriate category for each case. For example, there are only two classes of the nominal-level variable life status—living or deceased. These categories are clearly exhaustive and mutually exclusive, as every person can be classified as fitting into one of the categories (exhaustiveness), but *only* one (exclusiveness)—assuming, of course, that some medical or other single definition is universally applied.

In nominal measurement, numerals (or other symbols, such as letters) may be assigned for convenience to distinguish one category from another. Suppose we have divided a variable, type of treatment, into three categories: individual treatment, group treatment, and family treatment. We could then assign the label Treatment 1 to individual treatment, the label Treatment 2 to group treatment, and the label Treatment 3 to family treatment. The numerals we have used are merely labels and serve only to classify. It would be meaningless in this case to say that 1 is more or less treatment than 2 or 3, or to make any other statement that implies that the categories have any quantitative connotation. In describing nominal-level data, all we can do is to make counts of the numbers of cases falling into each category.

Ordinal Measurement

Ordinal-level measurement not only separates the different categories of a variable but also makes it possible to rank-order them consistently from high to low or from most to least. That is, it places them in categories that have a greater-than, less-than relationship to one another. Examples of variables that can be viewed as ordinal-level are social class, occupational prestige, educational degrees received (bachelor's, master's, doctoral), ratings of change (considerable, some, little, none), agreement on problem definition (high, moderate, low), ratings of treatment effectiveness (very effective, somewhat effective, somewhat ineffective, very ineffective), ratings of clients' satisfaction with treatment (very satisfied, somewhat satisfied, somewhat dissatisfied, very dissatisfied), and rankings of problem severity (very severe, severe, mild, very mild).

Value labels used at the ordinal level of measurement make it possible to identify not only differences between variable subclasses but also their relative positions. With a nominal-level measurement, we can say only that one value is different from another. In ordinal measurement, we can say that one value is not only different from another but reflects a greater or lesser quantity of the variable.

It is important to note that ordinal-level value labels for data do not indicate absolute quantities and do not assume equal intervals between the ranks. We also would not know the exact range encompassed by all the ranks. For example, we might have a social position scale that purports to rank social class according to a set of categories ranging from Class I (upper) to Class V (lower). Since the classes do not necessarily represent equal intervals, we cannot say that Class I is exactly two class intervals higher than Class III or that this interval is exactly the same distance as the one that separates Class IV from Class II.

Thus, ordinal measurement goes a step beyond nominal measurement by adding a quantitative difference to categories and by making it possible to rank-order observations. The different values of an ordinal-level variable, however, do not indicate their absolute quantities or the exact distances from one another.

Interval Measurement

Interval measurement also classifies and rank-orders properties of variables; in addition, it places them on an equally spaced continuum. Unlike ordinal scales, interval-level scales have a uniform unit of measurement, such as one year, one degree of temperature, and so on. Therefore, value labels indicate exactly how far apart one value is from another. With an interval-level variable, we can say that an object has "more" or "less" of a given property than another object; we can also specify how many units more or less.

With equal distances between the units, a 1 will be the same distance from a 4 as a 6 is from a 9, and so on. On a test designed to measure intelligence, generally assumed to be quantified at the interval level, the difference between IQ scores of 100 and 105 *should* reflect the same difference in intelligence as between IQ scores of 115 and 120. Two individuals with achievement test scores of 50 and 60 *should* have the same difference in achievement as exists between two individuals with scores of 80 and 90. In addition to intelligence and achievement, variables often claimed to be measured on an interval-level scale include anomie, group morale, and certain social attitudes. Their claim to interval-level status is based, in part, on the fact that researchers have spent many years in developing instruments for their measurements. These instruments have undergone a long series of refinements designed to increase their precision.

Interval-level scales do not have an absolute zero (that is, we cannot identify a point at which no quantity of the variable exists). This means that we cannot say that a 2 is twice as much as a 1—only that it is one unit more. Since a reading of zero degrees on a Fahrenheit (F) thermometer does not represent the absence of heat, a temperature of 60 degrees is not twice as high as a temperature of 30 degrees. Zero degrees Centigrade (C) is nothing more than a point (the temperature at which water freezes) arbitrarily chosen to receive the value label zero. Fahrenheit and Centigrade thermometers can generate only interval-level data (unlike a Kelvin thermometer, which has an absolute zero point).

Interval measurement indicates how far apart the values of a variable are from one another. It does not indicate the absolute magnitude of a property possessed by any particular object or person. This is possible only with the most precise type of measurement, ratio-level.

Ratio Measurement

The existence of a fixed, absolute, and nonarbitrary zero point constitutes the only difference between interval-level and ratio-level measurement. Therefore, numbers on a ratio-level scale indicate the actual amounts of the property being measured. With such a scale we can say not only that one object has so many units more of a property than a second object but that the first object has so many times more or less of the variable. Examples of ratio scales are birth or divorce rates; number of children in a family; and number of behaviors observed during a particular time period.

The absolute zero point has empirical meaning. All arithmetic operations are possible—addition, subtraction, multiplication, and division. This permits the valid use and meaningful interpretation of ratios formed by two scores. For example, a country with a birth rate of 4.8 children per couple has twice as high a birth rate as a country with a rate of 2.4 children per couple. Similarly, a family with an income of $15,000 has twice as much income as a family with $7,500.

Most of the data used in social work practice and research do not generate ratio-level measurements. One way to test for the existence of a ratio-level measurement is to think about the possibility of negative values. If negative values can logically be assigned (for instance, a temperature of −25°F), then the measurement of the variable cannot be considered to be more than interval-level.

MEASUREMENT PRECISION AND STATISTICS

As discussed in more detail in Chapter 8, the level of data we have helps determine the statistical test to be used. Normally, we want to apply the statistical test specifically appropriate to the level or levels of measurement available, since we then can utilize the data to the fullest. However, sometimes statistical techniques appropriate for interval-level data, for instance, also require other assumptions about those variables and the way in which their values are distributed. If these assumptions cannot be met, statistical tests normally designed for use with ordinal-level or even nominal-level data can be employed.

It is not possible to move in the other direction in the measurement hierarchy, from the less precise to the more precise. If a variable is measured only at the nominal level, we cannot treat it at the ordinal level, since it lacks a natural ordering of the variable's categories. Thus, it is not correct to apply statistical tests designed for ordinal-level measurement to variables considered to be only nominal-level. Similarly, it is not appropriate to apply statistical tests intended for interval-level measurement to variables considered to be only nominal- or ordinal-level.

One should be aware that the various levels of measurement refer to the way in which we conceptualize and measure social phenomena and usually not to inherent characteristics of the phenomena themselves. Depending on how it is conceptualized and measured in a given research study, a single variable, such as place of residence, may be used to indicate the geographic place name of one's residence (nominal), the distance of that residence from a specific point on the globe (ratio), or the size of one's community (ordinal or interval).

Consider the variable number of treatment sessions a client attends in a given month. If we are interested in the number, or amount, of treatment attendance per se, then we could claim a ratio-level variable, since it can take on the values zero, 1, 2, 3, and so on. However, this same variable could be used as an indicator of the amount of therapeutic help a client needed. The concept of needing help and the frequency of treatment sessions attended are not exactly the same. Just because Jane attended four treatment sessions in a given month, whereas Tom attended only two, we cannot justifiably say that Jane needed twice as much help as Tom. The variable could not be considered ratio-level. It is not interval-level either, because the difference in amount of help two clients needed, as reflected in the difference between three and four visits, is not the same as that reflected in the difference between six and seven visits. It is probable, though, that a difference in number of treatment sessions reflects some quantity difference in the need for therapeutic help. Therefore the variable can be considered as ordinal-level.

DIFFERENT USES OF STATISTICS

The general field of statistics involves methods for (1) designing and carrying out research studies, (2) describing collected data, and (3) making decisions, predictions, or inferences about phenomena observed within the data. In this book we deal primarily with the latter two uses of statistics. This is not to imply that the first aspect of the research process is unimportant. Statistics are used, for example, to assist in the design, evaluation, and revision of data collection instruments.

As we have suggested before, if a study is poorly designed, if measurement is not performed well, or if the data are not properly collected and/or reported, then conclusions drawn from them may be worthless or misleading, no matter how good a statistical analysis is performed. In our study of statistics that follows, we will generally *assume* that these research tasks have been performed well and that all that is now needed is knowledgeable statistical analysis of the data.

Two general categories are used to describe the two data analysis functions of statistics: descriptive statistics and inferential statistics. *Descriptive statistics* are used to summarize the characteristics of a sample or, if all cases were studied, of a population. After data on the members of a particular sample or population are collected, the original measurements, or scores (called *raw data*), are organized and summarized using techniques such as those described in Chapters 2 through 6. Descriptive statistics enable us to derive summaries of information from raw data measurements that only tersely describe a sample or population. In fact, it is this type of measure, once removed from the raw data, that is often of great interest to us.

Descriptive statistics are based on measurements actually taken of the sample or population. Our concern does not extend beyond our particular research subjects that we have studied. Graphs, tables, and descriptive numbers, such as averages and percentages, are easier to comprehend and interpret than a long list of data reporting the results of measurements of each variable for every case. The main purpose of descriptive statistics is to reduce the whole collection of data to simple and more understandable terms without distorting or losing too much of the valuable information collected.

Inferential statistics are procedures for determining whether it is possible to make generalizations about characteristics of a population based on data we have collected from a sample. Inferential statistics are relevant when we have access to only a randomly drawn *sample* from a population and when we do not have in our possession *all* the raw scores that could theoretically exist in the total population.

To compare the two types of statistics, we can say that descriptive statistics provide information about a sample or population from data actually collected, while inferential statistics consist of procedures that tell us how much we may generalize to a population from cases actually studied and what kind of statements we may make. Only inferential statistics allow us to draw certain conclusions from a randomly selected sample about a larger population that we have not measured but that yielded the sample. Both types of statistics are valuable to the social work researcher. We will examine some commonly used examples of both in the chapters that follow.

SUMMARY

Application of sound measurement principles and insights are a prerequisite to meaningful statistical analysis of data. This chapter has reviewed certain key concepts that are vital to an understanding of measurement.

Statistical procedures are methods for making decisions in the face of uncertainty. They are also methods for summarizing, analyzing, and evaluating information. The chapters that follow are aimed at developing an understanding of the basic statistical concepts and methods and the ways they are used to organize, analyze, and interpret data. In fact, statistical methods are little more than the application of common sense reasoning to the analysis of data.

STUDY QUESTIONS

1. Discuss how good statistical analysis can be negated by the use of poor measurement procedures. Provide social work examples in your discussion.

2. Explain how a variable differs from a characteristic.
3. What term describes the variable whose variations we are most interested in explaining in a given research study?
4. Provide an example of a variable that might be the dependent variable in one research study but the independent variable in another.
5. What do we call the process of carefully delineating the meaning of a variable?
6. What do we call the process of selecting and specifying devices for measuring variables?
7. What additional criterion must be met for a variable to be considered ordinal-level that is not a requirement of a nominal-level measure?
8. What is present in ratio-level measurement that is not required for a variable to be considered interval-level?
9. Explain how a variable, "client presenting problem," can be regarded as nominal-level in one research study and as ratio-level in another research study.
10. What do inferential statistics tell researchers that descriptive statistics do not tell them?

FURTHER READING

Bostwick, G. J., & Kyte, N. S. (1985). Measurement. In R. M. Grinnell, Jr. (Ed.), *Social work research and evaluation* (2nd ed., pp. 149–160). Itasca, IL: F. E. Peacock.

Reid, W. J., & Smith, A. D. (1981). *Research in social work* (Ch. 2). New York: Columbia University Press.

Schuerman, J. R. (1983). *Research and evaluation in the human services* (Ch. 2). New York: Free Press.

PART I

ORGANIZING DATA INTO MEANINGFUL INFORMATION

2

TABULAR PRESENTATION OF DATA

After data have been collected, they must be organized and summarized. These procedures can be done in both numerical and tabular form. Before tabular presentations of some data can be made, the information must be arranged in such a way as to make it more meaningful. This chapter will describe the most useful ways of tabulating data.

ARRAYS

Frequently, the first step in this process is to construct an array. Suppose, for example, that a social work agency administrator wonders whether the agency is serving older persons in the community. (We have operationally defined older people as 50 years of age or older.) The administrator decides to record the ages of new clients who apply for services every Tuesday over a one-month period (the sample). Twenty clients apply for services on Tuesdays during October. The records of these clients are examined to obtain ages. The names and ages of all 20 clients are then listed (see Table 2.1). Since the data are not presented in any particular order, they are considered to be raw data. The data in Table 2.1 indicate that the first client was named Janice, who was 32 years old, the second client was Mary, 27 years old, and so on.

To make the raw data more meaningful, they would then be placed in an array. An array displays raw data in order from the high value to the low value or from the low value to the high value. Table 2.2 is an example of an array that uses the raw data from Table 2.1. It presents these data from the lowest value (21) to the highest value (69). Table 2.2 demonstrates that two of the 20

Table 2.1
Raw Data: Clients' Ages and Names

Client's Age	Client's Name	Client's Age	Client's Name
32	Janice	37	Lynne
27	Mary	49	Pat
26	Brad	31	Leslie
21	Chuck	27	Peter
37	Richard	37	Sue
31	Kathy	26	Karen
32	Bill	49	Becky
69	David	21	Tony
26	Herb	27	Robert
31	Don	31	John

clients were 21 (low) years old (Chuck and Tony) while only one was 69 (high) years of age (David). In short, Table 2.2 orders the raw data from Table 2.1 to make them more useful for further study. The data in Table 2.2 provide a beginning answer to the research question about clients served; only one client (David) meets our definition of "older."

Table 2.2
Array: Clients' Ages and Names (from Table 2.1)

Client's Age	Client's Name
21	Chuck
21	Tony
26	Brad
26	Herb
26	Karen
27	Mary
27	Peter
27	Robert
31	Kathy
31	Don
31	Leslie
31	John
32	Janice
32	Bill
37	Richard
37	Lynne
37	Sue
49	Pat
49	Becky
69	David

FREQUENCY DISTRIBUTIONS

Frequency distribution tables, such as Tables 2.3 to 2.7, further organize data to make them more meaningful. There are five basic forms of frequency distributions: absolute frequency distributions, cumulative frequency distributions, percentage distributions, cumulative percentage distributions, and frequency and percentage distributions. We will describe each one in turn.

Absolute Frequency Distributions

To construct an absolute frequency distribution, we simply count the number of times each value for a particular variable occurs. Tallying the frequencies of each value provides a group picture of the data. It allows us to identify the range of values that occurred, a typical observation, and the variation among frequencies of the values. An absolute frequency distribution permits us to see at a glance how certain values of a variable are distributed. An absolute frequency distribution may be constructed for data at any level of measurement.

The left side of Table 2.3 indicates that the clients' ages range from 21 (Chuck and Tony) to 69 (David) and that the age most frequently reported is 31 (Kathy, Don, Leslie, and John). The absolute frequency column on the right side of the table indicates the number of times each value occurred. For instance, Chuck and Tony were 21 years old, and as a group they constitute a frequency of 2—that is, the absolute frequency for the value 21 is 2. Similar data are given for each age group through 69.

Table 2.3
Absolute Frequency Distribution Table:
Clients' Ages and Names (from Table 2.2)

Client's Age	Client's Name	Absolute Frequency
21	Chuck + Tony	2
26	Brad + Herb + Karen	3
27	Mary + Peter + Robert	3
31	Kathy + Don + Leslie + John	4
32	Janice + Bill	2
37	Richard + Lynne + Sue	3
49	Pat + Becky	2
69	David	1
	Total number of clients	20

Cumulative Frequency Distributions

If our data are of at least ordinal level (that is, if an array can be made), we can convert the absolute frequency table (Table 2.3) into a cumulative frequency distribution table. A cumulative frequency distribution table, such as Table 2.4, is in fact an extension of an absolute frequency distribution table. Table 2.4 differs from Table 2.3 only in that the far right-hand column represents the cumulative frequencies of the clients' ages from low (21) to high (69). As Table 2.4 shows, two clients were 21 years old and three clients were 26. Thus, the cumulative frequency of the clients' ages 26 and under is five (2 + 3). Another example is that 17 clients (2 + 3 + 3 + 4 + 2 + 3) are 37 years old and under.

Percentage Distributions

Table 2.5 presents a percentage distribution table that utilizes the data from Table 2.4. Its form is identical to that of an absolute frequency distribution table, such as Table 2.3; the only difference between the two types is that a percentage distribution table displays percentages rather than frequencies.

Since 20 clients were selected to be studied, each client represents 5 percent of our sample (100/20 = 5). As Table 2.5 indicates, two people (Chuck and Tony) were 21 years old, and, *together*, they represent 10 percent of the total number of clients (5 percent for Chuck + 5 percent for Tony). Similarly, Brad, Herb, and Karen *together* represent 15 percent of the total sample (5 percent for Brad + 5 percent for Herb + 5 percent for Karen). The total, then, is 100 percent.

Table 2.4
Cumulative Frequency Distribution Table:
Clients' Ages and Names (from Table 2.3)

Client's Age	Client's Name	Absolute Frequency	Cumulative Frequency
21	Chuck + Tony	2	2
26	Brad + Herb + Karen	3	5
27	Mary + Peter + Robert	3	8
31	Kathy + Don + Leslie + John	4	12
32	Janice + Bill	2	14
37	Richard + Lynne + Sue	3	17
49	Pat + Becky	2	19
69	David	1	20

Table 2.5
Percentage Distribution Table:
Clients' Ages and Names (from Table 2.4)

Client's Age	Client's Name	Percent
21	Chuck + Tony	10
26	Brad + Herb + Karen	15
27	Mary + Peter + Robert	15
31	Kathy + Don + Leslie + John	20
32	Janice + Bill	10
37	Richard + Lynne + Sue	15
49	Pat + Becky	10
69	David	5
Total		100

Cumulative Percentage Distributions

A cumulative percentage distribution table, such as Table 2.6, is constructed exactly like a cumulative frequency distribution table. However, a cumulative frequency distribution table (Table 2.4) presents frequencies of individual values, whereas a cumulative percentage distribution table gives percentages. As shown in Table 2.6, for instance, two clients (Janice and Bill) were 32 years old, and, together, they represent 10 percent of all clients (5 percent for Janice + 5 percent for Bill). Additionally, 70 percent of all clients were 32 years of age or younger.

Frequency and Percentage Distributions

A frequency and percentage distribution table, such as Table 2.7, is a combination of two tables: a cumulative frequency distribution table (Table 2.4) and a cumulative percentage distribution table (Table 2.6).

GROUPED FREQUENCY DISTRIBUTIONS

It may sometimes be difficult to interpret frequency distribution tables because of the unequal range between the ordered values of many variables. In our example, the variable age is distributed in such a way that there are confusing "gaps" (21 to 26; 27 to 31; 32 to 37; 37 to 49; and 49 to 69). Conclusions would be more obvious if these data were categorized (for instance, 20–29; 30–39, and so on) and summarized in a grouped frequency distribution,

Table 2.6
Cumulative Percentage Distribution Table:
Clients' Ages and Names (from Table 2.5)

Client's Age	Client's Name	Absolute Percent	Cumulative Percent
21	Chuck + Tony	10	10
26	Brad + Herb + Karen	15	25
27	Mary + Peter + Robert	15	40
31	Kathy + Don + Leslie + John	20	60
32	Janice + Bill	10	70
37	Richard + Lynne + Sue	15	85
49	Pat + Becky	10	95
69	David	5	100

as in Tables 2.8 to 2.12. Grouping the values displays variations among the data more easily.

Grouped frequency distributions are also useful when there are too many possible values for a variable to list each of them in the form of a table or an array. This is often the case with variables that are at the interval or ratio levels. Annual incomes of all students in social work graduate schools, for example, would comprise a lengthy list, especially if income was measured for each student in dollars and cents. Transforming the observations into *meaningful* categories makes it easier for us to visualize and summarize the data. For example, the students' income might be grouped into four ranges: under $6,000; $6,001–9,000; $9,001–12,000; and $12,001 or more.

Table 2.7
Frequency and Percentage Distribution Table:
Clients' Ages (from Tables 2.4 and 2.6)

	Frequencies		Percentages	
Clients' Ages	Absolute Frequency	Cumulative Frequency	Absolute Percentage	Cumulative Percentage
21	2	2	10	10
26	3	5	15	25
27	3	8	15	40
31	4	12	20	60
32	2	14	10	70
37	3	17	15	85
49	2	19	10	95
69	1	20	5	100

As in frequency distributions, there are also five basic forms of grouped frequency distributions: grouped absolute frequency distributions, grouped cumulative frequency distributions, grouped percentage distributions, grouped cumulative percentage distributions, and grouped frequency and percentage distributions. Again, we will take a look at each type.

Grouped Absolute Frequency Distributions

For most interval-level variables that have a large number of values, the categories are grouped into intervals (for instance, 20–29, 30–39) rather than single, discrete values (such as 32) of the variable. These intervals are usually of equal width, and they must be exhaustive—that is, set up to include all possible values of the variable in question. In addition, they must be mutually exclusive; any possible value must fit into one and *only* one interval.

Table 2.8 is an example of a grouped frequency distribution table that utilizes the data from Table 2.2. As can be seen, eight clients were between 20 and 29 years of age, while nine clients were between 30 and 39 years of age. The rest of the table provides information on the other age groups.

The width of the intervals in all grouped frequency distributions, such as *10* in Table 2.8, depends both on our judgment as to what makes sense and on the number of observations to be classified. Usually, the larger the number of observations, the greater the number of intervals that can be used. If too many intervals are used (say, more than 15), they are so narrow that the information presented is difficult to digest, and an overall pattern in the results may be obscured. On the other hand, if very few intervals are used, too much information may be lost through the

Table 2.8
Grouped Absolute Frequency Distribution Table:
Clients' Ages (from Table 2.2)

Client's Age	Absolute Frequency
20–29	8
30–39	9
40–49	2
50–59	0
60–69	1
Total number of clients	20

pooling together of dissimilar observations. Intervals should not be so wide that two measurements included in it have a difference between them that is considered important. For example, if a difference of $2,000 in annual family income is not considered important but a difference of $3,000 is important, we might choose the following intervals: under $2,000; $2,001 to 4,000; $4,001 to 6,000; and so forth.

Grouped Cumulative Frequency Distributions

Grouped frequency distributions can easily be converted into grouped cumulative frequency distributions, as in Table 2.9. The process is exactly the same as converting an absolute frequency distribution table (Table 2.3) into a cumulative frequency distribution table (Table 2.4). Table 2.9 is a grouped cumulative frequency distribution table that utilizes the data from Table 2.8.

Grouped Percentage Distributions

Grouped percentage distribution tables present the frequency of each value of the variable along with the percentage of the total represented by the cases in that category. Thus, as Table 2.10 indicates, eight clients were in the age range from 20 to 29; these eight clients represent 40 percent of the total sample. Grouped percentage distributions clarify the presentation of data by indicating the proportion of the total number of cases that were observed for a particular range of values. As will be discussed shortly, such a presentation is particularly useful when we are comparing the values for a variable for two or more groups of unequal size.

Table 2.10, which presents a grouped percentage distribution

Table 2.9
Grouped Cumulative Frequency Distribution Table:
Clients' Ages (from Table 2.8)

Client's Age	Absolute Frequency	Cumulative Frequency
20–29	8	8
30–39	9	17
40–49	2	19
50–59	0	19
60–69	1	20
Total number of clients	20	

Table 2.10
Grouped Percentage Distribution Table: Clients' Ages (from Table 2.9)

Client's Age	Absolute Frequency	Relative Percent
20–29	8	40
30–39	9	45
40–49	2	10
50–59	0	0
60–69	1	5
Total		100

utilizing the data from Table 2.9, shows how helpful such a table can be. As we noted, Table 2.10 depicts the proportion or percentage of clients within each age category. It indicates that 45 percent, or 9, of the clients ranged between 30 and 39 years of age. Additionally, 85 percent (40 percent + 45 percent) reported ages between 20 and 39. The data presented in this table indicate that the original concern of the agency is substantiated. That is, the majority (95 percent) of clients who request service are 49 years old or younger. This conclusion is much more precise and convincing than a statement that "more" of the clients ranged between the ages of 20 and 39 than between 40 and 69.

Grouped Cumulative Percentage Distributions

We can further summarize data by converting a grouped percentage distribution table into a grouped cumulative percentage distribution table, such as Table 2.11. A grouped cumulative percentage distribution table is constructed exactly like a grouped cumulative frequency distribution table, such as Table 2.9, except

Table 2.11
Grouped Cumulative Percentage Distribution Table:
Clients' Ages (from Table 2.10)

Client's Age	Absolute Percentage	Cumulative Percentage
20–29	40	40
30–39	45	85
40–49	10	95
50–59	0	95
60–69	5	100

Table 2.12
Grouped Frequency and Percentage Distribution Table:
Clients' Ages (from Tables 2.9 and 2.11)

	Frequencies		Percentages	
Client's Ages	Absolute Frequency	Cumulative Frequency	Absolute Percentage	Cumulative Percentage
20–29	8	8	40	40
30–39	9	17	45	85
40–49	2	19	10	95
50–59	0	19	0	95
60–69	1	20	5	100

that percentages rather than frequencies are given. As can easily be seen in Table 2.11, for instance, 85 percent of the clients were 39 years old or younger.

Grouped Frequency and Percentage Distributions

A grouped frequency and percentage distribution table is constructed exactly like a cumulative frequency and cumulative percentage distribution table, only the values are grouped. Table 2.12 is a combination of Tables 2.9 and 2.11.

USING CUMULATIVE FREQUENCY AND PERCENTAGE DISTRIBUTIONS FOR COMPARISONS

Cumulative frequency distributions are useful when we are interested in the cumulative standing for a particular value. Suppose, for example, that the administrators of a large social service organization want to study the problem of unauthorized staff absenteeism. They would like to identify seasonal patterns that may exist and that could possibly be reduced through new policies on vacations and annual leave. A cumulative frequency distribution table, such as Table 2.13, or a cumulative percentage distribution table, such as Table 2.14, might be used.

These two tables indicate that in April, absenteeism occurred 30 times (Table 2.13), or only 15 percent (Table 2.14) of the total amount of absenteeism for the four-month period. The cumulative amount of absenteeism was 200 days (Table 2.13). Only 35 percent (Table 2.14) occurred during the late spring, while the other 65 percent (100 − 35) occurred during the summer months of

Table 2.13
Cumulative Frequency Distribution Table:
Staff Days Lost by Month at XYZ Agency

Monthly Totals	Absolute Frequency	Cumulative Frequency
April	30	30
May	40	70
June	60	130
July	70	200

June and July. Thus, from the two tables the agency administrators were able to pinpoint a seasonal pattern of absenteeism.

USING GROUPED CUMULATIVE FREQUENCY DISTRIBUTIONS FOR COMPARISONS

Grouped cumulative frequency distributions are especially useful if we want to compare measurements of one or more variables between two groups or data subsets. They could be used, for example, to get a beginning assessment of the possible success of a state merit examination study guide. (Later we will discuss how statistical testing can provide us with more definitive answers about the study guide's effectiveness.) We might look at the respective scores of persons who used the study guide (experimental group) and persons who did not use it (control group). Cumulative distribution tables displaying the differences between outcome measures for the two groups are shown in Tables 2.15 and 2.16. For example, in Table 2.15, 120 persons in the experimental group scored between 70 and 79 on the examination, and 150 persons scored 79 or less.

Table 2.14
Cumulative Percentage Distribution Table:
Staff Days Lost by Month at XYZ Agency (from Table 2.13)

Monthly Totals	Absolute Percentage	Cumulative Percentage
April	15	15
May	20	35
June	30	65
July	35	100

Table 2.15
Grouped Cumulative Frequency and Percentage Distribution Table: Experimental Group's Scores on the XYZ State Merit Examination (N = 300)

	Frequencies		Percentages	
Scores	Absolute Frequency	Cumulative Frequency	Absolute Percentage	Cumulative Percentage
50–59	0	0	0	0
60–69	30	30	10	10
70–79	120	150	40	50
80–89	90	240	30	80
90–100	60	300	20	100

We can summarize from Table 2.16 that 20 percent of the social workers (40) in the control group scored 69 or lower on the examination. Table 2.15 indicates that 10 percent of the social workers (30) who used the study guide scored accordingly. Notice that the two groups are comprised of unequal size (N), 300 for the experimental group and 200 for the control group. Using percentages facilitates drawing comparisons between two or more groups that have unequal N sizes.

From a research perspective, the two groups of 200 and 300 research subjects were reasonably comparable in size. Percentage comparisons drawn from them would make the data easier to interpret. But a word of caution is in order about drawing percentage comparisons between groups of vastly unequal sizes. Such a practice can actually distort rather than clarify the data for the reader. The practice example below will explain how this could happen.

Table 2.16
Grouped Cumulative Frequency and Percentage Distribution Table: Control Group's Scores on the XYZ State Merit Examination (N = 200)

	Frequencies		Percentages	
Scores	Absolute Frequency	Cumulative Frequency	Absolute Percentage	Cumulative Percentage
50–59	10	10	5	5
60–69	30	40	15	20
70–79	80	120	40	60
80–89	70	190	35	95
90–100	10	200	5	100

Suppose one social worker has a caseload of ten clients, while another has a caseload of 100 clients. The one with ten clients terminates two cases during one month; the other one terminates six cases. The first social worker reports a 20 percent (2/10 = 20 percent) termination rate, while the other reports only a 6 percent (6/100 = 6 percent) termination rate. The percentage figures alone (20 percent versus 6 percent) suggest that a meaningful difference exists between the termination rates for the two social workers (20 is more than 3 times 6). Yet is the difference really all that meaningful?

To avoid giving a false impression, the actual numbers on which percentages are based should always be reported along with percentages if the number of cases in both groups is large but the groups are not of equal size. Generally, percentages are meaningless, if not totally misleading, in reporting data from small samples. It might be best not even to report them, since small numbers are quite comprehensible by themselves.

Getting back to our state examination example, we can note that cumulative percentages also make it possible to calculate at least approximate percentile ranks for individuals. Percentile ranks are indicators of the percentage of the cases within a group whose values fall above or below a particular value. In using the data in Table 2.15, suppose that a particular individual in the experimental group scored a 90 on the examination after using the study guide. A review of Table 2.15 would indicate that the person scored higher than at least 80 percent of all persons in the experimental group—that is, the test taker scored at approximately the 80th percentile. Percentile ranks enable us to put an individual score in perspective relative to the other scores in a group. In Chapter 6 we will explain a more precise method to figure the percentile for a given value within a group of values.

SUMMARY

In this chapter, we have suggested several basic methods in which large quantities of data can be organized in order to reveal patterns that may exist and to facilitate statistical analysis for hypothesis testing. The tabular presentation of data and the compiling of frequency distributions are often prerequisites to more sophisticated analysis. In fact, if we use a computer, we will generally observe that different forms of frequency distributions are a part of the printout from statistical analysis, a useful byproduct. Researchers must, however, be able to interpret the tables discussed in this chapter and to select the most useful type of tables for communicating findings to the reader.

STUDY QUESTIONS

1. How does an array differ from raw data?
2. What factors determine the width of intervals that are used in grouped frequency distributions?
3. What additional information is conveyed in a cumulative frequency distribution that is not present in an absolute frequency distribution?
4. What type of frequency distribution would quickly tell us what percentage of 369 students is 25 years old or younger?
5. What type of frequency distribution would tell us how many AFDC clients in a county agency have fewer than four children?
6. What is wrong with grouped age frequency distributions that use the age categories 20–30, 30–40, 40–50, 50–60, 60–70, and over 70?
7. In a study attempting to relate type of counseling to employment, why would it be inadvisable to group the variable "number of interviews" as 1–10, 11–20, and over 20?
8. Why are grouped cumulative percentage distributions superior to grouped percentage distributions for drawing comparisons between two subsamples of a population?
9. What does a score that falls at the 73rd percentile say about the score relative to other scores in the group?
10. Why is it misleading to report a 50 percent success rate in a treatment program for alcoholics when there were 20 people in the research sample?

FURTHER READING

Craft, J. L. (1985). *Statistics and data analysis for social workers* (Chs. 2 and 3). Itasca, IL: F. E. Peacock.

Grinnell, R. M., Jr. (Ed.). (1981). *Social work research and evaluation* (Ch. 21). Itasca, IL: F. E. Peacock.

MacEachron, A. E. (1982). *Basic statistics in the human services: An applied approach* (Chs. 5, 6, 9, and 10). Baltimore: University Park Press.

Reid, W. J., & Smith, A. D. (1981). *Research in social work* (Ch. 10). New York: Columbia University Press.

Schuerman, J. R. (1983). *Research and evaluation in the human services* (Ch. 3). New York: Free Press.

3

GRAPHIC PRESENTATION OF DATA

It is sometimes difficult to grasp the overall meaning of a table, but a picture can communicate it almost immediately. When graphic presentations of data are effectively performed, data are seen, rather than studied; they are grasped as a totality, rather than as fragments, as can happen even when statistical tables are examined carefully. For this reason, graphic presentations are especially useful for displaying the findings of a quantitative research study that involves a statistical argument. It is also true, however, that pictorial representations can easily be modified to produce misleading statements. But this caution should only alert, not discourage, us in contemplating their use. The fact that graphic data displays (and all other forms of data presentation) *can* be slanted does not mean that they *have* to be.

Another drawback of graphic representations is that they generally sacrifice detail and, sometimes, accuracy in an effort to improve communication. The sacrifice is justifiable if, and only if (1) the point at issue is important; (2) the point is one that can be effectively captured in pictures; (3) the audience is not research-oriented and would be unlikely to understand a table as well as a pictorial representation; or (4) if it is essential to get the point across quickly, because it is anticipated that the audience may become impatient or uninterested.

As discussed earlier, one of the first steps we take in data analysis is to describe the data we have collected. To accomplish this, we have several procedures at our disposal. Graphs, charts, diagrams, and figures can provide our readers with a visualization of the data we have gathered. They enable us to present, in an easy-to-grasp format, the variables that we have conceptualized and operationalized.

Graphic presentations of data involving more than one variable (and most graphs that reflect the frequencies for values of a single variable) are based on two perpendicular lines, as illustrated in Figure 3.1. The vertical line is known as the *y*-axis, and the horizontal line is known as the *x*-axis. In graphs showing a relationship between two variables that can be identified as either dependent or independent, the *y*-axis is used to represent the values for the dependent variable, and the *x*-axis is used to represent the values for the independent variable. The values for each variable (dependent and independent) are marked off in a uniform grid along their corresponding axes.
The point where *x*- and *y*-axes meet is the "point of origin." Starting with the point of origin, the values of the dependent and independent variables are placed along their respective axes in a hierarchical continuum at equal intervals. The values for the dependent and independent variables for a particular graph may or may not be of identical intervals. The values for the dependent variable may be marked off at five-space intervals, for example, while the values for the independent variable may be marked off at ten-space intervals.

If a graph is used to present a description of the values observed for only one variable, the *y*-axis is used to indicate frequencies for each value. The graph may extend to the left of the *y*-axis if there are negative case values.

While there are many types of graphs, we will discuss only six commonly used in social work research: bar graphs, line diagrams, histograms, pie charts, frequency polygons, and scattergrams. The first three will be discussed together, because they are used in a similar manner.

BAR GRAPHS, LINE DIAGRAMS, AND HISTOGRAMS

A basic method for organizing nominal-level data and representing them in pictorial form is the bar graph. Bars of equal width are drawn so that they do not touch (see Figure 3.2), to suggest the qualitative (not quantitative) differences in values of nominal-level data.

If lines rather than the thicker bars are used, and they are drawn so that their length reflects the frequencies with which given values occur, we refer to the graph as a line diagram. Line diagrams are frequently constructed so that the lines run parallel to the *x*-axis with different nominal level values placed along the *y*-axis (see Figure 3.2). The choice of whether to use a bar graph or a line diagram is pretty much up to the aesthetic preference of the researcher.

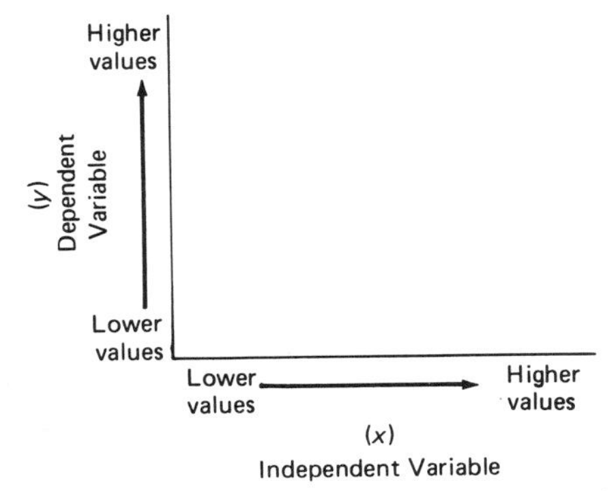

Figure 3.1 Basic Outline of a Graph for Depicting Scores from Two Variables

Sometimes ordinal data are displayed effectively in a similar way using a graph called a histogram. A histogram looks much like a bar graph except the bars are allowed to touch. Histograms are used when presenting data for a variable whose values can be rank-ordered and reflect differences in quantity. The ordering of categories is determined by the quantity of the variable reflected in the variable label—that is, the rank order of categories. The bars are also of equal width (see Figure 3.3). Figure 3.3 is an example of a histogram, derived from Table 3.1, for displaying an ordinal-level variable—discharge status of all patients discharged during February.

A histogram, like a bar graph, associates the frequency of a value for a given variable with the height of a bar. The graph is inherently comparative; if a bar of one length represents one frequency, a bar twice as long on the same graph represents twice that frequency.

A histogram may also be used to display interval- or ratio-level data. While the bars are usually of equal width reflecting equal

Table 3.1
Frequency Distribution Table: Client Discharge Status at XYZ Agency

Outcome	Frequency
Worse than at Admission	15
Unchanged	30
Improved	10
Greatly Improved	35
Total	90

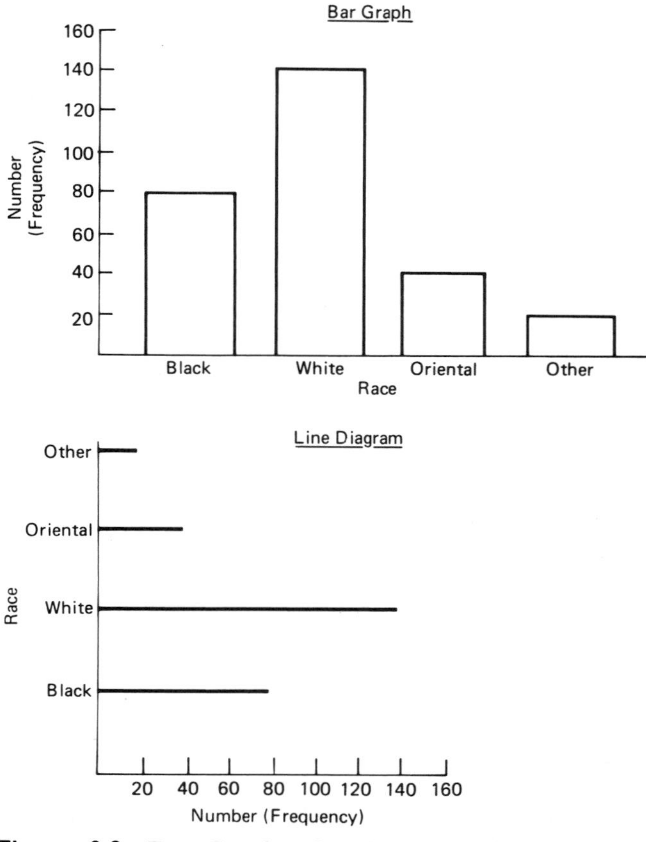

Figure 3.2 Two Similar Graphs: Bar Graph and Line Diagram Portraying Race of Active Clients in XYZ Agency.

category intervals (for instance, 20–29, 30–39, 40–49, and so on), they may be constructed so that their different widths correspond to the size of different intervals used for grouped data. Figure 3.4 reflects this variation on the usual form of the histogram. Bars of different widths are designed to communicate more accurately what the data looked like. They use the measurement precision available for interval- or ratio-level data, but not present in ordinal-level data.

Bar graphs and histograms can become an exercise in creativity. Unfortunately, as they become more creative, they can also become more difficult to interpret. The horizontal bars in bar graphs may be extended to the left or to the right, or in both directions simultaneously, but the graph quickly becomes more difficult to understand when more data are included, as the bar

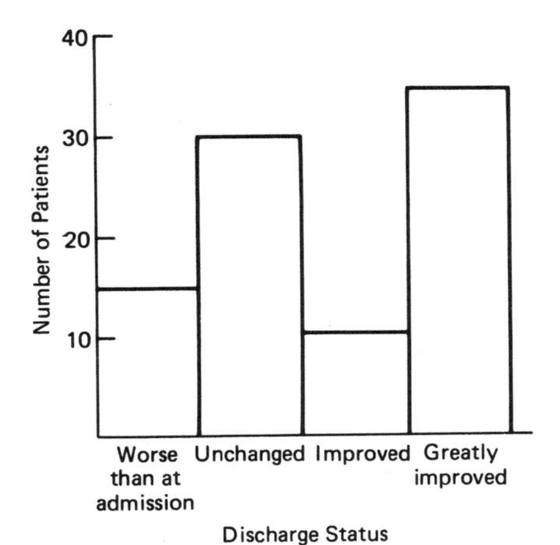

Figure 3.3 Histogram: Frequency of Discharge Status at XYZ Agency During February (from Table 3.1)

graph of Figure 3.5 shows. Figure 3.5 actually displays data relative to three variables. It illustrates the percent (relative frequency) of clients who experience three specific problems (environmental, psychological, and social) identified by social workers at XYZ agency. The graph portrays the realities of a situation in which (1) a given client may have more than one type of problem, and (2) not all clients have all three types of problems. The x-axis represents the percentage of each problem area occurring (right side) and not occurring (left side) for clients. Each problem area must equal 100 percent, since the problem either has, or has not, occurred for every client. Thus the right side of the figure plus the left side must total 100 percent for each row. Figure 3.5 indicates

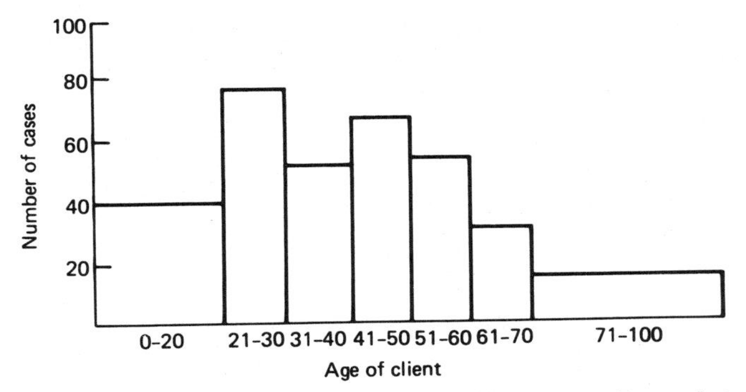

Figure 3.4 Histogram: Ages of Clients on Record in XYZ Agency During October.

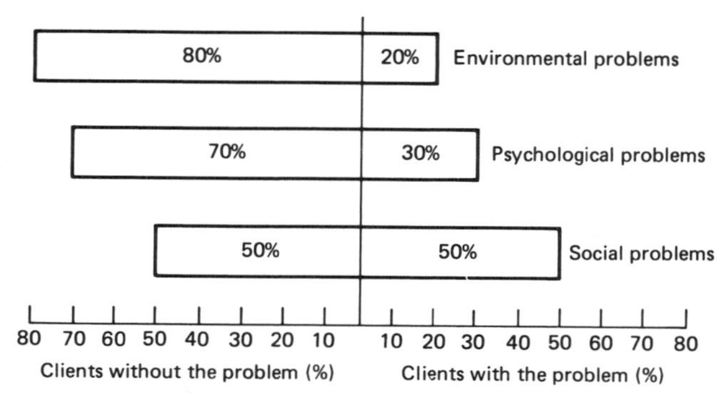

Figure 3.5 Bar Graph: Types of Client Problems at XYZ Agency

that 20 percent of the clients had environmental problems and 50 percent had social problems. We can also see that 70 percent did not have psychological problems, and 50 percent did not have social problems.

As we are tempted to use more intricate and creative bar graphs and histograms, we must always ask ourselves, will the graph really help the reader to understand our data? Or will it have the undesirable effect of confusing the reader of a research report?

PIE CHARTS

At times, when the various values of a single variable add up to a whole, such as that displayed in Figure 3.6, the categories can best be pictured as segments of the whole. If we were showing how a client's family budget was divided into sums for food, shelter, clothing, and recreation, we could display the budget as a whole—as a circle, or even as a bag of money—with food, clothing, and other budget items as a part of this whole. Pie charts are usually circle graphs divided into wedges representing fractions of the total circle. Because pie charts can portray the distribution of only one variable, they do not use the *x*- and *y*-axes. Figure 3.6 is an example of a pie chart showing the percentage of time taken by different methods of treatment in XYZ agency in October. Note that the segments of the circle are proportional to the percent of total time devoted to a given type of treatment (50 percent of the circle, 180 degrees, is set aside for individual treatment, which occupied 50 perce t of all treatment time for the month).

Figure 3.7 is an example of a pie chart from which we can easily ascertain various percentages of students enrolled in the different schools at XYZ University. According to Figure 3.7, 25.7 percent

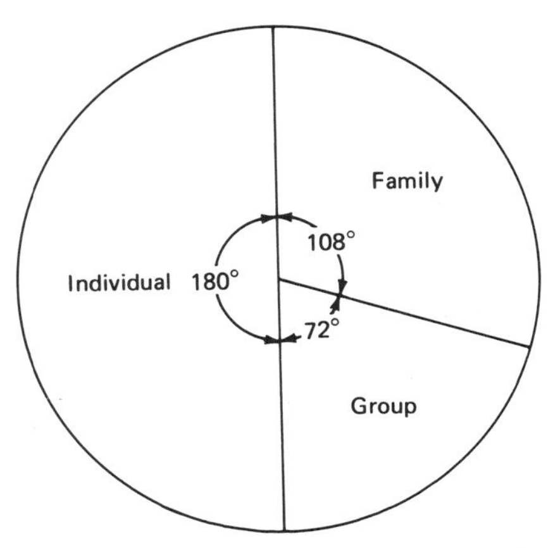

Figure 3.6 Simple Pie Chart: Percent of Treatment Time at XYZ Agency Used for Different Types of Treatment During October

of the students at XYZ University were enrolled in the School of Humanities, while 3.0 percent were enrolled in the School of Agriculture.

Pie charts also have assumptions identical to those for bar graphs. Any data that can be nominally categorized (into discrete, mutually exclusive categories) can be displayed in pie charts. Their chief advantage is that they provide a rapid visual appraisal of data that can make a discussion of findings more meaningful. Their disadvantage is that they cannot easily accommodate many

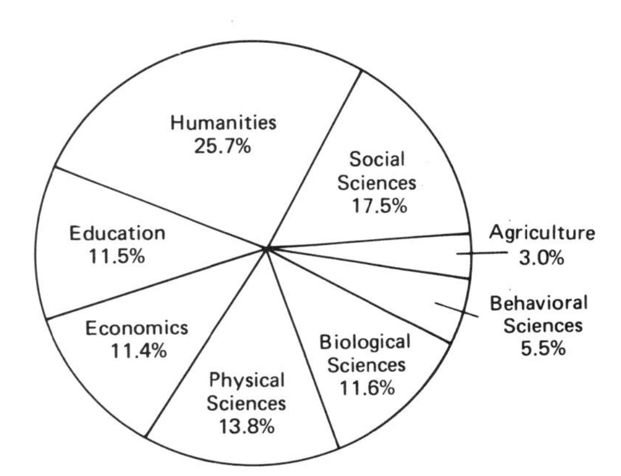

Figure 3.7 Complex Pie Chart: Percentage of Students Enrolled in Various Schools at XYZ University

different values for a variable; they often become too complicated or even illegible if more than five or six divisions of the circle or similar figure are necessary. A quick glance at Figures 3.6 and 3.7 will make this point clearer.

FREQUENCY POLYGONS

Frequency polygons are similar to histograms and are designed to portray the shape of a distribution of scores or values. If we were to take a pencil and place a dot at the top and in the middle of each vertical bar in a histogram and then connect the dots with straight lines, we would have a frequency polygon. Figure 3.8 is a frequency polygon displaying data that might have been collected at intake and stored in an agency computer-assisted data base.

Before we draw the shape of the graph, we would follow the steps for constructing a histogram. Midpoints of each interval are used, and straight lines are drawn to connect the dots. Lines that close the graph are drawn at each end of the distribution of values along the horizontal axis. These lines are attached to the midpoints of the intervals immediately preceding and following the distribution of values. In Figure 3.8, lines are drawn to the midpoints of the spaces that would represent values 0 and 30 even though there are no frequencies recorded for them. These lines simply close the graph.

The data of Figure 3.8 are at the interval level, but we have, in rounding them off, treated them as ordinal. It is possible to plot a frequency polygon for ordinal data, but it must be remembered

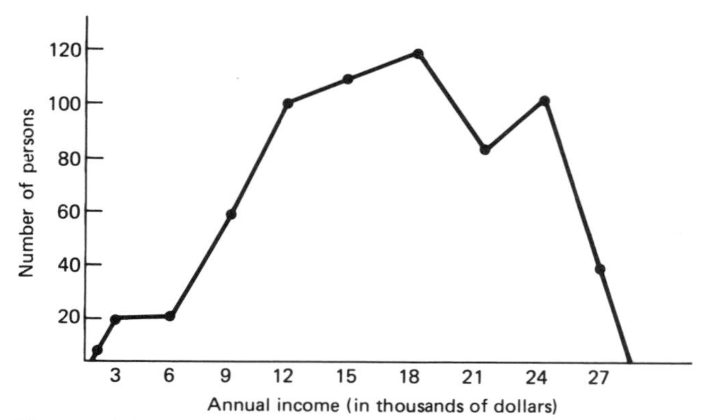

Figure 3.8 Frequency Polygon: Annual Income of Families Receiving Family Counseling at XYZ Agency (Rounded to Nearest Category)

that the distances between ordinal measurements are indeterminate. Figure 3.8 is not really a very accurate portrayal of the data. To show the problem this introduces, consider how we should picture the ordinal-level data in Table 3.1.

If it is assumed that all four client discharge statuses are about the same distance from one another, then Figure 3.9 would result. In other words, if we conceptualized and then operationalized that the client discharge status "unchanged" is the same distance from "improved" as "improved" is from "greatly improved," then we would produce a graph something like Figure 3.9.

If it is assumed, based on practice experience, that the client discharge status of "greatly improved" is twice as far from "improved" as "improved" is from "unchanged," then Figure 3.10 would result. In situations where it is virtually impossible to make such a determination, it might be preferable to use a bar graph, which does not suggest interval relationships, to represent these data. As we have suggested before, graphing should display data as accurately as possible. We want to communicate all that we can about our findings. But we also want to avoid suggesting more (in this case, higher measurement precision) than what actually occurred.

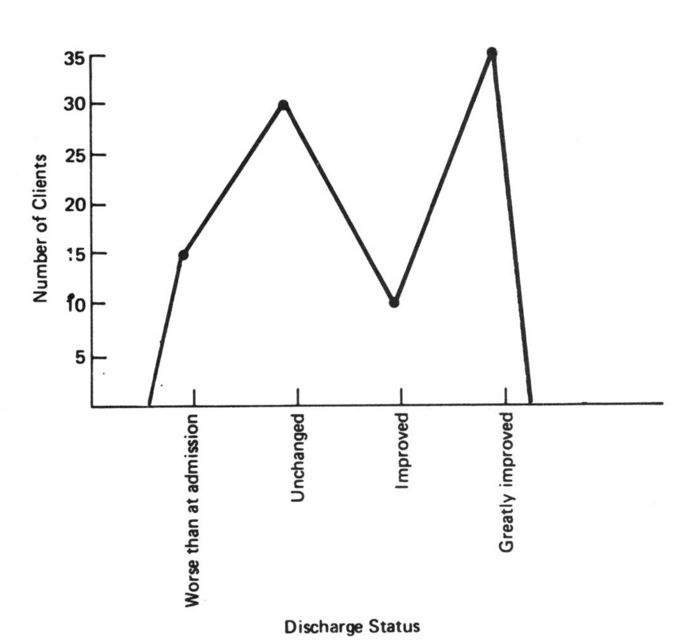

Figure 3.9 Frequency Polygon: Client Discharge Status at XYZ Agency (from Table 3.1)

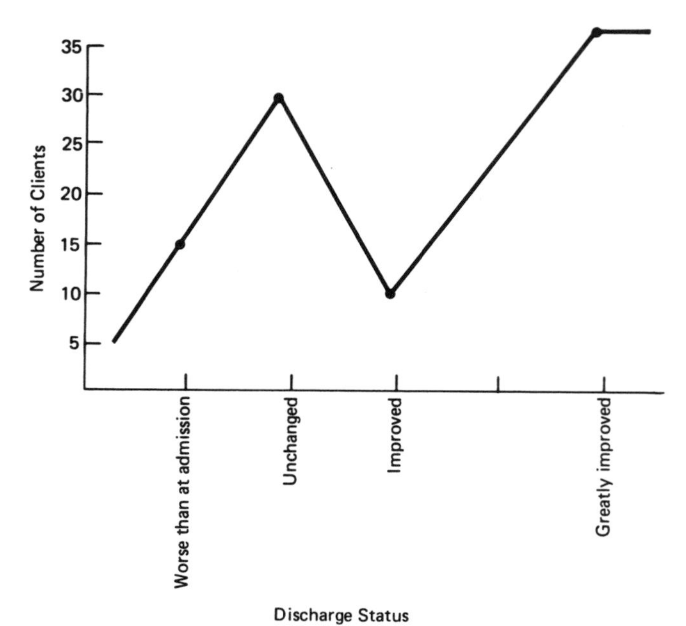

Figure 3.10 Frequency Polygon: Client Discharge Status at XYZ Agency (from Table 3.1)

SCATTERGRAMS

Scattergrams differ from the previous five graphic presentations in that they reflect individual frequency scores rather than grouped data. The scores or observations for two variables for various individuals are graphed. This type of graphic presentation is often used to suggest a possible association between two interval- or ratio-level variables or to underline graphically the existence of a relationship that has been demonstrated through the use of higher-powered statistical analyses.

For example, we may be interested in examining the relationship between self-concept and the number of treatment sessions our clients attend. We might hypothesize that among clients who began counseling with low self-concepts (a score of 20 or below on a test given at intake), there would be a direct association between current self-concept scores and number of treatment sessions—that is, persons seen more often would have higher self-concepts than those seen fewer times. We can measure self-concept by one of the many available scales designed for this purpose. The number of treatment sessions attended and the scores each client achieves on the self-concept scale could then be displayed, as in Figure 3.11. Each dot represents, for an individ-

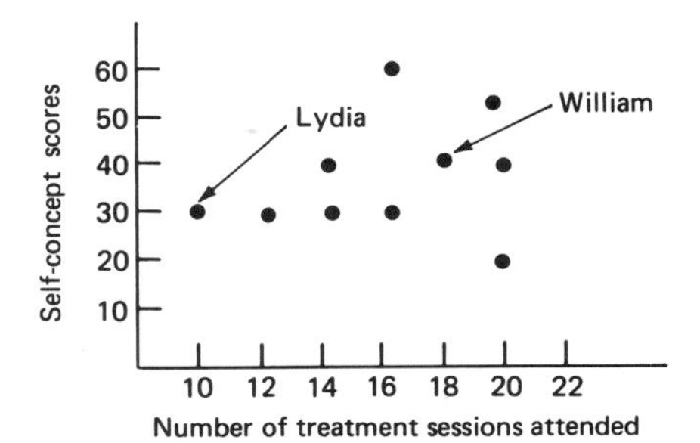

Figure 3.11 Scattergram: Self-Concept Scores and Number of Treatment Sessions Attended.

ual client, the union of his or her score on the test (y) and the number of treatment sessions attended (x). Notice that Lydia, who attended 10 treatment sessions, scored 30 on the self-concept scale, but William, who attended 18 sessions, scored 40.

The scattergram has two special features. Sometimes, as in our example, the respective variables may be shown on either coordinate axis, since neither may be clearly indicated as the independent variable. (Did self-concept affect number of treatment interviews, or vice versa?) We are looking only at the association between values of the two variables. Moreover, lines are not used to connect the plotted points. A scattergram simply shows all the data collected on the two variables. In Figure 3.11, we can easily see that there were ten clients (dots on the graph) who were in treatment.

Frequently, the points representing cases on a scattergram appear to be distributed in a way that suggests a pattern (a straight line, a "U" shape, a "J" shape, and so on). This can be important to understanding and drawing conclusions from research data. We will be returning to scattergrams and the patterns that emerge within them in Chapter 10.

SUMMARY

In this chapter we have discussed various methods for displaying data to summarize general patterns in the distribution of values of a variable and, in some cases, to illustrate a possible relationship between variables. Graphs may sometimes take the place of tables in presenting research findings. In other instances, they are used along with frequency distributions or tables to provide further clarification.

In selecting a graph for inclusion in a report, researchers

should keep in mind the limitations and specialized uses for the different graphs we have discussed. Sometimes more than one type of graph might be appropriate. Clarity and honesty of presentation for maximum communication should be the guiding principles for choosing the graph to be used.

STUDY QUESTIONS

1. What types of situations are best suited to graphic presentations of data?
2. In graphs that portray the values of two variables, where should values of the dependent variable be plotted?
3. How does a bar graph differ from a histogram?
4. What level of data is most appropriately displayed on a bar graph?
5. If an agency with a $360,000 annual budget allocates $90,000 for travel expenses, what portion of a pie chart would be reserved for the travel segment?
6. Why are frequency polygons an accurate portrayal of data only if data are of interval or ratio level?
7. Of the graphs discussed, which has the potential to suggest a possible relationship between two variables?
8. Why must both variables be of interval or ratio level for a scattergram to be an accurate reflection of the data?
9. What kind of graph(s) might be used to suggest the presence of sex discrimination in salaries within a social agency?
10. How might we display changes in the ethnic composition of an agency's professional staff between 1976 and 1986?

FURTHER READING

Grinnell, R. M., Jr. (Ed.). (1981). *Social work research and evaluation* (Ch. 21). Itasca, IL: F. E. Peacock.

MacEachron, A. E. (1982). *Basic statistics in the human services: An applied approach* (Chs. 5, 6, 9, and 10). Baltimore: University Park Press.

Reid, W. J., & Smith, A. D. (1981). *Research in social work* (Ch. 10). New York: Columbia University Press.

4

MEASURES OF CENTRAL TENDENCY

As presented in Chapters 2 and 3, tabular and graphic presentations of data can tell us what our research findings look like. There will be times, however, when we want to go beyond graphically displaying the data—when we want to direct the reader's attention to some specific characteristic of them. In particular, we may be summarizing the data or reporting on what is a "typical" attribute of them.

The word *typical* is a common part of our vocabulary. We speak of the "typical client" or the "typical starting salary for MSW social workers," often without being very specific as to exactly what the term means. The use of *typical* represents an attempt to find a single number or characteristic to describe what is representative of a whole group of numbers or values.

In statistics there are several different ways to summarize a "typical" value for a variable. Therefore, the use of precise terminology is essential. Every term must be used and labeled correctly to avoid ambiguity and confusion. We group the different descriptions of typical responses found in data under the term *central tendency*. Each measure of central tendency conveys only a limited amount of information about a group of values, and each tells us something quite different about the data. To understand differences among the various measures of central tendency, we must consider the computational basis of each. Interpretation requires knowledge of how the value of the statistic is determined.

Measures of central tendency are more widely used than any other statistical measures, largely because they are easily computed and are very useful. They have two basic uses.

1. They provide a summary of data. They represent an attempt to find one value, or number, that tells more about the characteristics of the distribution of the variable than any other. For example, an agency that hires several hundred social workers a

year may have an average monthly starting salary of $1,500. This one number helps summarize the agency's policy toward beginning social workers as far as pay is concerned.

2. They provide a common denominator for comparing two groups of data. If two figures are obtained—of the average monthly number of clients receiving family services (Department A) and of the average monthly number of clients receiving financial assistance (Department B)—a quick and easy comparison of the two departments can be made.

In this chapter we will examine the most frequently used measures of central tendency—the mode, the median, and the mean.

THE MODE

The mode is a measure of central tendency that tells us which value in the distribution of values is observed most frequently. For data in ungrouped form, we refer to the mode as the value, or score, that occurs most often. In the ten values presented in the array below, 7 is the mode because it occurs more frequently than any of the other numbers; the number 7 occurs three times.

$$2 \quad 4 \quad 5 \quad 6 \quad \underbrace{7 \quad 7 \quad 7}_{\text{mode}} \quad 8 \quad 8 \quad 9$$

For grouped data, we refer to the mode as the midpoint of the interval containing the greatest frequency. In Table 4.1, we have portrayed the grouped job-satisfaction scores of 50 social workers. For these grouped data, the interval containing the greatest relative frequency is 48–50, inclusive of the scores 48, 49, and 50. Since the midpoint of this interval is 49, then 49 is said to be the mode for the distribution.

Sometimes in ungrouped data, more than one value will occur most frequently. If two or more values occur most frequently, as when each occurs five times, each of these values is given as the mode for the data. When two values occur most frequently, the distribution is said to be *bimodal*. The eight values presented in the array below contain two modes.

$$4 \quad \underbrace{5 \quad 5}_{\text{mode 1}} \quad \underbrace{6 \quad 6}_{\text{mode 2}} \quad 7 \quad 8 \quad 9$$

The values 5 and 6 are given as the modes; 5 and 6 occur the most frequently—two times each.

If the same thing occurs for grouped data, the midpoints of the

Table 4.1
Grouped Cumulative Frequency Distribution: Job-Satisfaction Scores for Social Workers at XYZ Agency

Scores	Absolute Frequency	Cumulative Frequency (High–Low)	Cumulative Frequency (Low–High)
81–83	3	3	50
78–80	1	4	47
75–77	5	9	46
72–74	6	15	41
69–71	1	16	35
66–68	5	21	34
63–65	4	25	29
60–62	1	26	25
57–59	1	27	24
54–56	4	31	23
51–53	3	34	19
48–50	7	41	16
45–47	1	42	9
42–44	4	46	8
39–41	2	48	4
36–38	2	50	2

intervals containing the largest number of cases are both given as the modes for the data. The data in Table 4.2 are bimodal. The modes are the midpoints of the intervals that contain the largest frequencies. In this case, the modes are 55 and 52, midpoints for the respective intervals of 54–56 and 51–53, which contain eight cases each.

Assumptions of the Mode

Of the three measures of central tendency discussed in this chapter, the mode is the most unrestricted—that is, it has the fewest assumptions. It is appropriate for data of the nominal level or higher.

Advantages and Disadvantages of the Mode

The mode gives us an idea of the most "popular" value in a distribution of scores by identifying the value occurring most frequently. But the mode is not used as often as the other measures of central tendency, because it lacks the precision that the

Table 4.2
Grouped Cumulative Frequency Distribution: Job-Satisfaction Scores for Clerical Staff at XYZ Agency

Scores	Absolute Frequency	Cumulative Frequency (High–Low)	Cumulative Frequency (Low–High)
57–59	4	4	31
54–56	8	12	27
51–53	8	20	19
48–50	7	27	11
45–47	4	31	4

other measures possess. The most common or frequent value of a distribution of scores is not necessarily the most accurate description of a typical value. For example, Table 4.3 presents a frequency distribution in which the mode is clearly not in the center of the distribution, but rather toward the end of it (57–59 group). For ordinal-, interval-, or ratio-level data, we can usually obtain more accurate and representative descriptions by using other measures of central tendency.

THE MEDIAN

The median is the measure of central tendency that divides any distribution of values into two equal parts or proportions. In the 11 values presented in the array below, the median is 15 because

Table 4.3
Grouped Cumulative Frequency Distribution: Job-Satisfaction Scores for Social Workers at XYZ Agency

Scores	Absolute Frequency	Cumulative Frequency (High–Low)	Cumulative Frequency (Low–High)
57–59	10	10	33
54–56	6	16	23
51–53	7	23	17
48–50	3	26	10
45–47	2	28	7
42–44	1	29	5
39–41	4	33	4

15 coincides with the point that divides the values into two equal parts. There are just as many values, or cases, above 15 as there are below 15; five above (16, 17, 18, 19, and 20) and five below (14, 13, 12, 11, and 10).

10 11 12 13 14 15 16 17 18 19 20
↑
median

A preliminary step in determining the median for any distribution of values is to arrange them in an array like the one presented in Table 2.2 in Chapter 2. If an even number of values occurs, the median is defined as the midpoint along a line drawn alongside the array or, generally, the average of the two most central values. In the six values in the array below, 14.5 is the median. It is the average of the two central values (14 and 15).

12 13 14 15 16 17
↑
median

It should be noted that in this array the median (14.5) does not coincide with the value of any case. This phenomenon underlines the fact that—contrary to a common misconception—the median is *not* simply the value of the middle case. While it sometimes does coincide with the value of the middle case, as in our earlier example, it is likely to be a fraction of a whole value. This happens because the true median (midpoint of an array) is influenced by such factors as even numbers of cases, case values near the center of the array with a frequency of more than one, values with a frequency of zero, and so on. The median usually must be calculated using a formula especially designed for this purpose.

Assumptions of the Median

Because the median divides a distribution of values into two equal parts that are different in a quantifiable way, a ranking of values is required. For this reason, data at least equivalent to the ordinal level of measurement are needed for using the median.

Advantages and Disadvantages of the Median

Of the three measures of central tendency discussed in this chapter, the median is the most stable—meaning, in part, that it is least affected by extreme values occurring in a distribution. The following two sets of thirteen values contain identical medians, but notice the values at the extremes.

Distribution A

1 14 15 16 17 18 19 20 21 22 23 24 **50**

↑ median (19)

Distribution B

13 14 15 16 17 18 19 20 21 22 23 24 25

↑ median (19)

In Distribution A, the extreme values, 1 and 50, are quite different from the other values. In Distribution B, the extreme values, 13 and 25, are much closer to the other values. The fact that both distributions have the same median of 19 demonstrates that the extreme values can occur at either end of a distribution but have little or no effect upon the median. This quality of stability makes the median a highly useful measure of central tendency.

By comparison, the mode can fluctuate more widely than the median. The mode defines only the most popular value in a distribution of values; it does not necessarily appear in the center of the distribution.

The major disadvantage of the median is that it is more difficult to compute than either the mode or the next measure we will discuss, the mean. Duplicate values and other factors frequently require the use of a rather complicated formula. Fortunately, since most data analysis is now computer-assisted, this characteristic creates fewer problems than it once did.

THE MEAN

More sophisticated measures of central tendency than the mode and the median are possible when data are at the interval or ratio level. As explained in Chapter 1, the interval scale has an arbitrary zero, and the ratio scale has a true zero. If a variable can be justified as either interval- or ratio-level, the use of the mean as a measure of central tendency should be considered.

Because it is easily understood, the best known, and the most useful, the mean is often employed as a measure of central tendency. The arithmetic mean, the type most commonly used, is nothing more than the sum of all the values of a variable divided by the number of values. The mean is closest to what we refer to in everyday speech as the *average*. We can express this as a formula.

$$\text{Mean} = \frac{\text{Sum of all values in a distribution}}{\text{Total number of values in the distribution}}$$

For data in ungrouped form, such as the following five values, we can obtain the mean by summing the values and dividing the total by the number of values.

4 4 5 7 10

We do not have to place these values in an array, as we did to compute the median. For these data we can carry out the following operations.

$$\text{Mean} = \frac{4 + 4 + 5 + 7 + 10}{5}$$

$$= \frac{30}{5}$$

$$= 6 \text{ (Mean)}$$

Assumptions of the Mean

The primary assumption for using the mean is that the data must be of at least the interval level. Means computed for nominal- or ordinal-level data are "meaningless." For instance, it is not always appropriate to compute the means for ranks. A student may rank third in one class, fourth in another, and second in yet another. The sum of the ranks is 3 + 4 + 2, or 9, and the "average" rank is 3 (9/3 = 3). Interval-level data assume that there is an equal distance between each interval or rank. When that is the case, the computation of a mean is valid. But when the ranking scale is not an interval-level measurement, the average or mean should not be performed.

A second assumption for use of the mean relates to sample size. Because extremely large or extremely small values can easily distort the mean, it is best used with relatively large samples in which aberrant scores will cause less distortion. It also requires a distribution that is basically symmetrical or "normal." We will explore the concept of normal distributions in detail in Chapter 6.

Advantages and Disadvantages of the Mean

The mean is frequently used. Most of us are familiar with it. But primarily because of its popularity, we should be especially aware of its overuse and misuse. The mean also employs more precision than does either the mode or the median. It uses the precise value of *every* score in its computation (not just some of the scores in an array or their frequency). This characteristic can promote accuracy or distortion, depending on how similar the scores are.

One major disadvantage of the mean is that it can be used only for data of the interval or ratio level of measurement. This limitation rules out the possibility of using the mean for data of the nominal or ordinal level. This disadvantage is a restrictive one, particularly in social work research. There are many instances in our research studies when means simply cannot be used. For example, many instruments for measuring attitudes generate a numerical attitude score for each case, yet they are not sufficiently precise to justify treating the data as interval- or ratio-level. Because of the popularity of the mean, some of us have erroneously insisted on applying it to such phenomena. The use of some less stringent measure of central tendency, such as the median, is recommended when the data cannot be justified as interval- or ratio-level.

Another disadvantage of the mean is that it is affected by extreme scores. We can illustrate this disadvantage by averaging the ages of clients. Suppose we have ten clients with the following ages.

25 26 27 28 30 31 32 32 33 **76**

The mean for these data is the sum of ages (values) divided by the number of clients, 340/10, or 34. However, nine of the clients in this example are 33 years of age or younger. It is apparent that one person, age 76, is primarily responsible for distorting the "average age" for the group. (Note that a frequency polygon created to display these data would be very asymmetrical.) In this case, the deviant observation of 76 raised the overall mean considerably. Thirty-four does not offer a measurement of central tendency that accurately reflects what is typical. The mode and the median for these data are 32 and 30.5 respectively, values certainly more descriptive in the sense of being more central. This illustration suggests that when distributions are found containing a few deviant scores (observations departing markedly from the rest of the score) and the sample is not especially large, the median is ordinarily to be preferred to the mean. Sometimes for a particular distribution we may report both the mean and the median or even all three measures of central tendency—a practice that provides an even better picture of the distribution.

THE MODE, THE MEDIAN, OR THE MEAN?

The question of which measure or measures of central tendency to use is not always easily resolved. While, as we have indicated, certain general rules apply, the final decision is often more an ethical issue. Above all, researchers want to use central tendency to provide their readers with a mental image, a shorthand description of what the data looked like. Yet in some situations no value of a variable is typical, and the use of any of the measures of central tendency would be equally misleading. An example using case closing data from XYZ agency will illustrate this point.

Figure 4.1 is a frequency polygon that describes the number of interviews for all cases closed during December. It has been constructed from the data in Table 4.4. The variable "number of interviews" is at the ratio level, and the large number of cases suggests that the mean might be the best central tendency measure to use. However, as we noted earlier, the mean requires a distribution that is basically symmetrical. The shape of the polygon is our first warning that the mean, or at least the mean alone, may not be an appropriate choice. The mean number of interviews in Table 4.4 is actually 4.37.

It is apparent from Figure 4.1 that a client interviewed four or five times (rounding down or up) would not really be typical of clients in the agency. There are actually four other values (1, 2, 3, and 10) that occurred as frequently as, or more frequently than,

Table 4.4
Frequency Distribution: Number of Interviews for Cases Closed in XYZ Agency During December

Number of Times Seen	Absolute Frequency
1	55
2	35
3	55
4	40
5	25
6	15
7	10
8	20
9	5
10	35
Total number of cases	295

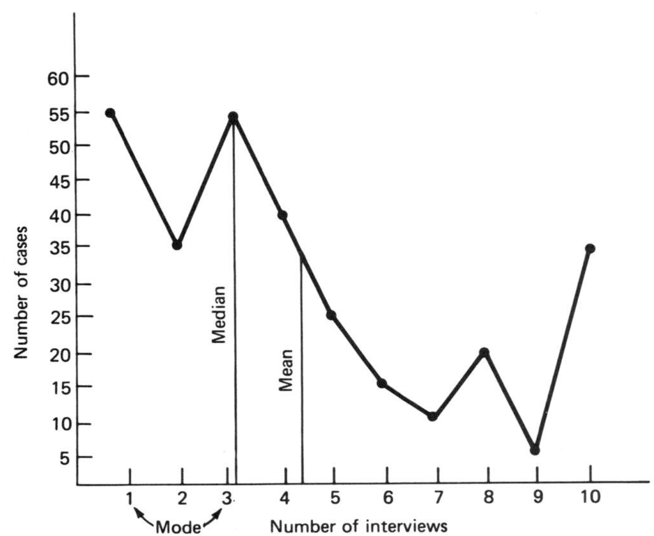

Figure 4.1 Frequency Polygon: Number of Interviews for Cases Closed at XYZ Agency During December (from Table 4.4)

either 4 or 5. Since three of the values (1, 2, and 3) are all clustered well to the left of the mean, the mean appears to be too high to reflect what is typical.

If the mean would not be a representative portrayal of the data, what about the median? It falls between the numbers 3 and 4 and very close to one of the most common values (3). As a choice for a single measure of central tendency to represent the data, it is fairly good. But it does not even hint that a fairly sizable group of clients (35) were interviewed ten times, a fact that may be a little surprising and possibly valuable for an agency that is generally believed to engage in short-term crisis intervention. It also does not confirm the more predictable finding that a large number of clients (55) were interviewed only once. In short, the median may be better than either the mean or the mode for presenting what is typical, but it is far from perfect for these data.

The distribution is bimodal, with the two modes falling at one and three interviews. But if we were to use only the mode, we would be suggesting that one or three interviews (both small numbers) is typical of a case when, in fact, fewer than half of all cases were seen four times or less. As with the median, the mode alone provides no hint of the possibility that "crisis intervention cases" may be interviewed a fairly large number of times. As we noted above, the mode is really most appropriate for nominal-level data. It treats different values of a variable as if they were differences of kind only; it does not take into account that (as in this example) they may really indicate a difference in quantities as well.

Sometimes no measure of central tendency is ideal for displaying what is typical of the data. Figure 4.1 points out the need for something like central tendency to summarize what the data look like, but our example illustrates a situation in which any one measure would have the potential to mislead. Yet all three—the mode, the median, or the mean—would contribute something to a visualization of how the data must have looked. The fact that the data were bimodal, with modes at one and three interviews, indicates that short-term treatment remains a common approach in the agency. Yet the median best reflects what is typical. It uses some of the available precision of measurement, more than the mode but less than the mean. It at least suggests that very short-term treatment may not be as typical of the agency as one might think. If the mean is presented, the fact that it is over 4 is even stronger evidence that a sizable number of clients *must* have been interviewed more frequently than we might expect.

The example using the data from Table 4.4 and Figure 4.1 underlines the suggestion that we must consider reporting more than one measure of central tendency. An experienced reader of research reports, or even one with a good understanding of the mode, the median, and the mean, would be able to compare the three and piece together a reasonably good picture of what the data must have looked like. Any one might mislead; all three would present an accurate communication—which is, after all, a goal of descriptive statistics.

SUMMARY

In this chapter we have discussed various measures of central tendency and the ways in which they can be used to summarize what is a typical value for a variable in a group of data. We have emphasized that such factors as level of measurement, sample size, and the presence or absence of very deviant scores all should be considered in the selection of the one or more measures of central tendency to be employed.

Central tendency is a kind of shorthand that is not a substitute for comprehension of the individual variations within a data set. But it is a way of quickly and simply communicating characteristics of subjects when minimal specificity is required. As is the case with tabular presentation and graphing of data, research ethics require that the choice of a measurement of central tendency place high priority on honesty in communication.

STUDY QUESTIONS

1. Why is the mode most appropriately used with nominal-level data?
2. What does a frequency polygon look like when the distribution can be described as bimodal?
3. Why is the median more likely to be an accurate description of ordinal-level data than the mode?
4. What makes the median more stable than the mode?
5. Why would the mean probably be inappropriate for the variable grade point ratio in a class of 12 students?
6. Why do we consider the mean to be a more precise indicator of central tendency than either the median or the mode?
7. How do a few extremely high or extremely low values of a variable tend to distort the mean?
8. If all the criteria for use of the mean cannot be met, what is the alternative choice for a measure of central tendency?
9. Why may only one measure of central tendency be an inadequate description of a data set?
10. In what situation might the use of more than one measure of central tendency provide a better description of the values of a variable than any one measure?

FURTHER READING

Craft, J. L. (1985). *Statistics and data analysis for social workers* (Chs. 4 and 5). Itasca, IL: F. E. Peacock.

Grinnell, R. M., Jr. (Ed.). (1981). *Social work research and evaluation* (Ch. 22). Itasca, IL: F. E. Peacock.

MacEachron, A. E. (1982). *Basic statistics in the human services: An applied approach* (Ch. 7). Baltimore: University Park Press.

Reid, W. J., & Smith, A. D. (1981). *Research in social work* (Ch. 10). New York: Columbia University Press.

5

MEASURES OF VARIABILITY

In Chapter 4, three measures of central tendency were discussed. If we were to stop our analysis of data at this point, however, our description of any given distribution of values would be inadequate or even misleading. True, Chapter 4 described the points around which all other values in a distribution tend to focus, but it did not explain the way in which the values were distributed around these points.

Distributions A and B below have an identical mean of 3. However, the way in which each set of values is distributed around the mean is different.

Distribution A

0 2 3 4 6

Distribution B

2 3 3 3 4

Roughly describing these two distributions of five values each, we could say that the values in Distribution B closely cluster around the mean of 3, while the values in Distribution A are more widely scattered around the same mean.

The way in which values scatter themselves around a measure of central tendency in a distribution is summarized in what we refer to as *measures of variability*. In short, measures of variability describe the spread of a distribution of values around the mean or other measure of central tendency. There are seven commonly used indicators of variability: the minimum value, the maximum value, the range, the interquartile range, the semi-interquartile range, the mean deviation, and the standard deviation.

THE MINIMUM VALUE

The minimum value in any distribution is simply the lowest value relative to all the other values in the distribution. Consider the nine values below.

1 1 1 1 2 2 3 3 4

The minimum value in this distribution is 1. The minimum value can occur any number of times in a distribution; it is simply the smallest value in a distribution—*not* the lowest frequency of a specific value (in this case, 4).

THE MAXIMUM VALUE

The maximum value in any distribution is simply the highest value relative to all the other values in the distribution. Consider the 11 values below.

1 2 3 3 4 5 8 9 10 11 12

The maximum value in this distribution is 12. Like the minimum value, the maximum value can occur any number of times in a distribution; it is simply the largest value in a distribution—*not* the highest frequency of a specific value (in this case, 3).

THE RANGE

The range is a measure of variability that determines the distance between the maximum value (largest) and the minimum value (smallest) in a distribution. We can express this as a formula.

$$\text{Range} = \text{Maximum value} - \text{minimum value} + 1$$

Consider Distributions C and D below.

Distribution C

1 5 5 5 5

Distribution D

1 5 5 5 **9**

The range of Distribution C is computed as

$$\text{Range} = \text{Maximum value} - \text{minimum value} + 1$$
$$= 5 - 1 + 1$$
$$= 5 \text{ (Range)}$$

The range of Distribution D is computed as

$$\text{Range} = \text{Maximum value} - \text{minimum value} + 1$$
$$= 9 - 1 + 1$$
$$= 9 \text{ (Range)}$$

Since Distributions C and D have the same number of scores and the same intervals, the larger range in Distribution D indicates the greater amount of variation among scores in that distribution.

Assumptions for the Range

The range can be used in statistical analyses only when the data are at the interval level or higher. This assumption is frequently violated when the range is used to construct distributions for ordinal-level data. The range assumes that there are equal distances between all values in a distribution. As we noted in Chapter 1, when we have ordinal-level data, we do not really know how great the distance is between any two values. We know only that one value is higher (or lower) than another, but not how much higher (or lower).

Advantages and Disadvantages of the Range

The range is a useful measure of variation in that it can be computed quickly and easily from an array, as Table 2.2 in Chapter 2 shows. Once we have identified the upper and lower limits (values) of a set of values, we can more easily construct a frequency distribution. Calculating the range enables us to determine the number of intervals to employ in the grouped frequency distribution as well as the most appropriate interval size.

The range is an unstable measure of central tendency, however. It is computed on the basis of the maximum and the minimum values in a distribution, and one deviant value can increase the range considerably. For example, consider Distributions E and F below.

Distribution E
10 11 12 13 14 15 16 17 **90**

Distribution F

10 11 12 13 14 15 16 17 18

In Distribution E, the range is 81 (90 − 10 + 1 = 81). In Distribution F, the range is 9 (18 − 10 + 1 = 9). The differences in ranges, 81 and 9, is due to the one extreme score of 90 in Distribution E. This property is an undesirable one. It makes the comparison of ranges from two or more distributions potentially misleading.

THE INTERQUARTILE RANGE

Instead of measuring the distance between the maximum and minimum values to obtain a range, we can measure the distance between the 75th and 25th percentiles, the third and first quartiles, respectively. This distance is known as the *interquartile range*. As a measure of variability, it is more stable than the range because a few extremely high or low scores cannot distort it as they would distort the range. When the 75th percentile and the 25th percentile have been determined (either by construction of an array, by computation, or by estimation from a cumulative graph), the interquartile range is found by direct subtraction. We can express this as a formula.

$$\text{Interquartile range} = \text{75th percentile} - \text{25th percentile}$$

Consider the 12 values in Table 5.1. The 25th percentile falls between 3 and 4, and the 75th percentile falls between 9 and 10. Thus the interquartile range for the data presented in Table 5.1 is

$$\text{Interquartile range} = \text{75th percentile} - \text{25th percentile}$$

$$= 9.5 - 3.5$$

$$= 6 \text{ (Interquartile range)}$$

The interquartile range is similar in some respects to the median. Like the median, it is particularly useful in skewed distributions of interval- or ratio-level data where a few extreme values might distort the value of other variability indices such as the standard deviation (to be discussed).

Table 5.1
Values and Their Percentiles

Values	Percentiles
1	
2	
3	
25th percentile = 3.5	
4	
5	
6	
50th percentile = 6.5	
7	
8	
9	
75th percentile = 9.5	
10	
11	
12	

Assumption for the Interquartile Range

The only assumption necessary for the computation of the interquartile range is that we have interval- or ratio-level data.

Advantage and Disadvantage of the Interquartile Range

The main advantage of the interquartile range is that it is a more stable measure of variability than the range. Unlike the range, it is not as easily influenced by the extreme values in a distribution of its values. It does, however, take longer to compute than the range.

THE SEMI-INTERQUARTILE RANGE

The semi-interquartile range is half the interquartile range. We can write this as a formula.

$$\text{Semi-interquartile range} = \frac{\text{75th percentile} - \text{25th percentile}}{2}$$

For the distribution of values in Table 5.1, the semi-interquartile range is

$$\text{Semi-interquartile range} = \frac{\text{75th percentile} - \text{25th percentile}}{2}$$

$$= \frac{9.5 - 3.5}{2}$$

$$= \frac{6}{2}$$

$$= 3 \text{ (Semi-interquartile range)}$$

The assumptions, advantages, and disadvantages of the interquartile range apply to the semi-interquartile range. But the semi-interquartile range is rarely used anymore. Naturally, a question could be asked, "Why bother to discuss the semi-interquartile range?" The answer is simple: Since it is seen in the older professional literature, we thought the reader ought to know what it is and how it relates to the more common interquartile range, which, by convention, is now the preferred choice.

Frequently we find ourselves doing things merely because of custom or convention. The same is true in statistical practice. Through continued usage, some statistical procedures have become popular and widely accepted. The way we have chosen to approach the study of statistics in this book is often a reflection of convention. We have selected certain statistics for inclusion, and we may present material in a particular form because most people are familiar with it that way. Convention plays an important role in how we structure and interpret the statistical world as well as other worlds—including our own personal experiences and professional practices.

THE MEAN DEVIATION

The range, interquartile range, and semi-interquartile range each have advantages and are useful in certain situations, but none of the three uses *every* value in the distribution to determine the statistic. When we want a measure of variability that is determined by *all* the values, or observations, we may choose the mean deviation.

Instead of looking only at two extreme values in a distribution, we can approach the problem of describing variability by indicating the degree to which all the group's values differ (or deviate) from the mean of the distribution. The more the values tend to be scattered from the mean, the more they will tend to differ from each other. The group's mean is the ideal reference point for a mathematical reason; the sum of the deviations about the mean is zero (which says that the mean is, in effect, the distribution's center of gravity). This property is important because it ensures that the value of our variability statistic will reflect only differences among group members and not their absolute values.

Table 5.2 lists five values, their mean, and deviation scores. A deviation score for any value is simply the difference between the observation and the group mean.

$$\text{Deviation score for value} = \text{value} - \text{mean}$$

To compute the mean deviation for the data in Table 5.2, we would proceed as follows.

$$\text{Mean deviation} = \frac{\text{Sum of deviation values (ignoring } - \text{ or } + \text{ sign)}}{\text{Number of values in the distribution}}$$

$$= \frac{(2) + (1) + (0) + (1) + (2)}{5}$$

$$= \frac{6}{5}$$

$$= 1.25 \text{ (Mean deviation)}$$

The value of 1.25 is the typical deviation of the values from the mean in Table 5.2. Most people easily understand the concept of mean distance of the values for a distribution from the mean. It is relatively easy to compute and interpret. However, the mean deviation is rarely used. We usually need a measure of variability that will provide a more complete visual picture of the distribution of values of a variable around the mean—the standard deviation.

Table 5.2
Deviations from the Mean

Value	–	Mean	=	Deviations from the Mean
1	–	3	=	−2
2	–	3	=	−1
3	–	3	=	0
4	–	3	=	1
5	–	3	=	2
		Total		0

THE STANDARD DEVIATION

The standard deviation is a widely used indicator of dispersion. It is an important part of the formulas that examine the relationships between variables (some of which are discussed in later chapters of this book). Like the mean deviation, it takes all case values into consideration in its computation. Although it does not simply ignore the sign of the difference between each score and the mean, as the mean deviation does, it has its own way of dealing with minus values (by squaring them).

While the mean deviation can tell us what is a typical deviation of values from the mean, the standard deviation can do much more. When used with the mean in appropriate situations, it allows us (1) to have a picture of where a given score falls relative to other scores, (2) to know what percentage of scores in a distribution falls within specified distances from the mean, and (3) to reconstruct the distribution of all the values of a variable.

Assumptions for the Standard Deviation

The standard deviation requires data that are regarded as interval- or ratio-level. It also is most appropriately used with fairly large samples and with variables that, if graphed, would form a symmetrical frequency polygon that has a particular shape, the normal distribution (discussed in detail in Chapter 6).

When the Standard Deviation Is Useful

The mean may suggest what is a typical value for a variable in our data, but it does not tell us how all the rest of the values disperse around the mean. The standard deviation does. For example, the average score on a depression scale for a specific group of clients receiving a new type of group treatment (Group A) may be the same as for all other clients receiving group treatment for depression, but we do not know, and cannot assume, that the total distribution of their scores would also be the same. Table 5.3 presents the scores on a depression scale for 20 clients in Group A alongside the scores for all other clients receiving group treatment for depression. They have an identical mean of 74.

Notice that the scores for Group A include scores from 60 to 90, whereas for all other treatment groups, the distribution includes scores as low as 50 and as high as 100. We can easily observe that Group A has a range of 31 ($90 - 60 + 1 = 31$) points, whereas all other treatment groups have a range of 51 ($100 - 50 + 1 = 51$) points.

Table 5.3
Frequency Distribution of Depression Scores

Scores	Frequencies: Treatment Group A	Frequencies: Other Treatment Groups
50	0	10
60	4	10
70	8	25
80	4	45
90	4	5
100	0	5
Totals	20	100

We could also have two distributions that have identical means, the same number of values, but different variabilities, such as Distributions G and H.

Distribution G
8 9 10 10 13

Distribution H
1 5 10 16 18

Figures 5.1 and 5.2 represent the respective five values for each of the two distributions. Figures 5.1 and 5.2 visually depict the values of the two distributions as weights on a plank. We can easily see from Figures 5.1 and 5.2 that Distribution H is more variable than Distribution G. Sometimes, however, we cannot visualize which of two distributions is more variable. Consider Distributions I and J.

Distribution I

1 4 10 11 14

Distribution J

2 5 8 12 13

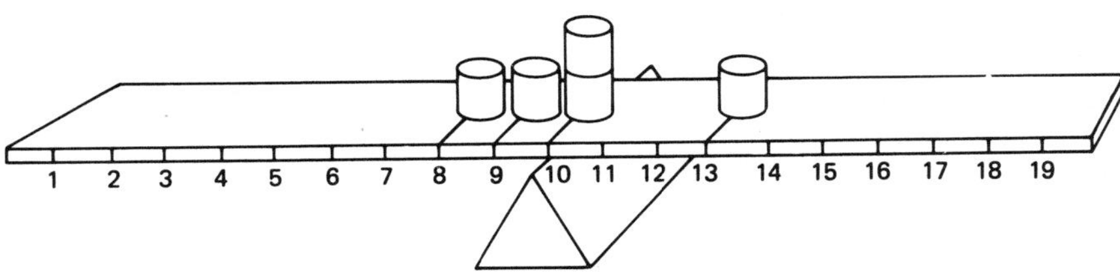

Figure 5.1 Frequency Distribution G

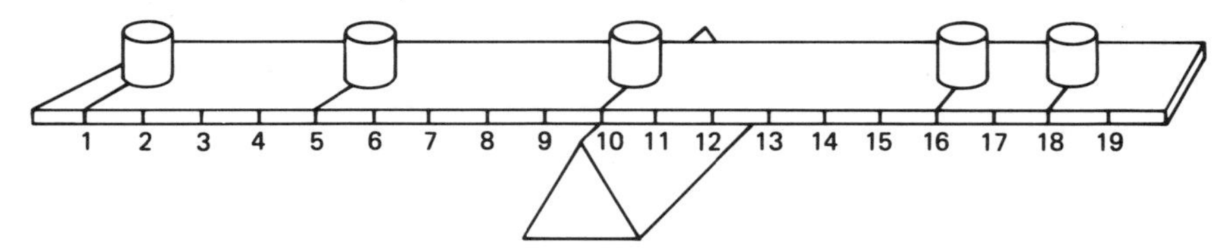

Figure 5.2 Frequency Distribution H

When we graphically plot the values of the two distributions, we still may be at a loss to determine which distribution is more variable, as Figures 5.3 and 5.4 reveal. It is at this point that we would rely on the standard deviation.

Meaning and Computation of Standard Deviation

In order to decide which distribution is more variable, we would have to compute the standard deviation for both distributions. We would then compare the two; the larger standard deviation would indicate greater variability in its distribution. Conceptually, the standard deviation represents the distance between the mean and a given point on the frequency polygon for a frequency distribution. A comparison of two standard deviations computed from their respective distributions indicates which distribution (the one with the larger standard deviation) has a greater spread between that point and the mean.

The standard deviation suggests the degree to which case values tend to vary from the mean for any distribution. The actual values of the mean and of the scores are used in its computation but are not implied in the size of the standard deviation itself. The mean is usually reported along with the standard deviation in a research report so that the reader can get a better picture of what the actual scores looked like.

Adding a fixed amount to all values of a distribution will affect the mean (by increasing it that amount) but will not affect the standard deviation for that distribution. This phenomenon occurs, for example, when a $5,000 raise is given to all employees of

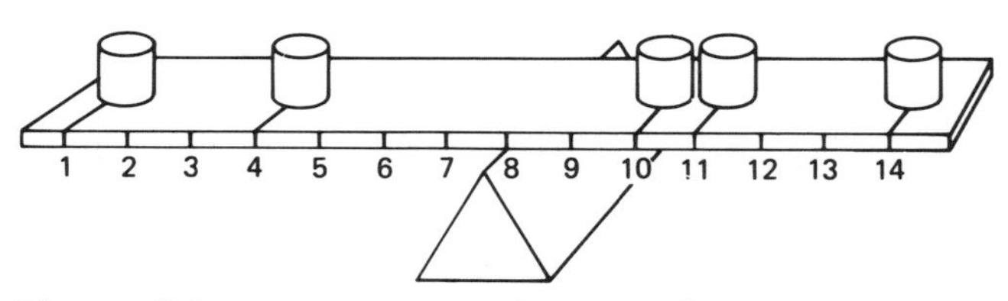

Figure 5.3 Frequency Distribution I

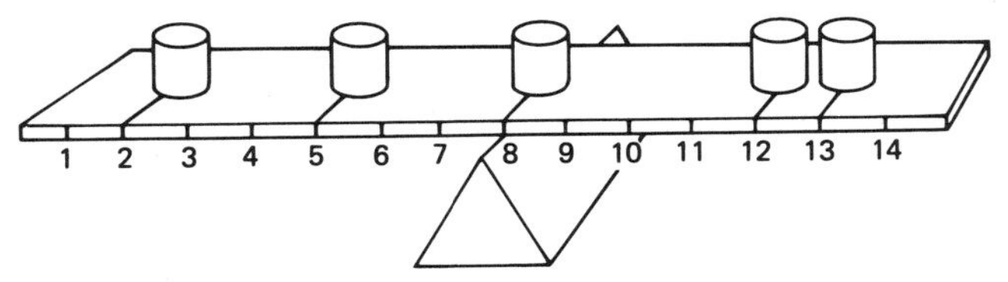

Figure 5.4 Frequency Distribution J

a social agency. The mean salary would be $5,000 higher, but the amount of variation in salary among employees would remain exactly the same.

The standard deviation may be computed by the following eight steps.

1. List the values in a distribution in column *a*.
2. Obtain a mean of the values in column *a*.
3. List the mean in column *b*.
4. Subtract the mean from each value in column *a*, and place this value in column *c*.
5. Square each value in column *c*, and place this value in column *d*.
6. Add column *d*.
7. Divide the sum of column *d* by the total number of values in column *a*.
8. Obtain the square root of the number in Step 7. This number is the standard deviation of the values in column *a*.

Let us compute the standard deviation for the six values in Distribution K.

Distribution K

5 6 6 6 7 8

Now, utilizing the eight steps to compute the standard deviation for a given distribution, we can determine Distribution K's standard deviation (Table 5.4).

The representation of Distribution K's six values can be visualized as weights on a plank, as shown in Figure 5.5.

Let us take a distribution that is more varied than Distribution K. Consider Distribution L, which also has six values.

Distribution L

1 2 4 7 9 12

Utilizing the eight steps to compute the standard deviation, we can determine Distribution L's standard deviation (Table 5.5).

The representation of Distribution L's six values as weights on a plank is shown in Figure 5.6. It is evident from a comparison of

Table 5.4
Determining the Standard Deviation for Distribution K

Step 1 (*a*) Value	−	Step 3 (*b*) Mean	=	Step 4 (*c*) Deviations from Mean		Step 5 (*d*) Squared Differences from Mean	
5	−	6.3	=	−1.3		1.69	
6	−	6.3	=	− .3		.09	
6	−	6.3	=	− .3		.09	
6	−	6.3	=	− .3		.09	
7	−	6.3	=	.7		.49	
8	−	6.3	=	1.7		2.89	
					Step 6	5.34	
					Step 7	$\frac{5.34}{6}$	
					=	.89	
					Step 8	$\sqrt{.89}$	
					=	.94	(Standard deviation)

Figures 5.5 and 5.6 that Distribution L reflects more variation than does Distribution K. This is also reflected in their respective standard deviations.

The actual calculation of the standard deviation is a rather lengthy process. Fortunately it is usually unnecessary to compute one by hand, since many pocket calculators are programmed to calculate it. However, it is important to understand what the standard deviation means. To look at the values of a given distribution graphically (Figures 5.1 through 5.6) may help a great deal. If you do not yet have a clear grasp of the concept of standard deviation, Chapter 6 provides further clarification.

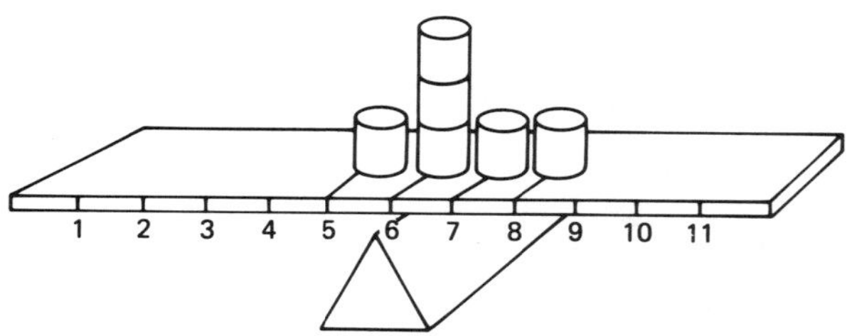

Figure 5.5 Frequency Distribution K (from Table 5.4)

Table 5.5
Determining the Standard Deviation for Distribution L

Step 1 (a) Value	−	Step 3 (b) Mean	=	Step 4 (c) Deviations from Mean		Step 5 (d) Squared Differences from Mean	
1	−	5.8	=	−4.8		23.04	
2	−	5.8	=	−3.8		14.44	
4	−	5.8	=	−1.8		3.24	
7	−	5.8	=	1.2		1.44	
9	−	5.8	=	3.2		10.24	
12	−	5.8	=	6.2		38.44	
					Step 6	90.84	
					Step 7	$\frac{90.84}{6}$	
					=	15.14	
					Step 8	$\sqrt{15.14}$	
					=	3.89	(Standard deviation)

SUMMARY

In this chapter, we have taken the process of summarizing and describing research data a step further. Variability, along with central tendency, clarifies the picture of what any given data set looks like. Measures of variability such as the range or interquartile range are easily computed, but they can still be misleading. Their formulas do not take into consideration all scores in the data collected. If there are few if any really deviant scores, and if data are of interval or ratio level, the standard deviation is the measure of variability of choice. Readers of a research report who are provided with the mean and standard deviation of values of a

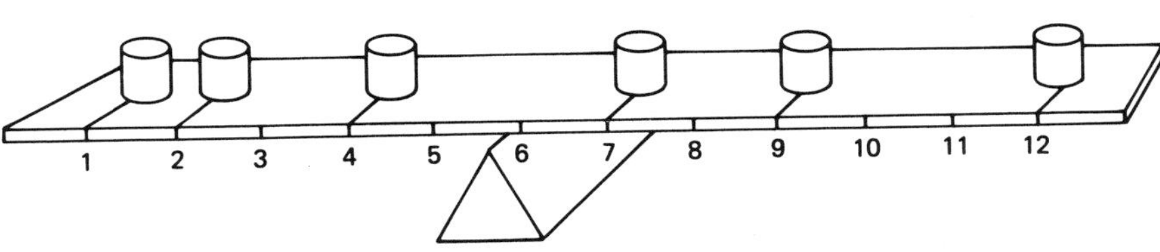

Figure 5.6 Frequency Distribution L (from Table 5.5)

variable will be able to reconstruct a complete picture of the values that were found to exist. As explained in Chapter 4, if the criteria for use of the mean cannot be met, we must consider using a less stable measure of central tendency. Similarly, if all criteria for use of the standard deviation cannot be met, we may have to settle for a less stable measure of variability, such as the interquartile range or the range.

STUDY QUESTIONS

1. How do measures of variability help to complete the description of what data look like?
2. Why is the range an especially unstable measure of variability?
3. What makes the interquartile range a more stable measure of variability than the range for use with interval- or ratio-level data?
4. Which measures of variability consider all values of a variable in their computation?
5. How would an especially deviant value (very high or very low) tend to distort the mean deviation for a group of data?
6. How would adding the number 10 to each of the values for a variable affect the standard deviation?
7. How would a frequency polygon for data with a mean of 10 and a standard deviation of 3 compare with a frequency polygon for other data with a mean of 10 and a standard deviation of 12 displayed on the same grid?
8. If a few deviant high values of a set of interval-level data would badly distort the standard deviation, what measure of variability should be used?
9. If the interquartile range is often used when the median is most appropriate, what measure of variability is often used when the mean is most appropriate?
10. How would knowing the mean deviation or standard deviation help a social worker to decide whether to apply for a job that advertises a mean caseload of 25?

FURTHER READING

Craft, J. L. (1985). *Statistics and data analysis for social workers* (Chs. 4 and 5). Itasca, IL: F. E. Peacock.

Grinnell, R. M., Jr. (Ed.). (1981). *Social work research and evaluation* (Ch. 22). Itasca, IL: F. E. Peacock.
MacEachron, A. E. (1982). *Basic statistics in the human services: An applied approach* (Ch. 7). Baltimore: University Park Press.
Reid, W. J., & Smith, A. D. (1981). *Research in social work* (Ch. 10). New York: Columbia University Press.

6

THE NORMAL DISTRIBUTION

Chapters 4 and 5 presented the main characteristics of frequency distributions: central tendency and variability. However, there is a special form of frequency distribution known as the *normal distribution*. Knowledge of the normal distribution is a fundamental prerequisite to an understanding of subsequent discussions of statistical inference and to the testing of hypotheses presented in Part II of this book.

Consider a frequency distribution such as Table 6.1. As we demonstrated in our discussion of frequency polygons in Chapter 3, frequency distributions can be displayed graphically. Such graphs can assume many different shapes. For example, some may show distributions of values in which a large number of frequencies focus around lower values and taper off toward the higher values. Such is the case with the frequency distribution as presented in Table 6.1.

The frequency distribution in Table 6.1 can easily be converted to a histogram, as in Figure 6.1. The continuous line joining the

Table 6.1
Cumulative Frequency Distribution

Scores	Absolute Frequency	Cumulative Frequency (High–Low)	Cumulative Frequency (Low–High)
1	60	60	210
2	50	110	150
3	40	150	100
4	30	180	60
5	20	200	30
6	10	210	10

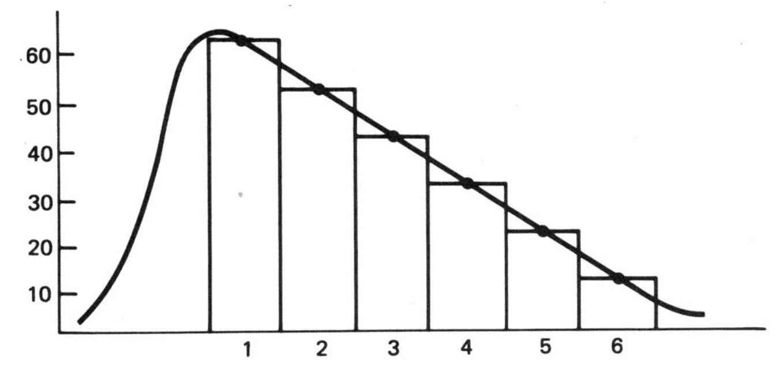

Figure 6.1 Positively Skewed Histogram (from Table 6.1)

midpoints of the tops of the intervals in the histogram is called a *curve*.

Distributions like Table 6.1 and Figure 6.1 are said to be *skewed*. *Skewness* means that the distribution is not symmetrical—that their tails or ends do not taper off equally in both directions. The curve in Figure 6.1 is skewed to the right because the frequencies taper off to the right. A curve that is skewed to the right is called *positively skewed*.

If we were to completely reverse the frequencies, or the values, in Table 6.1 and rearrange them as shown in Table 6.2, we would have a frequency distribution represented by the curve in Figure 6.2. This distribution is also said to be skewed. This time, however, the frequencies taper off to the left. A curve that is skewed to the left is termed *negatively skewed*.

When a curve is free of skewness, such as Figure 6.3, it is said to be *symmetrical*, and the frequency distribution from which it was drawn is symmetrical. In addition, Figure 6.3 is described as *normal*. Not all symmetrical curves are normal, but all normal curves are symmetrical. The word *normal* refers to a specific type

Table 6.2
Cumulative Frequency Distribution

Scores	Absolute Frequency	Cumulative Frequency
1	10	10
2	20	30
3	30	60
4	40	100
5	50	150
6	60	210

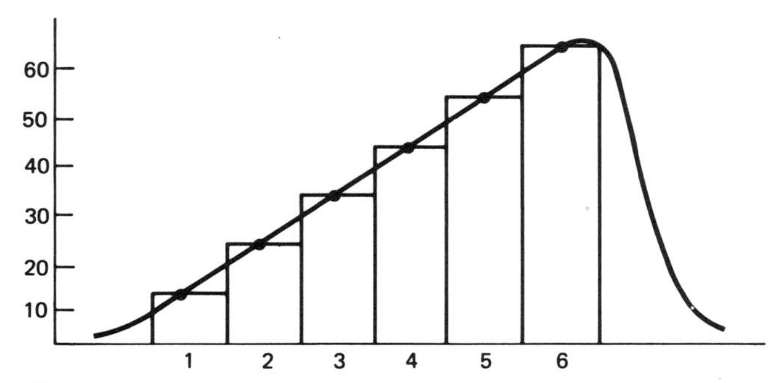

Figure 6.2 Negatively Skewed Histogram (from Table 6.2)

of curve and a distribution having certain mathematical properties. Another term for a normal distribution is *bell-shaped curve*. This shape, as distinguished from other symmetrical frequency polygons, can be seen in Figure 6.3.

PROPERTIES OF THE NORMAL DISTRIBUTION

The properties of a normal distribution are constant, which means that they are the same in all normal distributions. The normal distribution contains about six standard deviations (three on either side of the mean). Figure 6.4 presents a normal distribution showing this property. As we shall see shortly, we need to compute the standard deviation if we are to compare two scores taken from two different distributions.

The mean, the median, and the mode (three central tendency measures) of the normal distribution all occur at the same point—that is, at the highest point of the curve in the center of the distribution. As Figure 6.5 shows, however, different normal curves may have variations in their means and standard deviations. In skewed curves, the mean, the median, and the mode occur at different points, as presented in Figure 6.6.

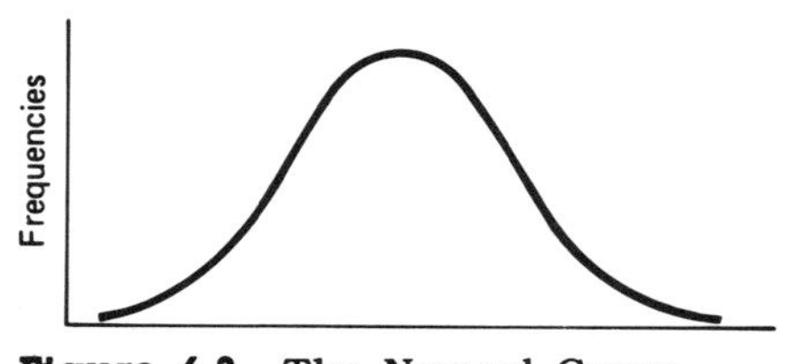

Figure 6.3 The Normal Curve

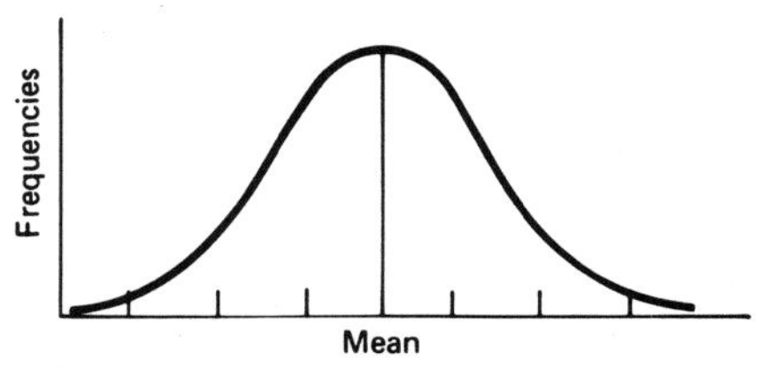

Figure 6.4 The Normal Distribution

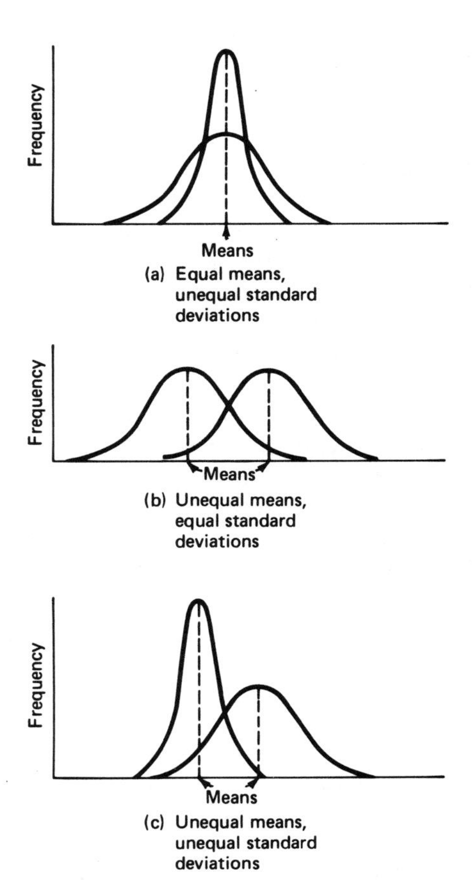

Figure 6.5 Variations in Normal Distributions

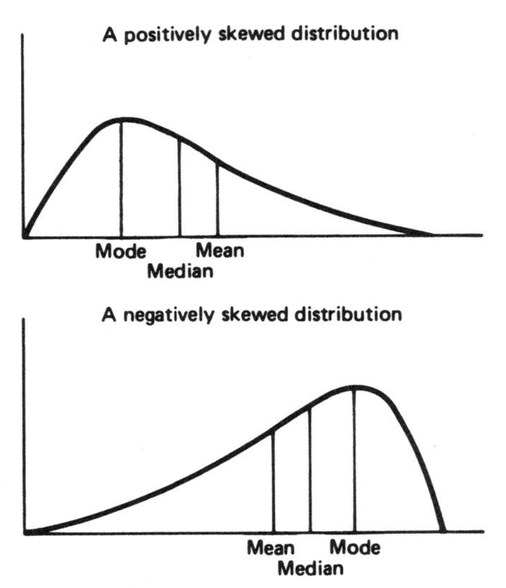

Figure 6.6 Skewed Distributions

The total area underneath the curve and contained within the normal distribution is equal to one (1.0). *One*, as we are using the term here, refers to the fact that there is a 100 percent certainty that all scores or values for the normally distributed variable will fall within the normal distribution. Parts of one (sometimes referred to as *unity*) are represented as proportions of the total area underneath the curve and within the distribution. For example, the 50 percent of the area of a normal curve to the left of the mean represents that half of the scores or values that fall below the mean. In a distribution like that of Figure 6.7, all scores or values are found underneath the curve.

As we noted, the normal distribution is symmetrical and bell-shaped. The ends of the distribution extend toward infinity—the ends of the distribution always approach the horizontal axis but never quite touch it. For this reason, the ends of the normal curve in all the figures in this book are shown as not touching the horizontal axes of the distributions. This property represents the possibility that a very small number of scores may occur beyond three standard deviations from the mean. It also reflects the fact that at a higher level of abstraction a total universe (or population) never exists, because it is always subject to change as cases are added or deleted over time. That is, populations are never static; they always are evolving.

The area of a normal curve between a point on the horizontal axis and the mean is equivalent to the area of the curve between a

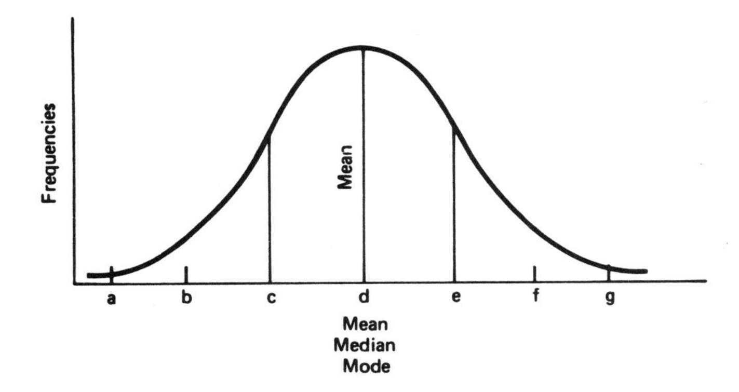

Points	Standard deviation point	Distance from mean
a	−3	3 SD
b	−2	2 SD
c	−1	1 SD
d	0 (Mean)	0
e	+1	1 SD
f	+2	2 SD
g	+3	3 SD

Figure 6.7 Normal Distribution Showing Positive and Negative Standard Deviation Points

point on the axis the same distance on the other side of the mean. For example, a distance of one standard deviation to the left of the mean is equal to a distance of one standard deviation to the right of the mean, and the area of the curve corresponding to these distances on either side of the mean is identical. This equality is a property of the symmetry of the curve. Figure 6.8 illustrates this more clearly.

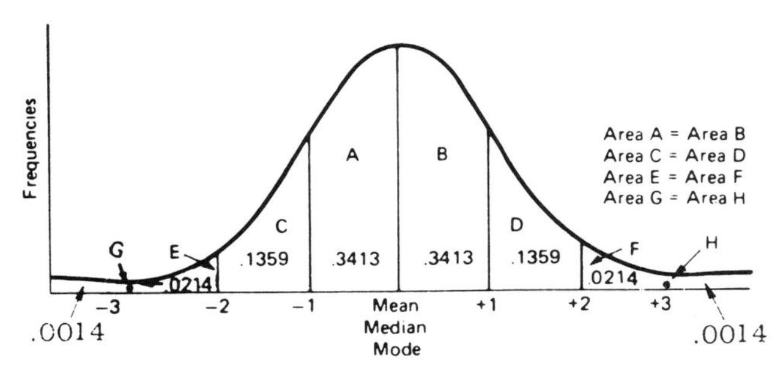

Figure 6.8 Normal Distribution Showing Standard Deviations from the Mean

Z Scores and the Normal Distribution

Whenever we encounter values of some variable based on measurements taken from two different populations, we may be unable to make direct comparisons. For example, we cannot directly compare the socioeconomic class of two individuals if we know only their dollar income earned in two different countries. Comparison is possible only when we know where the dollar income for each case stands relative to other cases in their respective groups. This additional information is necessary unless the means and the standard deviations of the two populations are identical to one another. Such is seldom the case in actual social work research.

We can overcome the difficulty by converting the values taken from different populations to a common standard. Such a standard is found with the normal distribution in the form of *z* scores. Comparing scores from different populations after such conversion poses no problems, because each population is reduced to virtually the same standard of measurement, units of standard deviation (*z* scores).

Z scores are really raw scores converted to units of standard deviation. Every raw score can be given an equivalent *z* score that tells us how many standard deviation units from the mean it falls. The relative positions of two *z* scores taken from two different normal distributions can then be compared.

Because of the nature of the normal distribution, *z* scores can be converted to an even more familiar mathematical term, *percentile.* A score at the 75th percentile would be higher than about three quarters of the scores in its distribution and lower than about one quarter of the scores. If, for example, we know that Bill's test score on the statistics exam in his section fell at the 82nd percentile and Mary's score on a different statistics test in her section fell at the 92nd percentile, Mary can be assumed to have done better, at least in one sense, than Bill, despite the fact that both received a grade of 75 on their respective exams.

To change a raw score into a *z* score, the following formula is used.

$$z \text{ score} = \frac{\text{Raw score} - \text{mean}}{\text{Standard deviation}}$$

As long as we know the mean and the standard deviation of the distribution from which any raw score is obtained, we can compute a *z* score.

As suggested above, a *z* score can be perceived as the number of standard deviation units that measures its distance from the mean of the distribution. A z score of 1 is one standard deviation above the mean, a z score of 2 is two standard deviations above the mean, and so on. A z score may be either positive or negative, according to which side of the mean the particular value is found. A positive z score is a value above the mean; a negative z score is a value below the mean.

As Figure 6.8 shows, the area of the normal distribution directly above the portion of the axis between $z = +1$ and the mean is equal to that area of the curve above the portion of the axis between $z = -1$ and the mean (34.13 percent). The percentage of the curve between any two points (z scores) is also the same as the percentage of cases whose z scores for the variable fall between the points. For example, 34.13 percent of all scores in a normal distribution fall between the mean and $z = +1$; 34.13 percent between the mean and $z = -1$; 13.59 percent between $z = +2$ and $z = +1$, 13.59 percent between $z = -2$ and $z = -1$, and so on.

A large percentage of the area of the curve and, therefore, of cases in the distribution (68.26 percent) falls in the center (between the z scores -1 and $+1$). Only a small percentage of the curve and of cases in a normal distribution (less than half of one percent) falls beyond z scores of -3 and $+3$. This means that, in a normal distribution, scores that fall beyond three standard deviations from the mean are very rare.

If a z score corresponding to a given raw score is not a whole number ($z = -3$, $z = +2$, and so on), the data on areas of normal distributions as provided in Figure 6.8 are not adequate to convert a z score to a percentile. Fortunately, there are tables to assist us in converting fractional z scores ($z = .28$, $z = 2.15$, and so on) to percentiles. Table 6.3 covers whole and fractional z scores. It tells us the corresponding areas of the normal curve between the whole or fractional z score and the mean in any normal distribution.

The whole number digit and first fractional digit of the z score are line labels in the left-hand (z) column in Table 6.3, while the second fractional digit is a column heading across the top of the table. The number at the point where the line and column intersect in the body of the table is the proportionate area of the normal curve included between the mean and the z score. The examples in Table 6.4 will make the use of Table 6.3 clearer.

The sign (+ or −) simply indicates whether a z score is above or below the mean. The proportionate area included by z scores of the same size, regardless of the sign, is the same. For raw scores above the mean (and, therefore, having a positive z score), we *add* the area included between the mean and the z score to 50.00 to

Table 6.3
Areas of the Normal Curve

Area Under the Normal Curve Between
Mean and z score

z	.00	.01	.02	.03	.04	.05	.06	.07	.08	.09
0.0	00.00	00.40	00.80	01.20	01.60	01.99	02.39	02.79	03.19	03.59
0.1	03.98	04.38	04.78	05.17	05.57	05.96	06.36	06.75	07.14	07.53
0.2	07.93	08.32	08.71	09.10	09.48	09.87	10.26	10.64	11.03	11.41
0.3	11.79	12.17	12.55	12.93	13.31	13.68	14.06	14.43	14.80	15.17
0.4	15.54	15.91	16.28	16.64	17.00	17.36	17.72	18.08	18.44	18.79
0.5	19.15	19.50	19.85	20.19	20.54	20.88	21.23	21.57	21.90	22.24
0.6	22.57	22.91	23.24	23.57	23.89	24.22	24.54	24.86	25.17	25.49
0.7	25.80	26.11	26.42	26.73	27.04	27.34	27.64	27.94	28.23	28.52
0.8	28.81	29.10	29.39	29.67	29.95	30.23	30.51	30.78	31.06	31.33
0.9	31.59	31.86	32.12	32.38	32.64	32.90	33.15	33.40	33.65	33.89
1.0	34.13	34.38	34.61	34.85	35.08	35.31	35.54	35.77	35.99	36.21
1.1	36.43	36.65	36.86	37.08	37.29	37.49	37.70	37.90	38.10	38.30
1.2	38.49	38.69	38.88	39.07	39.25	39.44	39.62	39.80	39.97	40.15
1.3	40.32	40.49	40.66	40.82	40.99	41.15	41.31	41.47	41.62	41.77
1.4	41.92	42.07	42.22	42.36	42.51	42.65	42.79	42.92	43.06	43.19
1.5	43.32	43.45	43.57	43.70	43.83	43.94	44.06	44.18	44.29	44.41
1.6	44.52	44.63	44.74	44.84	44.95	45.05	45.15	45.25	45.35	45.45
1.7	45.54	45.64	45.73	45.82	45.91	45.99	46.08	46.16	46.25	46.33
1.8	46.41	46.49	46.56	46.64	46.71	46.78	46.86	46.93	46.99	47.06
1.9	47.13	47.19	47.26	47.32	47.38	47.44	47.50	47.56	47.61	47.67
2.0	47.72	47.78	47.83	47.88	47.93	47.98	48.03	48.08	48.12	48.17
2.1	48.21	48.26	48.30	48.34	48.38	48.42	48.46	48.50	48.54	48.57
2.2	48.61	48.64	48.68	48.71	48.75	48.78	48.81	48.84	48.87	48.90
2.3	48.93	48.96	48.98	49.01	49.04	49.06	49.09	49.11	49.13	49.16
2.4	49.18	49.20	49.22	49.25	49.27	49.29	49.31	49.32	49.34	49.36
2.5	49.38	49.40	49.41	49.43	49.45	49.46	49.48	49.49	49.51	49.52
2.6	49.53	49.55	49.56	49.57	49.59	49.60	49.61	49.62	49.63	49.64
2.7	49.65	49.66	49.67	49.68	49.69	49.70	49.71	49.72	49.73	49.74
2.8	49.74	49.75	49.76	49.77	49.77	49.78	49.79	49.79	49.80	49.81
2.9	49.81	49.82	49.82	49.83	49.84	49.84	49.85	49.85	49.86	49.86
3.0	49.87									
3.5	49.98									
4.0	49.997									
5.0	49.99997									

Source: The original data for Table 6.3 came from *Tables for statisticians and biometricians*, edited by Karl Pearson, published by Cambridge University Press, and are used here by permission of the publisher. The adaptation of these data is taken from Lindquist, E. L., *A first course in statistics* (revised edition), with permission of the publisher, Houghton Mifflin Company.

Table 6.4
Examples of z scores and Their Corresponding Areas

z Score	Row	Column	Area Included Between Mean and z Score
.12	0.1	.02	04.78
1.78	1.7	.08	46.25
−2.90	2.9	.00	49.81
1.15	1.1	.05	37.49
−1.15	1.1	.05	37.49

learn at what percentile the raw score falls. For raw scores below the mean, we *subtract* the area included between the mean and the *z* score from 50.00 to learn at what percentile the raw score falls. For example (see Table 6.4), a raw score that converts to a *z* score of .12 would fall at about the 55th percentile (50.00 + 04.78 = 54.78). As Table 6.4 shows, a *z* score of 1.78 would fall at about the 96th percentile (50.00 + 46.25 = 96.25); a *z* score of −1.15 would fall at about the 13th percentile (50.00 − 37.49 = 12.51), and so on.

Advantages and Disadvantages of z Scores

The primary advantage of *z* scores is that they may be used to compare raw scores taken from different distributions. The data, however, must be at least of the interval level of measurement, and the sample sizes should be fairly large.

The major disadvantage of *z* scores is that a normal distribution must be assumed. When this assumption is not met, a *z* score cannot be interpreted in terms of a standardized proportion of the distribution from which it was computed. When the distribution is skewed, the area within one standard deviation to the left of the mean is not equal to the area within the same distance to the right of the mean. For example, the distribution in Figure 6.9 is positively skewed. Area A is not equal to Area B, even though each area corresponds to one standard deviation from the mean.

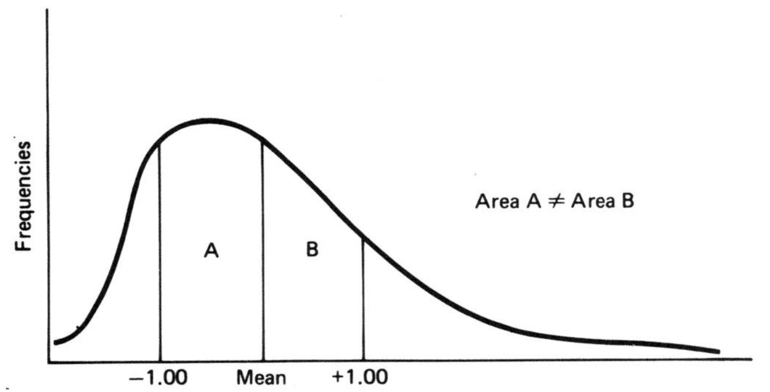

Figure 6.9 Comparing Areas of the Curve of a Skewed Distribution

USE OF NORMAL DISTRIBUTIONS IN STANDARDIZED TESTS

A common use of the normal distribution can be seen in standardized tests such as IQ tests, Scholastic Aptitude Tests (SATs), or Graduate Record Exams (GREs). Over many years, these tests have been repeatedly refined to the point that the scores of large numbers of persons taking the tests will tend to fall into patterns having consistent means and standard deviations. They would also form normal distributions. IQ tests generally are structured so that they have a mean of 100 and a standard deviation of either 15 or 16, depending on the test. If we understand the principles and characteristics that relate to normal distributions, it is possible, given these data, to convert raw IQ scores to *z* scores and then to percentiles using Table 6.3. For example, a score with a *z* score of +1 (115 or 116) would fall at about the 84th percentile. It would also be possible to reverse this process to convert a percentile into a raw score.

SAT and GRE scores were originally designed so that combined verbal and math scores for large numbers of students would form a normal curve with a mean of 1000 and a standard deviation of 200. Because virtually all scores would fall between +3 and −3 standard deviations from the mean, the lowest score would be three times 200, or 600, below the mean (that is, 400). The highest score (the 100th percentile) would fall at 1600. In fact, because of declining SAT and GRE scores in recent years, the mean has fallen considerably below 1000 for a given year, but the scores continue to form a distribution that is nearly symmetrical and still regarded as normal.

USE OF *z* SCORES: A PRACTICE EXAMPLE

Z scores are especially useful for comparing raw scores of two different cases when two different measurement indices of the same variable were used. They allow us to compare the relative position of one case (its percentile rank for its measurement) with the relative position of another case (its percentile rank for its measurement). Assuming that the two groups are essentially comparable in regard to the distribution of the variable, a valid comparison of the two cases can be made. An example will help illustrate this usage.

Deborah, a social worker in a family service agency, has been leading a group of college students diagnosed as experiencing acute anxiety. In the past, members have been selected for the group on the basis of their scores on Anxiety Scale A, a test given to all students as part of intake screening. The scale has a mean of 70 and a standard deviation of 10. Only clients scoring over 80 on Anxiety Scale A are eligible to join the group.

A vacancy occurred in the group. Deborah checked the files of active cases in her agency and noted that the highest score among potential group members was 78 (Gina). However, Deborah had just received a referral from another family agency. The new client (Tom) had recently moved to her city and needed further assistance. The transfer letter indicated that Tom, who suffered from anxiety, received a score of 66 on Anxiety Scale B—a scale that was different from the one Deborah had been using. The letter further stated that Anxiety Scale B has a mean of 50 and a standard deviation of 12.

Both anxiety scales were standardized tests. Based on her knowledge of normal distributions and the information received in the referral letter, Deborah saw no need to retest Tom. She decided to use *z* scores to determine whether Gina or Tom was a better candidate for the group vacancy.

To simplify her decision, Deborah constructed a table with comparative data (Table 6.5). She then computed the *z* score for both potential clients, which allowed her to compute the percentile for each score.

Table 6.5
Comparative Data: Two Indices and Clients' Scores

Data	Anxiety Scale A (Gina)	Anxiety Scale B (Tom)
Raw score	78	66
Mean	70	50
Standard deviation	10	12

$$z \text{ score (Gina)} = \frac{\text{Raw score} - \text{mean}}{\text{Standard deviation}}$$

$$z \text{ score} = \frac{78 - 70}{10} = \frac{8}{10} = .80$$

z = .80 (corresponds to 28.81, Table 6.3)

$$\begin{array}{rl} 28.81 & \text{(area between score and mean)} \\ +\ 50.00 & \text{(area left of mean)} \\ \hline 78.81 & = \text{79th percentile (scale A)} \end{array}$$

$$z \text{ score (Tom)} = \frac{\text{Raw score} - \text{mean}}{\text{Standard deviation}}$$

$$z = \frac{66 - 50}{12} = \frac{16}{12} = 1.33$$

z = 1.33 (corresponds to 40.82, Table 6.3.)

$$\begin{array}{rl} 40.82 & \text{(area between score and mean)} \\ +\ 50.00 & \text{(area left of mean)} \\ \hline 90.82 & = \text{91st percentile (scale B)} \end{array}$$

Based on her comparative analysis using z scores, Deborah chose Tom for the group. His relatively high level of anxiety (based on his scale) made him an obvious candidate. Furthermore, she saw no need to relax the group criteria to admit Gina (79th percentile), which required a score of 80 (84th percentile) or above (based on her scale). Figures 6.10 and 6.11 illustrate the comparison that Deborah was able to make using z scores. Note that the score of 80 (cutoff point on Scale A) is comparable to a score of 62 on Scale B because both fall at the point $z = +1$ (the 84th percentile). Tom's score was above this point (Figure 6.11) and, of course, Gina's (Figure 6.10) was below it.

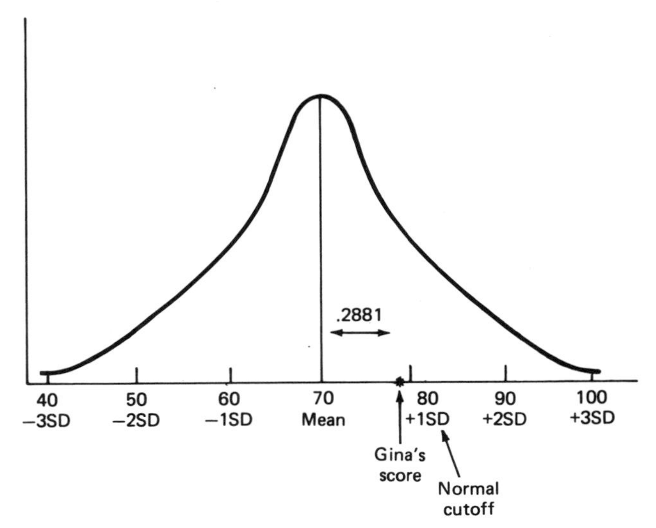

Figure 6.10 Distribution of Scores on Anxiety Scale A (Mean = 70; Standard Deviation = 10)

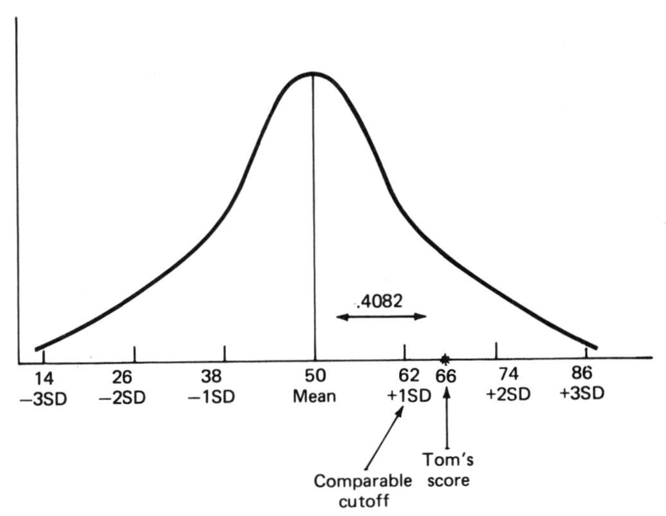

Figure 6.11 Distribution of Scores on Anxiety Scale B (Mean = 50; Standard Deviation = 12)

SUMMARY

In this chapter we have looked at special kinds of data analysis that can be performed when the values of a variable form a normal distribution. By converting raw scores of normally distributed variables into z scores, we can compare individual scores in two different data sets or subsets by seeing how each score compares to others in its own group of scores. Understanding the normal distribution also enables us to visualize where a given score falls relative to others in a very large sample or population. Through the use of percentiles, which we can calculate, we can determine about what percent of scores fall above or below a given score.

The principle of the normal curve is useful to us in many ways. It is especially critical to hypothesis testing, as we shall see in the later chapters of this book.

STUDY QUESTIONS

1. How does a positively skewed distribution differ in appearance from a negatively skewed one?
2. What are the characteristics of a normal, or bell-shaped, frequency polygon?
3. In a frequency polygon for the variable "number of children among AFDC cases," is the distribution likely to be normal, positively skewed, or negatively skewed?
4. In a positively skewed distribution, where is the median relative to the mean?
5. With a variable that is normally distributed, approximately what percentage of all scores falls within one standard deviation of the mean?
6. What is the z score for an anxiety score of 79 when the mean for the sample is 84, with a standard deviation of 5?
7. In a normal distribution, how frequently would a score occur that is more than three standard deviations above or below the mean?
8. On an IQ test with a mean of 100 and a standard deviation of 16, at approximately what percentile will an IQ of 132 fall?
9. Which z score reflects a higher score, -1.62 or 1.50?
10. If a woman has a z score of $-.71$ for weight and 1.95 for height based on normative data for all women in her country, what is her body build likely to be?

FURTHER READING

Grinnell, R. M., Jr. (Ed.). (1981). *Social work research and evaluation* (Ch. 22). Itasca, IL: F. E. Peacock.

MacEachron, A. E. (1982). *Basic statistics in the human services: An applied approach* (Ch. 15). Baltimore: University Park Press.

Reid, W. J., & Smith, A. D. (1981). *Research in social work* (Ch. 10). New York: Columbia University Press.

PART II

ANSWERING QUESTIONS THROUGH DATA ANALYSIS

7

SEEKING TO CONFIRM HYPOTHESES

Part I of this book presented the procedures we use to organize, display, and summarize the characteristics of data we have collected. These summarization procedures are mainly concerned with displaying data in a form that readily communicates them to readers who are interested in knowing what our data looked like in regard to particular variables. While, to the careful observer, graphic displays and descriptive statistics may suggest relationships between or among variables, they cannot be regarded as anything approaching confirmation or verification of such relationships. They do not allow us to generalize beyond the immediate sample that we studied. For such generalization, we need to develop hypotheses and test them according to scientific principles.

TESTING HYPOTHESES

This book cannot overstress the importance of hypothesis construction in social work practice and research. It is, after all, from hypotheses that we gain an understanding of the field and of our own contribution to it. Whether ultimately supported or not, hypotheses allow us to take a more scientific and informed approach to social work practice.

Hypotheses are usually formulated after a thorough review of the literature has been conducted. They are formulated through the process of synthesizing existing qualitative and quantitative knowledge on a particular subject: from experience gained in personal practice, from the writings of scholars in the profession, and from many other sources of expertise in the field, including legislation, unpublished documents, and persons who "ought to know." After an examination of the literature, we can narrow, partially answer or refine a general research question. As the evidence in the literature review starts to accumulate, we try to express our tentative impressions, or conclusions, in the form of a hypothesis. We would then test our hypothesis with a suitable research design.

Many different definitions of hypotheses have been stated, but they all suggest the same concept—a *hypothesis* is a tentative answer to a research question derived from a thorough review of the literature. It is, at the same time, a statement of a relationship between or among variables. A hypothesis, whether ultimately supported by data analysis or not, must be a logical extension of previously existing knowledge. Any other method used to formulate hypotheses is nothing more than "plucking" relationships out of thin air and has the potential to weaken the credibility of the research study.

After collecting, organizing, and summarizing data using statistics such as those presented in Part I of this book, we may begin to sense whether or not our hypothesis is supported by the data we collected. Suppose, for example, that after a thorough literature review, we had hypothesized that alcoholic clients receiving group work treatment are more likely to have abstained from drinking after three months of treatment than are alcoholic clients receiving individual treatment. Frequencies and percentages might seem to provide support for the hypothesis, particularly if the number of clients was small and it was easy to visualize a trend in success for one treatment method (that is, group treatment) as opposed to the other (individual treatment). Perhaps 70 percent of the alcoholic clients receiving group work treatment abstained compared to 65 percent of those receiving individual treatment. There is, *apparently*, a relationship between the dependent variable (drinking/not drinking) and the independent variable (group treatment/individual treatment). However, only the most naive would conclude, on this evidence alone, that group work treatment is a better method for alcoholics than individual treatment. To test our hypothesis scientifically, we would now have to examine alternative explanations.

ALTERNATIVE EXPLANATIONS

At this point, as we said, our hypothesis *may* have been supported by the data we collected. However, it would be presumptive and premature to conclude that there is a true relationship between the two variables. A relationship can be verified only after all competing alternative explanations for the apparent relationship can be dismissed. The three major alternative explanations, besides the one that the hypothesis is indeed correct, are (1) bias, (2) other variables, and (3) chance. The first two are primarily related to research methodology; the third is directly related to statistical testing. A good social work research methods text will help us to minimize the effects of the first two alternative explanations—this book will help us with the third.

Bias

The first alternative explanation is bias. Bias is a systematic source of distortion that can affect the quality of data collected. It can result in erroneous research findings and, subsequently, erroneous conclusions drawn from our findings. Biases might relate to the fact that data were collected at an atypical time or that our study was influenced by some outside event, or to the conscious or unconscious tendency of the person collecting the data to get a less than true perception. If, for whatever reason or combination of reasons, data were biased, our dependent and independent variables could appear to be related when, in fact, they were not. The possibility that bias would explain an apparent relationship between two variables is usually minimized by careful measurement techniques.

Other Variables

The second alternative explanation is other variables. Factors besides the independent variable could also explain the differences in the dependent variable (drinking/not drinking, in our example). In this example, these may include differing amounts of family support for the method of treatment and differing skill levels of the social workers offering the two treatment methods. A true experimental design, through randomization, might have provided some level of control for other variables, but true experimental designs are rare in social work research. Appropriate methodological techniques can make us reasonably confident that other variables are not the real explanation of an apparent relationship between two variables. The specific ways in which research designs can help control for other variables are generally discussed in research methodology texts.

Chance

The third alternative explanation is chance, alternately referred to as probability, sampling error, a fluke occurrence—or just plain luck. Chance states that the likelihood of any event's occurring can range from 0 (never) to 1.0 (absolute certainty). It is based on the assumption that while certain patterns of events can be seen to exist in many repeated observations over time, individual, or short-term, observations tend to differ somewhat from the overall long-term patterns. For example, whenever we randomly draw a sample from a population, we may not select a sample that is identical in composition to (representative of) the population from which it was drawn. Probability theory relates directly to the concept of sampling error that is usually presented in methodology texts.

Probability states that if we flip a fair coin in the air, it has a 50–50 or .50 chance of landing on heads. Obviously, it has the same probability of landing on tails. Yet we know that if we flip the coin ten times, we are likely to get a result different from five heads. We would not be surprised if we obtained four, six, or even two or eight heads. We would simply blame it on chance (normal sampling error) and assume that, in the long run, if we repeated the coin tossing many more times, the number of heads would eventually approximate 50 percent.

When we analyze our data, we must determine that our findings are not a plausible and expected aberration from the normal pattern of events based on sampling error. We must be reasonably certain that an apparent relationship between variables is not a fluke that occurs from time to time but has no particular importance. We need to determine if chance might be the real explanation for the apparent relationship. A hypothesis can be supported only when chance, as well as bias and other variables, can be convincingly dismissed as alternative explanations. Chance is usually the final explanation that the skeptical consumer of a research report proposes as the *real* reason why two variables appear to be related. Unlike bias or other variables, solid research designs are not enough to eliminate chance as an alternative explanation for an apparent relationship between variables. Only statistical testing can do that.

REFUTING CHANCE THROUGH STATISTICS

All statistical tests attempt to discredit chance as an explanation of an apparent relationship between variables. However, they do it in different ways. Fortunately, there are more similarities between statistical tests than there are differences. This chapter examines the ways in which all statistical tests take a common approach to the task.

In attempting to gain support for a hypothesis, we can never totally eliminate chance as the explanation for an apparent relationship. Before we can claim a relationship, however, we must be *reasonably* certain that what we observe is not a fluke occurrence that can easily be explained by a normal sampling error related to chance. We do not want to report a relationship that appears to be true but is not. At the same time, we must never be so rigid or unreasonable that we will not allow research findings to claim support for a hypothesis that is *very unlikely* to be explained by chance. If researchers became obsessed with totally eliminating chance as an alternative explanation, few, if any, research findings would ever see the light of day.

Statistical tests determine the likelihood that apparent relationships between variables have occurred as a result of chance. If it is highly unlikely that chance lies behind the apparent relationship, and if bias and other variables have been eliminated as the other two probable alternative explanations, only one reasonable explanation is left; a true relationship is *believed* to exist. If the likelihood of chance is high, we cannot claim support for a hypothesis that predicts a relationship, even if the other two alternative explanations have been eliminated. In short, we must eliminate all three alternative explanations before a hypothesis can be considered to have been supported.

Types of Relationships Stated in Hypotheses

A hypothesis that states there is a relationship between variables, but does not indicate which values of one variable will cluster with which values of the other variable, is called a *non-directional*, or *two-tailed*, hypothesis. A hypothesis stating that there is a relationship between two variables *and* specifying the way (direction) in which they are believed to be related is called a *directional*, or *one-tailed*, hypothesis.

The example we used earlier in this chapter is a directional hypothesis. It clearly predicted that a higher rate of abstinence from alcohol would be found among alcoholic clients receiving group work treatment than among alcoholic clients receiving individual treatment. A nondirectional hypothesis for our example would have stated that the treatment method used is related to the rate of abstinence; it would not have predicted which treatment method would be associated with the higher or lower rate of abstinence.

There is, of course, a third possible description of a relationship between two variables—the prediction that they will be found to be unrelated. This is called the *null hypothesis*. The null hypothesis is occasionally the same as the research hypothesis—that is, the hypothesis we set out to prove. Although research hypotheses tend most frequently to be directional, sometimes nondirectional hypotheses are utilized if existing knowledge of the subject area is limited. Seeking support for a prediction that two variables are unrelated is relatively rare, but not without utility in social work practice and research. Researchers who sought to disprove that one race is intellectually superior to another did so by finding statistical support for the null hypothesis (race and intelligence are *not* related). Similarly, practice folklore may suggest that individual treatment is more effective than group work treatment for sexual dysfunction in clients. From our observations and our reading of the relevant literature, however, we may conclude that the method of social work treatment used makes no difference. Thus, we would choose the null hypothesis as our research hypothesis: success in treatment of sexual dysfunction is *unrelated* to the method of treatment.

The Null Hypothesis and Statistics

The three forms of hypothesis (directional, nondirectional, and null) are of interest to us in our early decisions related to hypothesis construction. All three, but especially the null hypothesis, are extremely important in understanding how statistics are used in hypothesis testing.

We should remember that the null hypothesis is consistent with chance. It maintains that two variables are unrelated even if they appear to be related in a given set of data. It stresses that the normal fluctuation of chance in the form of sampling error is the likely explanation for the apparent relationship between two variables. When the null hypothesis is not used as the research hypothesis, and the hypotheses are either directional or nondirectional, the concept of the null hypothesis plays an important part in testing. To confirm that two variables *are* related, we must first verify that they are *not unrelated*. To put it another way, we must demonstrate that chance (as expressed by the null hypothesis) is a very unlikely explanation of the apparent relationship.

When a hypothesis is directional or nondirectional, a kind of phantom null hypothesis exists. The null hypothesis states that an apparent relationship is really the result of chance. It would contend that we have drawn an atypical sample and that the apparent relationship that we observed in the sample is not really true of the population from which the sample was drawn. To overcome the null hypothesis, we need to demonstrate that chance is an unlikely explanation for the apparent relationship and that a true relationship is a more plausible conclusion. Statistical tests enable us to determine when we may justifiably claim statistical support for a directional or a nondirectional hypothesis.

Type I and Type II Errors

Two types of errors can be made in interpreting research findings —Type I and Type II. A Type I error is the rejection of the null hypothesis and the conclusion that a relationship between two variables exists when, in fact, no relationship exists. A Type II error is the failure to reject the null hypothesis and the consequent failure to identify a true relationship between two variables when one exists. The two types are compared in Table 7.1.

Several factors relate to research design decisions that can increase or decrease the likelihood of committing either Type I or Type II errors. These include selecting a biased sample, utilizing data collection instruments that are invalid and/or not reliable, and failing to control for the presence and effect of other variables.

Type I and Type II errors can also result from the use of inappropriate statistical tests. If we use a statistical test that requires extremely demanding conditions that are not met, or if we employ a test that requires few conditions for its use when conditions for a more powerful test are present, either a Type I or a Type II error can occur. In the first instance, the data were treated as if they possessed qualities they really lacked; in the latter case, the opportunity for more exacting analysis was not exercised. If the appropriate statistical test is not used, a statistical relationship may emerge based on faulty assumptions about the data and their collection. Or a true relationship may remain hidden.

We can never totally eliminate the possibility of committing an error in our decision as to whether or not the null hypothesis can be rejected. In fact, if we are overly careful not to commit a Type I error (mistakenly rejecting the null hypothesis), we increase the likelihood of committing a Type II error (mistakenly failing to reject the null hypothesis). Conversely, if we are overly careful to avoid committing a Type II error, we increase the likelihood of committing a Type I error. Researchers must ultimately decide which error, Type I or Type II, is more acceptable to them, should it occur. This is an ethical decision that requires a knowledge of

Table 7.1
Type I and Type II Errors

	Our Decision	
Real World	Reject Null Hypothesis	Accept Null Hypothesis
Null hypothesis false	No error	Type II error
Null hypothesis true	Type I error	No error

social work practice and the consequences of committing one error or the other. Fortunately, as we shall indicate below, there are also statistical conventions to guide us in this decision.

In a research study the consequences of such errors are, of course, potentially grave. For example, social work practitioners, not recognizing that misuse of a statistical test or some methodological error has resulted in a Type I error, may mistakenly conclude that there is a true relationship between a particular treatment method and an increased rate of treatment success. They may adjust their treatment approaches based on this "fact." Or they may respond to other research findings in which, for some reason, a Type II error was committed and discard a treatment method that was really effective but appeared not to be related to treatment success. Type I and Type II errors can be equally destructive when we apply research findings to social work practice situations. Both can mislead us, potentially harm our clients, or result in a wasteful expenditure of limited agency resources.

Even if research studies are well designed and if we understand and apply the criteria for appropriate selection of a statistical test, there is always some possibility, no matter how "acceptably" small, of committing an error in drawing research conclusions. It always remains possible that we have happened upon that one-time-in-a-billion sample that leads us to draw an erroneous conclusion about the relationship between variables in the population from which the sample was drawn. Or we may have made some obscure methodological error that introduced bias or other variables to our research design. This remote possibility should not, however, preclude us from taking reasonable risks in interpretation of research findings and in their application to practice. This is how we make progress in becoming knowledge-based practitioners.

SUFFICIENT EVIDENCE AND SIGNIFICANCE

If we return to our example of the two different types of treatments and their possible relationship to abstinence among alcoholic clients, we can see that the 70 percent rate of abstinence for those in group work treatment versus the 65 percent rate of abstinence for those in individual treatment really means little in itself. Even if we had as many as 50 clients in each treatment group, most of us would not presume that this 5 percent (70 percent − 65 percent = 5 percent) difference would be sufficient to reject the null hypothesis. (The null hypothesis in this example would be that treatment method and outcome are unrelated.) A difference of 40 percent between the two treatment methods, however, may have left us more hopeful of statistical support for the hypothesis.

Unfortunately, in the real world, the data rarely speak out so dramatically for support or rejection of the null hypothesis. They tend to fall somewhere in between, where we need assistance in the form of statistical tests to guide us (not rule us) in a decision as to whether or not we have statistical support to reject the null hypothesis. At what point would we feel comfortable in rejecting the null hypothesis and claiming statistical support for the directional hypothesis? If, by some fortuitous event, it were possible to repeat our research study (called *replication* in research terminology) 100 or even 200 times and in each individual study the clients in group treatment had a higher rate of alcohol abstinence, we would likely be convinced that the null hypothesis could safely be rejected. Unfortunately, in social work research we hardly ever have the opportunity to repeat a study many times. Thus, we need, within a single research study, some comparable evidence of the unlikelihood that the null hypothesis is valid. At what point can we be sufficiently certain that whatever apparent relationship we find cannot reasonably be dismissed as the work of chance? Here we must rely on common sense and convention.

Over the years, most researchers have settled on the 95 percent certainty level as the point at which they are sufficiently confident to be able to reject the null hypothesis. Expressed another way, they would feel safe in concluding that two variables are related if statistical analysis suggests that there is less than a 5 percent chance that if the null hypothesis were to be rejected, a mistake would be made. That much risk of committing a Type I error is acceptable for most research studies. Statistical convention would usually declare support for a directional or nondirectional hypothesis if the possibility of making a Type I error is less than 5 percent—referred to as the .05 level of significance or .05 confidence interval level. A decision to reject the null hypothesis does not totally rule out chance as the explanation of an apparent relationship. It takes the position that chance in the form of sampling error *may* have caused two variables to appear to be related when they were not related, but the likelihood of this is sufficiently remote.

There is nothing sacred about the .05 level of significance. While it is the most widely used level of statistical significance for rejecting the null hypothesis, other levels are also used. The decision to use levels other than .05 is based on the consequences of mistakenly rejecting the null hypothesis (or failing to reject it). A more demanding proof of a relationship between variables, such as .025 or .01, might be used when there must be even less possibility that we would reject the null hypothesis in error and conclude that a relationship exists between two variables when chance is the real explanation for the apparent relationship between them. This figure provides even less likelihood that sampling error caused the apparent relationship. If utilization of the research findings might be a matter of life and death, such as in research on a new drug, an even more demanding threshold for rejection of the null hypothesis might be used—for instance, .001. The .001 significance level means that the probability of erroneously rejecting the null hypothesis is 1 out of 1000.

In research studies in which the consequences of an error in rejecting the null hypothesis are less likely to be fatal or traumatic, we might consider a .10 (a 10 percent chance of error) confidence level as acceptable. A .10 confidence level allows for twice the possibility of committing a Type I error because of chance (in the form of sampling error) than does a .05 level. Sometimes a less demanding confidence level such as a .10 can be utilized as confirmation of a relationship between two variables if the research design includes replication. While one .10 level may be viewed as insufficient support for a relationship, a pattern or a series of them may lead us to the conclusion that the null hypothesis can be rejected.

While some flexibility is allowed in selecting the threshold at which chance is reasonably eliminated as the explanation for an apparent relationship, the choice of a confidence level should not be viewed as casual. A general convention states that the .05 level of statistical significance should be used unless we develop and state a convincing rationale for the use of another level. The selection of a confidence level must also be made before data are collected. It would be unethical to change the confidence level afterward because the decision could be construed as a manipulative effort to twist the findings to support the researcher's beliefs.

STATISTICALLY SIGNIFICANT RELATIONSHIPS AND SUBSTANTIVE FINDINGS

The word *significant* is widely and loosely used in our profession. We use it rather flippantly to emphasize the importance of something, such as a social worker's "significant contribution" to the passage of a licensure bill or the role of a "significant other" in the development of a client's self-esteem. As with other words we use daily, such as *value* or *interview*, it is best to set aside the meaning of *significance* as commonly used elsewhere in order to understand its specific meaning in statistics. *Statistical significance* is the demonstration, through the use of statistical testing, that it would be safe to reject the null hypothesis and that a real relationship between variables is believed to exist. A relationship between two variables that is declared to be statistically significant is one that we are reasonably certain (95 percent, in most instances) cannot be explained away as an idiosyncrasy of chance or sampling error. In statistics, this is the only relevant meaning of the word *significant* or *significance;* we must be careful to use the terms in this sense—and only in this sense.

A statistically significant relationship between variables may or may not suggest a research finding that is really important. We must be careful to evaluate every statistically supported relationship between variables in the context of the question, "So what?!" In social work practice, every statistically significant relationship is not a substantive finding that cries out for implementation. In fact, some statistically significant relationships are judged to be trivial in the absolute sense.

An example may help to illustrate this distinction. A social work administrator has conducted a research study to determine which type of treatment approach (A or B) produces higher scores among clients on a marital adjustment inventory. The administrator demonstrates that the mean score of 53 among couples receiving Treatment A is sufficiently different from the mean score of 57 among couples receiving Treatment B. The administrator feels safe in rejecting the null hypothesis and concludes that a statistically significant relationship between type of treatment and marital adjustment has been identified. But, after consideration, the administrator concludes that the findings are not substantive; a difference of four points (57 − 53) is really quite small. It is certainly not large enough to justify sending several staff members to expensive staff development programs to learn the knowledge and skills necessary to use Treatment B. Based on the lack of what can be viewed as a substantive finding (a trivial difference of four points on the inventory), the administrator decides not to implement the findings.

The existence of a statistically significant relationship between variables can be determined by statistical testing using laws of probability. Afterward, the determination of whether a finding is substantive or not must also be made. This decision requires insight into many different aspects of the social work practice milieu.

SUMMARY

This chapter has presented a rationale of the way chance and the laws of probability are involved in the testing of research hypotheses. Statistical testing is used to eliminate chance as an explanation of apparent relationships; research designs are used to eliminate other possible explanations, such as bias and other variables. We must always employ ethics, convention, and common sense in making the determination as to whether chance has been adequately dismissed as a competing explanation for an apparent relationship between variables. The decision as to whether or not statistical support for a relationship can be claimed must always be made with reference to the decision's potential to benefit or to harm social work clients. Finally, we must decide whether a relationship between variables that has been found to be statistically significant is substantive or meaningless.

STUDY QUESTIONS

1. Before we can claim a true relationship between variables, what three competing explanations for an apparent relationship must be eliminated?
2. Which of the competing explanations does statistics most often seek to discredit?
3. What competing explanations should be controlled primarily by the design of the research?
4. What four other terms for chance are used in hypothesis testing?
5. What is the difference between a Type I and a Type II error?
6. What is the null form of a statement of a relationship between age and political party preference?
7. What is the relationship between the null hypothesis and chance in hypothesis testing?
8. Does a "statistically significant" relationship between variables mean that there is no possibility that the variables are unrelated? Explain.
9. When might we use a level other than the conventional .05 to conclude whether statistical support exists for a hypothesis?
10. Which significance level, .01 or .10, suggests a greater likelihood of a true relationship between variables?

FURTHER READING

Reid, W. J., & Smith, A. D. (1981). *Research in social work* (Ch. 10). New York: Columbia University Press.

Schuerman, J. R. (1983). *Research and evaluation in the human services* (Ch. 3). New York: Free Press.

8

SELECTING A STATISTICAL TEST

Chapter 7 described how statistical tests are used to provide support for hypothesized relationships between or among variables; statistical tests attempt to determine whether chance is an unlikely explanation for apparent relationships. This chapter continues the discussion of statistical tests and presents the conditions that influence whether a given statistical test is appropriate for the needs of a specific data analysis situation.

THE IMPORTANCE OF SELECTING AN APPROPRIATE TEST

Many research-related decisions we make have the potential to harm the credibility of a research study. The selection of a biased data collection instrument, the use of inadequate sampling methods, or the compilation of an inadequate literature review can cause us to doubt any study's findings. Additionally, the credibility of a social work research study rests heavily on the appropriateness of the statistical analysis utilized. The use of the wrong statistical test can lead to erroneous conclusions and recommendations that, in turn, call into question the findings that result from even the best of research designs. With the possible exception of sampling methods, more research studies are probably discredited on the basis of the misapplication of statistical tests than by any other phase of the research process.

Why do we sometimes choose an inappropriate statistical test when more appropriate ones are available for almost any possible situation? One major reason is the "rule of the instrument." This idea states that most of us tend to see the solution to a problem as calling for what we do best—and for that with which we are most comfortable and familiar. For example, a caseworker may tend to respond to a client's problem as requiring casework services; a group worker may see the same client as needing group work services. Or a lawyer may tend to see legal services as the solution to most problems.

Few social workers have received any extensive training in the use of statistical testing. Their knowledge is often confined to a passing familiarity with only one or two statistical tests. Facing the necessity of choosing a statistical test under typical time constraints, we may apply the "rule of the instrument," turning to an "old friend" with which we are more familiar, rather than exploring the possibility of using a more appropriate statistical test that would require additional study.

There may also be a widely held misbelief that, because statistical tests have so much in common, it makes little difference which one is utilized. This fallacy would lead us to select one that is frequently used rather than one that is less widely known. After all, aren't the hundreds of different statistical tests little more than slight variations of one another? This kind of weak logic falsely excuses us from taking the time to examine the specialized uses of the various statistical tests that are available. It leads to the misapplication and discrediting of what would otherwise be useful and needed research in our field.

THE CONSEQUENCES OF SELECTING AN INAPPROPRIATE TEST

Every statistical test has certain conditions for its appropriate use. As we will see later, some tests are more demanding than others—that is, some statistical tests require more conditions to be met for their use than others. As a general rule, those tests that require more exacting conditions should be used rather than the less demanding ones *if* the conditions for their use can be met. They are less likely to lead us into Type I or Type II errors in formulating our research conclusions (see Chapter 7).

The Concept of Power in Statistics

Not all statistical tests are equal; some are inherently better than others. The better tests are more powerful than the less powerful tests. A more powerful test allows us to draw quite specific conclusions from the data; more general conclusions evolve from the use of less powerful tests. *Power* is a concept based on mathematical computations designed to assess the likelihood of committing an error in rejecting the null hypothesis if the test is used correctly.

A more powerful test, used appropriately, will have less likelihood of leading us into a Type II error—that is, it is more likely to detect a true relationship between variables. A less powerful test, by its very nature, is more likely to result in a Type II error, even if all criteria for its use are met.

As we have suggested, the more powerful tests are generally those which require that fairly demanding conditions for their use be met. They are more complex in that they generally use all the values for all cases in their formulas (directly or indirectly), rather than the values for only some cases (for instance, extremes or typical values). You will recall from Chapter 5 that the standard deviation is preferable to the range as an indicator of dispersion (where appropriate) and from Chapter 4 that the mean is a more precise indicator of central tendency (where appropriate) than is the median or mode. Why? Both the mean and the standard deviation require computations using every value; the less precise descriptive statistics do not. The same principle applies in understanding the greater or lesser power of a statistical test used in hypothesis testing. Generally, more powerful tests are more likely to use the values from the cases in the data set. They are also more likely to take advantage of measurement of a greater precision if it is available.

Generally, we should use the most powerful test that can be justified for any given situation. Data are wasted if a less powerful test is used when criteria for a more powerful test can be met. A too powerful statistical test for the conditions that exist, however, can mislead us into drawing false conclusions from the data analysis. We can avoid the selection of an overly powerful or underpowerful test only if we understand those factors relating to the criteria that are specific to the various tests.

CONSIDERATIONS THAT INFLUENCE THE CHOICE OF A TEST

The research methods employed and the resulting data directly affect the choice of a statistical test. It is critical that we be aware of the context of our research study, the specific research strategies we employ, and the level of measurement of the data collected. A thorough understanding of our research study and an ability to specify the whats, hows, and whys *prior* to data analysis will greatly facilitate our selection of a statistical test.

It is customary to specify the statistical tests to be used before beginning data collection. However, it is not unusual to encounter problems in data collection that may change the way these data are collected and the ways in which they can be measured and analyzed. If such situations arise, it is considered ethical and, in some cases, absolutely essential to select different tests from those anticipated. Three considerations directly influence the choice of a statistical test: (1) sampling methods used, (2) nature of the research population, and (3) level of measurement for the variables.

Sampling Methods Used

Various methodological choices that we make in the research process will begin the process of eliminating some statistical tests as we conclude that they are inappropriate for hypothesis testing. The choice of a sampling method quickly narrows the list of appropriate tests we can use. In selecting the correct test, we must be able to specify answers to three sampling-related questions.

1. Were the observations independent? Did the selection of one case in any way increase or decrease the likelihood that any other case within the population would also be selected?
2. Did the sampling method draw a single sample or more than one sample? How many?
3. If more than one sample was used, were the samples independent of each other, or were they related in any way?

If we can answer these three questions, we will be able to eliminate well over half the existing statistical tests because of their inappropriateness for the particular sampling method employed. The decision regarding the specific test that is most appropriate for a given situation has been simplified by various authors who have provided decision-making models and, more recently, flow charts for this purpose. In 1956, Siegel authored a text that continues to be widely used for the selection of a statistical test for data analysis in social work research. If the reader encounters a situation that precludes the use of tests described within this text, reference to Siegel or any one of several other later texts will be helpful in identifying the test that should be used.

Nature of the Research Population

A second major consideration in selecting a statistical test is the way in which the variables that we have selected to study are distributed within the population. Some of the most powerful tests require that a normal (bell-shaped) distribution of a variable exist within the population from which our sample was randomly drawn. As discussed in Part I in this book, a positively or negatively skewed distribution usually should preclude the use of the mean as a measure of central tendency or the standard deviation as a measure of dispersion. The absence of a normal distribution of a variable within our study's research population will similarly eliminate many otherwise useful and powerful tests from consideration.

A normal distribution is rarely perfect in its symmetry. Full descriptive data on a given variable within a population may not exist; if they do, the data may only approximate a bell-shaped curve. In research situations, we often depend on value judgments to help us make decisions. For example, we use a value judgment when we decide when enough literature has been reviewed, whether we can justify a directional hypothesis, or when we select a confidence level for rejection of the null hypothesis. Likewise, we make a value judgment when we determine whether a distribution is sufficiently "normal." Generally, a variable whose values approximate a bell-shaped curve when a frequency polygon for the population is imagined will be considered sufficiently normal for the use of some relatively high-powered statistical tests.

Level of Measurement for the Variables

A third major factor to consider in the selection of a statistical test is the level of measurement for the dependent and independent variables. As explained in Chapter 1, we can categorize variables as nominal-, ordinal-, interval-, or ratio-level. The well-planned construction of data collection instruments will allow us to obtain the highest possible level of measurement for any given variable. By carelessly constructing data collection instruments, we can throw away data precision by permitting a variable that could have been considered to be measured at the interval or ratio level to be measured less accurately. We then have to treat it as if it were only a crude indicator of quantity (at the ordinal level). Similarly, the choice of a measuring instrument that yields only ordinal-level categories of measurement instead of an index that yields interval-level measurements will automatically preclude the use of all statistical tests that require interval-level variables. Thus, the decisions we make in operationalization and questionnaire construction affect our research either by narrowing or expanding the choice of statistical tests that may be appropriate for hypothesis testing.

PARAMETRIC AND NONPARAMETRIC TESTS

The three factors above, sampling methods, nature of the research population, and the level of measurement of the variables, determine the most appropriate statistical test to use. Each test has its own specific requirements that relate to each of these three factors. However, to simplify the process of selecting an appropriate test, it should be pointed out that two mutually exclusive groups of tests exist that reflect two distinct clusterings of requirements. The two types of statistical tests are parametric and nonparametric tests.

Parametric Tests

Parametric tests are more powerful than nonparametric tests. Therefore, they are more desirable if conditions for their use can be met. They are tests that require (1) a normal population distribution of the variable(s) being studied, (2) the drawing of independent samples, and (3) at least one variable being studied to be at the interval or ratio level. Generally, they also require a larger sample size than nonparametric tests. As a rule of thumb, it is helpful to remember that if the mean and the standard deviation are appropriate descriptive statistics for summarizing findings, parametric statistics *may* be appropriate for examining relationships between variables.

Nonparametric Tests

Nonparametric tests are designed for research situations in which the conditions for the use of parametric tests do not exist. They are less powerful, as a group, than parametric tests. Unlike the parametric tests, they do not require a normal distribution. Some are intended for independent samples; others are not. The number of samples and the number of cases within each sample are important factors in selecting one test from the many that exist. Most of these tests require only nominal- or ordinal-level data, but some are more demanding, requiring greater measurement precision.

Because nonparametric statistics generally are designed for the analysis of nominal- or ordinal-level data that need not be normally distributed, they are often ideally suited for social work research. As noted earlier, many of the dependent variables of common interest to social workers are not at the interval or ratio level of measurement (for example, success or failure in treatment, rehospitalization or non-rehospitalization, and so forth).

Nonparametric tests are more than just a second-best choice designed for situations in which criteria for parametric statistics cannot be met, however. They also have some distinct advantages over parametric tests and are often the *only* test appropriate for addressing some of our statistical needs. For example, a nonparametric statistic is especially useful when

1. Samples have been compiled from different populations,
2. Data measurement consists primarily of rank ordering of several item response alternatives, or
3. Very small samples (as few as six or seven) are all that are available for study.

Fortunately, the lack of power of nonparametric tests as a group can be compensated for, at least in part. In many situations, two or more nonparametric tests would be appropriate for use; one may be potentially more powerful than the other(s). However, they may have different sample size requirements. As a general rule, the test requiring the largest sample size is likely to be the most powerful. If we anticipate the need for power in testing, we can frequently increase the size of our sample(s), thereby meeting the criteria for the use of the more powerful statistical test. While a larger sample is more likely to have positive effect on power in some tests than others, it never hurts to use as large a sample size as possible, if resources are available. In some instances, this strategy can have an important effect by making a nonparametric test just about as powerful as a parametric one.

BECOMING KNOWLEDGEABLE ABOUT STATISTICAL TESTS

Because so many statistical tests are available, we can never be fully knowledgeable about all of them. In fact, probably fewer than a dozen tests are commonly used in social work research; another group occurs rarely in the literature; and a third group includes a large number of obscure tests. Furthermore, new tests are constantly being created with assistance of the computer, while others become fashionable for a time and then drop out of favor.

Chapters 9, 10, and 11 focus on the use of only three statistical tests. They are tests that have been popular for many years and promise to remain popular because of their versatility and suitability for social work research data analysis. The emphasis will be on the *understanding* of how they perform their jobs. It is the authors' assumption that an understanding of factors that influence the choice of a test, as discussed in this chapter, and of the general principles of testing explained in Chapter 7 and elaborated in Chapters 9, 10, and 11, will prepare the reader to make the critical choice of a statistical test.

SUMMARY

This chapter has emphasized the importance of the careful selection of a statistical test for data analysis. It has presented the major factors to be considered in choosing the most suitable test for a given situation. Throughout the discussion, we have observed that the appropriate selection of a statistical test is critical to the credibility of the research study and will greatly influence the likelihood that the research findings will be of use to the social work practitioner.

STUDY QUESTIONS

1. How can the use of an inappropriate statistical test harm the credibility of the research?
2. How might a researcher's use of an inappropriate test ultimately have a negative effect on services to clients?
3. How does the "rule of the instrument" sometimes lead to selection of an inappropriate statistical test?
4. What do we mean when we say that one statistical test is more "powerful" than another?
5. What factors related to sampling methods used help to determine which statistical test is appropriate?
6. What two characteristics of the data also affect which statistical test should be used?
7. How does the operationalization of a variable performed before data are even collected serve to limit or expand the researcher's options of statistical tests that can be used?
8. What three criteria must be met for a parametric test to be used?
9. Why are nonparametric tests particularly useful in many social work research projects?
10. How can we increase power when it is necessary to use nonparametric tests?

FURTHER READING

Craft, J. L. (1985). *Statistics and data analysis for social workers* (Ch. 8). Itasca, IL: F. E. Peacock.

Reid, W. J., & Smith, A. D. (1981). *Research in social work* (Ch. 10). New York: Columbia University Press.

Siegel, S. (1956). *Nonparametric statistics for the behavioral sciences* (inner covers). New York: McGraw-Hill.

9

CROSSTABULATION

No statistical analysis is better known and more frequently misused than crosstabulation—commonly referred to as *chi-square*. Its popularity derives primarily from two factors. First, most of us who have been exposed to statistics as part of our professional social work education have spent some time studying this statistical test. There has been a kind of intergenerational learning whereby social work educators (who are more familiar with it than with other analyses) tend to suggest its usage to students, who, in turn, recommend it to others. Both social work educators and former students may smugly offer to assist others in using it because it is one statistic about which they are reasonably knowledgeable.

Crosstabulation analyses appear so frequently in our professional literature that we almost expect to see them used in statistically oriented journal articles. The fact that knowledge of crosstabulation procedure is so widespread definitely facilitates communication of research findings to social work practitioners who might read fewer quantitatively oriented journal articles in which *other* statistical procedures have been used. Statistical procedures that are widely understood are advantageous when we try to communicate knowledge for social work practice. However, crosstabulation, as is true of all other statistical analyses, is designed for specific types of data and for specific research situations. The researcher or the practitioner who is unaware of the conditions for its use runs the risk of making a serious error that could ultimately have a negative impact on social work practice. Consequently, crosstabulation's popularity can also be its greatest potential danger. Faith in it, and its widespread acceptance among researchers and practitioners alike, may compound the negative consequences of its misuse.

A second reason for the popularity of crosstabulation relates directly to its conditions for use: it requires only nominal-level data. The fact that only nominal-level variables are needed makes crosstabulation especially well suited for a number of social work research situations. Crosstabulation requires only that the values for each variable represent distinct categories and a difference of kind. It should be evident by now that if relationships between ordinal- or interval-level variables are to be examined, other, more powerful tests are generally more appropriate.

Social workers are often interested in seeking relationships between such variables as treatment effectiveness (success/failure) and other nominal-level variables such as type of treatment (group/individual). It is often difficult enough to say with reasonable certainty whether client success (improvement/nonimprovement) has occurred, without having the presumption to try to determine the exact *amount* of success. Similarly, we can easily find out whether a specific piece of social legislation passes in different states. However, we would probably not presume to measure the *amount* of involvement of client advocacy groups in the various states—only whether the advocacy groups were active or not. In social work practice and research situations, many of our variables have "yes–no" or other value categories that can only be considered to be at the nominal level. Since crosstabulation is most appropriately used when the variables under study are both considered to be at the nominal level, it is a legitimate statistical test for many of our data analysis projects.

WHAT CROSSTABULATION SEEKS TO DETERMINE

As discussed in Chapter 7, all statistical tests attempt to refute chance as an explanation for an apparent relationship between two or more variables. With crosstabulation, the specter of chance has certain characteristics. If, for example, we were seeking to find a relationship between a dependent variable such as client treatment success (success/failure) and an independent variable such as type of treatment (group/individual) in a follow-up evaluation of an alcoholism counseling program, chance would play the skeptic in a distinct way. The null hypothesis states that there is no relationship between whether clients abstained from alcohol for a given time (success) or not (failure) and whether they received group treatment or individual treatment. It may occasionally *seem* as if those clients who abstained tended to receive group treatment, and those clients who didn't abstain tended to receive individual treatment, or vice versa. However, according to the null hypothesis, this apparent relationship between the two variables may be best explained by the normal variations in characteristics that occur in using relatively small samples of people. It is only the result of normal sampling error. As discussed in Chapter 7, chance would contend that no *real* relationship exists between the two variables within the population.

We could legitimately claim a true relationship between the two variables only if we could demonstrate that the apparent relationship between them is so unlikely to occur just on the basis of chance, that any reasonable person would dismiss chance (and, of course, bias and other variables) as the likely explanation. Crosstabulation attempts to determine if there is a true relationship between two variables by examining whether specific values of one variable tend to be associated with specific values of the other variable to a greater degree than is likely to result from the effects of sampling error. When using crosstabulation, we are not so ambitious as to suggest that one variable may *cause* the variation in the other. We can only state, at best, that a pattern of clustering may exist. Crosstabulation is used when we wish to know whether this pattern is strong and consistent enough to claim that chance is an inadequate explanation of the pattern or apparent relationship.

Crosstabulation analysis is one of the simplest ways to determine if a true relationship exists between two variables. The example that follows illustrates how crosstabulation is used in examining the relative effectiveness of group treatment versus individual treatment with clients who were treated for alcoholism at a particular treatment center. To do this, a group of clients who have received group treatment are directly compared with a group of clients who have received individual treatment. The specific crosstabulation techniques presented in this chapter have been adapted and modified from Schuerman (1981).

THE LOGIC OF CROSSTABULATION

To understand crosstabulation procedures, it helps to begin with a table that is in a format like Table 9.1 or Table 9.2. The table has many names. It has been referred to as a crosstabulation, chi-square, crosstab, crossbreak, or contingency table. We will refer to it as a crosstabulation table. In the far right-hand column of Table 9.1 and Table 9.2, the totals (frequencies) for each row are entered. Likewise, the totals for each column are entered in the bottom line. These row and column totals are called marginal totals, or *marginals*. They indicate the total number of cases that were observed to possess a given value for one of the variables—that is, group treatment, individual treatment, success, or failure. The grand total number of cases (N) in the table is entered in the bottom right-hand corner. Note that the row totals added together equal the grand total, as will the column totals added together.

Table 9.1
Type of Treatment by Client Success

Type of Treatment	Success? Yes	No	Totals
Group Treatment	a	b	$a + b$
Individual Treatment	c	d	$c + d$
Totals	$a + c$	$b + d$	N

Source: Adapted and modified from Schuerman, J. R. (1981). Bivariate analysis: Crosstabulation. In R. M. Grinnell, Jr. (Ed.), *Social work research and evaluation* (p. 462). Itasca, IL: F. E. Peacock.

As can be seen, Table 9.1 contains two dichotomous (two-category) variables, type of treatment and client success. That is, clients vary as to what types of treatment they received (independent variable), *and* they vary as to whether they had successful outcomes (dependent variable). It is, of course, possible to have variables with more than two categories. The crosstabulation table would then have more rows and columns and, thus, more cells. Table 9.1 identifies the various cells in our example as *a*, *b*, *c*, and *d* for reference purposes.

The categories of the variables in crosstabulation tables can be assembled in any order because they are nominal; no rank ordering or any other quantitative difference is implied. It is mathematically possible to use crosstabulation analysis with ordinal-, interval-, or ratio-level variables. However, using crosstabulation with ordinal- or interval-level variables would not take full advantage of the precision of measurement these variables are capable of providing. It would treat their different values as if they reflect a qualitative, not a quantitative, difference in the variable.

Crosstabulations usually present frequencies for one independent variable and one dependent variable. Throughout this chapter, for all tables, the dependent variable will be displayed in the columns, and the independent variable will be displayed in the rows. This is not an established convention, however, and some researchers do it the other way around. Besides, in a given research study crosstabulation is "blind" to which variable is dependent and which is independent when computations are performed; it merely examines association between the variables. In some situations neither variable is clearly independent or dependent. They are just two variables whose relationship we want to study. Chi-square is also appropriate for this type of situation.

Observed Frequencies

Table 9.2 presents the actual, or observed, results of our hypothetical study involving the two treatment methods. The data in the four cells of Table 9.2 are the actual number of clients observed who possessed each combination of values for the two variables. We can observe that there was a total of 100 clients (N), of whom 60 received group treatment ($a + b$), and 40 received individual treatment ($c + d$). Fifty-five had a successful outcome, while 45 had an unsuccessful outcome. Additionally, of the 60 in group treatment, 40 clients had a successful outcome (cell a), and 20 had an unsuccessful outcome (cell b). Among clients seen individually, 15 were considered a success (cell c), and 25 were not (cell d).

In our example, we need to compare the clients who received group treatment with those who received individual treatment in regard to their respective outcomes. Such a comparison could not be easily observed in Table 9.2, as the two types of treatment groups have widely differing numbers of clients in them (60 and 40). We obviously cannot simply compare the 40 clients who had successful outcomes with group treatment (cell a) directly with the 15 clients who had successful outcomes with individual treatment (cell c) and conclude that group treatment is a better treatment method simply because 40 is larger than 15.

Despite the difference in the number of cases in the two groups, it is possible to make tentative comparisons between the two types of treatment by computing percentages. For example, we can find what percentage 40 clients is of 60 clients, and what percentage 15 clients is of 40 clients. Table 9.3 is a percentage table for the observed data in Table 9.2. It indicates that 66.7 percent of those clients who received group treatment had successful outcomes, compared with 37.5 percent of those clients who received individual treatment. The variables of type of treatment received and client success *may* therefore be related. If the percentages (cell a and cell c) were exactly the same, the two variables would clearly *not* be related. Yet at this point it is difficult to know whether the apparent relationship is anything more than a fluctuation of chance.

Table 9.2
Observed Frequencies for Type of Treatment by Client Success

Type of Treatment	Success? Yes	No	Totals
Group Treatment	40	20	60
Individual Treatment	15	25	40
Totals	55	45	100

Source: Adapted and modified from Schuerman, J. R. (1981). Bivariate analysis: Crosstabulation. In R. M. Grinnell, Jr. (Ed.), *Social work research and evaluation* (p. 463). Itasca, IL: F. E. Peacock.

Table 9.3
Percentages of Clients for Type of Treatment by Client Success (from Table 9.2)

Type of Treatment	Success? Yes	No	Totals
Group Treatment	66.7	33.3	100.0
Individual Treatment	37.5	62.5	100.0

Group Treatment = Cell *a*: 40/60 = 66.7%
Cell *b*: 20/60 = 33.3%
100.0%

Individual Treatment = Cell *c*: 15/40 = 37.5%
Cell *d*: 25/40 = 62.5%
100.0%

Source: Adapted and modified from Schuerman, J. R. (1981). Bivariate analysis: Crosstabulation. In R. M. Grinnell, Jr. (Ed.), *Social work research and evaluation* (p. 464). Itasca, IL: F. E. Peacock.

Although the two variables appear to be somewhat related, it could be asserted that they are "not very much related." The argument would imply that a 29.2 percent difference (66.7 percent − 37.5 percent = 29.2 percent) is not very great and probably just the result of sampling error. But is it? Much of statistical reasoning is concerned with helping us to decide *how much* of a difference is needed to rule out chance as a possible explanation of an apparent relationship between variables.

Expected Frequencies

How great a difference in percentages is large enough to be improbable? We can answer this question by focusing on how much the observed frequencies differ from those frequencies we would expect to occur most frequently if the null hypothesis were true—that is, the expected frequencies.

Let us return to Table 9.2 and focus only on the marginals. Of the total 100 clients, 55, or 55 percent, had successful outcomes. If type of treatment is not related to client success, we would expect about 55 percent of the clients in *both* treatment groups to have successful outcomes. Although the results from any particular sample would probably not turn out *exactly* that way very often, if we were to take a large number of samples from a population in which the null hypothesis were true (the variables really are unrelated) and found the "average result" for all those samples, the proportions' average would approximate 55 percent.

We can construct a table of the expected frequencies under the null hypothesis, such as Table 9.4. The way to arrive at this table is to take each column total for a cell, multiply it by the respective row total for that cell, and divide by the grand total (N). We can express this as a formula.

$$E = \frac{(R)(C)}{(N)}$$

Where E = Expected frequency in a particular cell
R = Total number in that cell's row
C = Total number in that cell's column
N = Total number of cases

Substituting values for letters, we get

$$\text{Cell } a\text{: } E = \frac{(60)\ (55)}{100} = 33$$

$$\text{Cell } b\text{: } E = \frac{(60)\ (45)}{100} = 27$$

$$\text{Cell } c\text{: } E = \frac{(40)\ (55)}{100} = 22$$

$$\text{Cell } d\text{: } E = \frac{(40)\ (45)}{100} = \underline{18}$$

Total of expected frequencies = 100

Observed Minus Expected Frequencies

The table of observed frequencies is now compared with the table of expected frequencies. This means that we closely examine the

Table 9.4
Expected Frequencies and (Percentages) for Type of Treatment by Client Success

	Success?		
Type of Treatment	Yes	No	Totals
Group Treatment	33 (55%)	27 (45%)	60 (100%)
Individual Treatment	22 (55%)	18 (45%)	40 (100%)
Totals	55	45	

Source: Adapted and modified from Schuerman, J. R. (1981). Bivariate analysis: Crosstabulation. In R. M. Grinnell, Jr. (Ed.), *Social work research and evaluation* (p. 468). Itasca, IL: F. E. Peacock.

differences between the observed frequencies (Table 9.2) and the expected frequencies (Table 9.4) for each cell. Table 9.5 presents the arithmetic differences between the observed frequencies and the expected frequencies in our example.

The Chi-Square Statistic

Some kind of summary of the differences presented in Table 9.5 is needed. Simply adding up the differences for all the cells will not work because the sum will *always* be zero. A better summary is provided by squaring the difference in each cell, dividing that square by the expected value for the cell, and adding the results for all the cells in the table. The resulting number is called *chi-square value*, represented by the lower-case Greek letter *chi* with a squared sign added to it. We can express this as a formula.

$$\chi^2 = \Sigma \frac{(O - E)^2}{E}$$

Where χ^2 = Chi-square value
O = Observed frequency
E = Expected frequency
Σ = Sum of (for all cells)

Substituting values for letters, we get

$$\begin{array}{lccccccc} & \text{Cell } a & + & \text{Cell } b & + & \text{Cell } c & + & \text{Cell } d \\ \chi^2 = & (40-33)^2 & + & (20-27)^2 & + & (15-22)^2 & + & (25-18)^2 \\ = & \frac{(+7)^2}{33} & + & \frac{(-7)^2}{27} & + & \frac{(-7)^2}{22} & + & \frac{(+7)^2}{18} \\ = & \frac{49}{33} & + & \frac{49}{27} & + & \frac{49}{22} & + & \frac{49}{18} \\ = & 1.5 & + & 1.8 & + & 2.2 & + & 2.7 \\ = & \multicolumn{7}{l}{8.2 \text{ (Chi-square value)}} \end{array}$$

If there are only four cells, as is the case in our example, we should also subtract .5 from the difference between the observed and expected frequencies for each cell before squaring it (referred to as the Yates Correction Factor). But for the sake of simplicity, and to demonstrate use of the customary formula, our example did not do this.

Table 9.5
Differences Between Observed and Expected Frequencies for Type of Treatment by Client Success (from Tables 9.2 and 9.4)

Cells	Observed (Table 9.2)	−	Expected (Table 9.4)	=	Difference (Table 9.5)
Cell *a*	40	−	33	=	+7
Cell *b*	20	−	27	=	−7
Cell *c*	15	−	22	=	−7
Cell *d*	25	−	18	=	+7
Totals	100	−	100	=	0

Type of Treatment	Success? Yes	No	Totals
Group Treatment	+7	−7	0
Individual Treatment	−7	+7	0
Totals	0	0	0

Source: Adapted and modified from Schuerman, J.R. (1981). Bivariate analysis: Crosstabulation. In R.M. Grinnell, Jr. (Ed.), *Social work research and evaluation* (p. 469). Itasca, IL: F.E. Peacock.

Degrees of Freedom

Before we can use a chi-square table to determine whether a statistically significant association exists between our two variables, we need to understand the concept of degrees of freedom. The likelihood of obtaining a large chi-square value is affected by the size of the crosstabulation table on which it is computed. Size here refers to the number of rows and columns (that is, number of cells) in the table. The larger the table, the more likely it is to have a large chi-square value. This should be evident from the fact that a chi-square value is the sum of figures derived from each of its cells. Thus the more cells in a table, the more figures there are to be added and the higher the chi-square value is likely to be.

Each chi-square value must be evaluated in relation to the size of the table, expressed in terms of its degrees of freedom. The degrees of freedom for any crosstabulation are equal to the number of rows minus one, times the number of columns minus one. We can write this as a formula.

$$df = (r - 1)(c - 1)$$

Where df = Degrees of freedom
r = Number of rows
c = Number of columns

Substituting values for letters in our example, we get

$$df = (2 - 1)(2 - 1)$$
$$= (1)(1)$$
$$= 1 \text{ (Degree of freedom)}$$

Thus, Table 9.2 has one degree of freedom, as will all two-by-two tables.

Determining Probability

To determine whether or not a statistically significant association between variables is suggested by the chi-square value for a given crosstabulation, we first find the row in Table 9.6 that corresponds to the degrees of freedom for our chi-square value. The six values in each of the rows in Table 9.6 are chi-square values that have probabilities indicated at the top of their respective columns. We read across to find where our chi-square value would fall within this row. If the exact number does not appear, we move to the number in the row which is to the *left* of where our chi-square value would fall. We then go to the heading (top) of the column in which that number appears to find the probability associated with it. If, for example, we set our probability level at .05, we would know that if we were to reject the null hypothesis, the statistical probability of making a Type I error would be less than 5 times out of 100.

For our example, the obtained chi-square value is 8.2, with one degree of freedom. We take our calculated chi-square value of 8.2 and find the two values in the first row in Table 9.6 that it would fall between. Our chi-square value of 8.2 would be located between the two values 6.64 and 10.83. Thus, if our hypothesis was directional (referred to as "one-tailed" in the table), such as "clients who received group work treatment would have a statistically significant higher success rate than clients who received individual treatment," we could state that, if we were to reject the null hypothesis, we would have only a .005 chance of making a Type I error (only 5 times out of 1000). In short, our directional hypothesis would be supported because .005 is much smaller than the conventional .05. On the other hand, if our hypothesis had been nondirectional (referred to as "two-tailed" in the table), we would still be able to claim support for the hypothesis because the probability would be less than .01, still smaller than the conventional .05.

Remember that it is the value to the *left* of our calculated chi-square value that we use to determine the correct probability level. For example, we would need to have a chi-square value of *at least* 2.71, with one degree of freedom, for a directional hypothesis to be supported at the customary .05 significance level.

Presentation of Results of Crosstabulation Analysis

The actual presentation of our findings using crosstabulation is quite simple. First, we display the crosstabulation table taken directly from the observed frequencies. We then place the chi-square value (χ^2), the degrees of freedom (*df*), and the probability of chance (*p*) associated with our χ^2 value at the bottom of the table. These three pieces of information would then be printed as

$$\chi^2 = 8.2,\ df = 1,\ p < .005$$

Tables 9.7, 9.8, 9.11, and 9.12 are examples of presentations of the results of crosstabulation analysis.

WHEN NOT TO USE CROSSTABULATION

Chi-square analysis can be very helpful to us. However, it also can be misleading. The probabilities it generates are not very accurate when there are small expected frequencies in some of a table's cells. Two situations occur in which crosstabulation procedures should definitely not be used.

1. When, in a two-by-two (four cells) table, one or more cells has an expected value of less than 5.
2. When, in a larger than two-by-two table, more than 20 percent of the cells have expected values of less than 5.

A handy check on whether there is a problem with small expected values in any crosstabulation table can be performed by locating the cell with the smallest expected value. To do this, locate the row with the smallest total and the column with the smallest total. The cell with the smallest expected value is at the intersection of that row and column. Then the cell's expected value is determined with the formula $(R)\ (C)\ /\ (N)$. If the expected frequency is 5 or more, it is safe to use crosstabulation analysis. If not, it may be necessary to combine certain adjoining cells (called "collapsing") so that the criteria for use of chi-square can be met,

Table 9.6
Critical Values of Chi-square

	Level of Significance for a One-Tailed Test					
	.10	.05	.025	.01	.005	.0005
	Level of Significance for a Two-Tailed Test					
df	.20	.10	.05	.02	.01	.001
1	1.64	2.71	3.84	5.41	6.64	10.83
2	3.22	4.60	5.99	7.82	9.21	13.82
3	4.64	6.25	7.82	9.84	11.34	16.27
4	5.99	7.78	9.49	11.67	13.28	18.46
5	7.29	9.24	11.07	13.39	15.09	20.52
6	8.56	10.64	12.59	15.03	16.81	22.46
7	9.80	12.02	14.07	16.62	18.48	24.32
8	11.03	13.36	15.51	18.17	20.09	26.12
9	12.24	14.68	16.92	19.68	21.67	27.88
10	13.44	15.99	18.31	21.16	23.21	29.59
11	14.63	17.28	19.68	22.62	24.72	31.26
12	15.81	18.55	21.03	24.05	26.22	32.91
13	16.98	19.81	22.36	25.47	27.69	34.53
14	18.15	21.06	23.68	26.87	29.14	36.12
15	19.31	22.31	25.00	28.26	30.58	37.70
16	20.46	23.54	26.30	29.63	32.00	39.29
17	21.62	24.77	27.59	31.00	33.41	40.75
18	22.76	25.99	28.87	32.35	34.80	42.31
19	23.90	27.20	30.14	33.69	36.19	43.82
20	25.04	28.41	31.41	35.02	37.57	45.32

The obtained value of χ^2 is significant if it is greater than or equal to the value listed in the table.

Source: From Table IV of Ronald A. Fisher and Frank Yates, *Statistical Tables for Biological, Agricultural and Medical Research*, published by Longman Group, Ltd., London (previously published by Oliver and Boyd, Ltd., Edinburgh) and by permission of the authors and publishers.

or to use an alternative statistical test (see Chapter 12). Of course, a two-by-two table cannot be collapsed.

Sample Size

In general, the larger the sample, the greater the chance of acquiring statistical support to reject the null hypothesis. The larger the sample size, the greater the power of the test. (This is true of all statistical tests.) In fact, with a very large sample, it is extremely likely that the null hypothesis will be rejected even if the absolute

Table 9.6
(Continued)

	Level of Significance for a One-Tailed Test					
	.10	.05	.025	.01	.005	.0005
	Level of Significance for a Two-Tailed Test					
df	.20	.10	.05	.02	.01	.001
21	26.17	29.62	32.67	36.34	38.93	46.80
22	27.30	30.81	33.92	37.66	40.29	48.27
23	28.43	32.01	35.17	38.97	41.64	49.73
24	29.55	33.20	36.42	40.27	42.98	51.18
25	30.68	34.38	37.65	41.57	44.31	52.62
26	31.80	35.56	38.88	42.86	45.64	54.05
27	32.91	36.74	40.11	44.14	46.96	55.48
28	34.03	37.92	41.34	45.42	48.28	56.89
29	35.14	39.09	42.69	46.69	49.59	58.30
30	36.25	40.26	43.77	47.96	50.89	59.70
32	38.47	42.59	46.19	50.49	53.49	62.49
34	40.68	44.90	48.60	53.00	56.06	65.25
36	42.88	47.21	51.00	55.49	58.62	67.99
38	45.08	49.51	53.38	57.97	61.16	70.70
40	47.27	51.81	55.76	60.44	63.69	73.40
44	51.64	56.37	60.48	65.34	68.71	78.75
48	55.99	60.91	65.17	70.20	73.68	84.04
52	60.33	65.42	69.83	75.02	78.62	89.27
56	64.66	69.92	74.47	79.82	83.51	94.46
60	68.97	74.40	79.08	84.58	88.38	99.61

difference in the expected and observed frequencies in each cell is fairly small. When people interpret a crosstabulation table, they often are misled by the chi-square statistic itself and its resulting probability level, unless they look carefully at the sample size (N). We must always keep in mind that a chi-square value, and hence its probability level, is *directly* related to the sample size on which it is calculated.

The previous statement may seem hard to understand, but a crosstabulation table can present a statistically significant relationship between two variables (via the chi-square statistic), and—believe it or not—it can also portray a statistically significant *weak* relationship. In short, we can almost always get a statistically significant chi-square value—regardless of the real magnitude of the relationship between two variables—if the sample is large enough. Thus, we must always look at the meaningfulness or strength of the relationship—not just the statistical significance level (p) of the chi-square value. This relates to our discussion in Chapter 7 in which we distinguished between (1) statistically significant relationships between or among variables and (2) substantive findings.

A continuation of our example will make our discussion here clearer. Let us suppose that in another study, 200 clients had received treatment in our alcoholic treatment program. The actual results of our study might have looked like those in Table 9.7. As can be seen from Table 9.7, p would be greater than .20 only if the direction of the relationship had not been predicted and greater than .10 if we had predicted the direction (see Table 9.6). Either way, we would lack sufficient statistical support at the .05 level to be able to reject the null hypothesis.

Now let's suppose that we had, not 200 clients, as in Table 9.7, but 10 times more—2000! And the proportion of the 2000 clients in all the cells is exactly the same as those of our smaller sample in Table 9.7. The results are displayed in Table 9.8.

A close look at Table 9.7 and Table 9.8 will reveal that the observed frequencies in both tables are exactly proportional to one another, but the differences in their chi-square values and probability levels are quite dramatic. The observed frequencies in Table 9.7 are not statistically significant, while the observed frequencies in Table 9.8 are statistically significant (at the .01 level for a two-tailed hypothesis and at the .005 level for a one-tailed hypothesis). If we had used 20,000 clients, our chi-square value would be 67.2; if we had 200,000 clients, it would be 672, and so on. However, the strength of the association is identical in Tables 9.7 and 9.8. The only thing that is different is the number of cases that we used to calculate the two chi-square values.

Table 9.7
Observed Frequencies and Percentages for
Type of Treatment by Client Success (N = 200)

	Success?					
	Yes		No		Totals	
Type of Treatment	Number	Percent	Number	Percent	Number	Percent
Group Treatment	30	60.0	20	40.0	50	100
Individual Treatment	80	53.3	70	46.7	150	100
Totals	110		90		200	

χ^2 = .672, df = 1, p > .20 (direction not predicted)

Table 9.8
Observed Frequencies and Percentages for
Type of Treatment by Client Success ($N = 2000$)

	Success?					
	Yes		No		Totals	
Type of Treatment	Number	Percent	Number	Percent	Number	Percent
Group Treatment	300	60.0	200	40.0	500	100
Individual Treatment	800	53.3	700	46.7	1500	100
Totals	1100		900		2000	

$\chi^2 = 6.72$, $df = 1$, $p < .01$ (direction not predicted)

CROSSTABULATIONS WITH THREE OR MORE VARIABLES

Frequently we are focusing primarily on the relationship between two variables. However, we may be concerned that a third variable might "explain" the apparent relationship in some way. In the example we have been using, we are dealing primarily with the relationship between the two variables, type of treatment and client success. It is possible, though, that a third variable, level of client motivation before entering treatment, may not have been methodologically controlled and might explain the apparent relationship between the dependent and independent variables. We will need to control for it to get a better picture of the true relationship between type of treatment and treatment success. The third variable, client motivation, is said to be a control variable.

One way to explore the effect of a third variable is to divide our clients into all the categories of the third variable and examine the relationship between the two main variables, controlling for the third variable. In our example, we could divide our sample into two subcategories, high motivation for treatment and low motivation for treatment. We would then construct two separate tables to look at the relationship between the two variables, type of treatment and client success. The results might come out as in Table 9.9 (high motivation for treatment) and Table 9.10 (low motivation for treatment). The relationship between type of treatment and client outcome has nearly disappeared, as we can see by examining the differences between observed and expected frequencies in the respective cells (they are nearly zero). Thus, controlling for the clients' motivation for treatment has caused our initial apparent relationship nearly to disappear. It is likely that the apparent relationship between the dependent and independent variables was not a real one.

Table 9.9
Observed Frequencies and Percentages for Type of Treatment for Clients Who Had a High Motivational Level for Treatment (N = 70)

	Success?					
	Yes		No		Totals	
Type of Treatment	Number	Percent	Number	Percent	Number	Percent
Group Treatment	21	52.5	19	47.5	40	100
Individual Treatment	16	53.3	14	46.7	30	100
Totals	37		33		70	

Source: Adapted and modified from Schuerman, J. R. (1981). Bivariate analysis: Crosstabulation. In R. M. Grinnell, Jr. (Ed.), *Social work research and evaluation* (p. 478). Itasca, IL: F. E. Peacock.

The original relationship will not always disappear when we control for a third variable, of course. It may remain essentially the same among all the values of the third variable. In such cases, we would conclude that the third variable probably does not play a role in explaining the original relationship. The relationship may also be decreased but may not disappear. In these cases, the third variable may explain part, but not all, of the original relationship. The relationship may also increase when the third variable is controlled. In such instances, the third variable is probably a suppressor variable (also called an obscuring variable) that has been hiding the real degree of association between the dependent and independent variables.

Still another result sometimes occurs when a third variable is introduced. The relationship between the two primary variables may be different among the different categories of the control variable. Although this is not a simple finding, it is often an important one. It is usually not possible to summarize the results easily;

Table 9.10
Observed Frequencies and Percentages for Type of Treatment for Clients Who Had a Low Motivational Level for Treatment (N = 30)

	Success?					
	Yes		No		Totals	
Type of Treatment	Number	Percent	Number	Percent	Number	Percent
Group Treatment	11	55	9	45	20	100
Individual Treatment	6	60	4	40	10	100
Totals	17		13		30	

Source: Adapted and modified from Schuerman, J. R. (1981). Bivariate analysis: Crosstabulation. In R. M. Grinnell, Jr. (Ed.), *Social work research and evaluation* (p. 478). Itasca, IL: F. E. Peacock.

rather, the primary relationship has to be described for each category of the control variable. The third variable is said to further specify the relationship between the first two variables and is called a specifying variable.

MICRO PRACTICE EXAMPLE

Impetus for the Study

Joan is a social worker performing readmission intake interviews with patients from a state in-patient hospital. She observed that a large number of patients being readmitted to the hospital had been previously discharged to live with their relatives. Knowing that her social work colleagues doing discharge planning made frequent use of boarding homes for discharged patients, she wondered why she was seeing very few readmissions among those patients who were discharged to boarding homes. She wondered if there might not be a relationship between patients being readmitted to the hospital and the place to which they had been discharged (boarding home/relatives).

The Hypothesis to Be Tested

Joan read all the literature on the topic that was available to her. Based on a general consensus among other social work practitioners, previous research findings, and her own subjective feelings and personal observations, she set out to design and implement a small-scale research study that would gather data to test her directional hypothesis.

Patients discharged to boarding homes will have a statistically significant lower rate of readmission than those patients discharged to relatives.

Overview of Methodology

Joan devised a simple research strategy to test her directional hypothesis. She gained permission from her supervisors to select a 10 percent random sample of all the patient files from patients discharged during the last 18 months. Using a standardized data collection instrument that she constructed, she gathered data on a wide variety of demographic variables on the 148 patients (10 percent of 1480 patients = 148 patients) who were discharged to boarding homes and the 250 patients (10 percent of 2500 patients = 250 patients) who were discharged to relatives. Her total sample was 398 patients (148 + 250 = 398). The dependent variable in her hypothesis was the admission status of the patients (readmitted/not readmitted). The independent variable was the patients' discharge status (to boarding homes/relatives).

Findings

Table 9.11 presents Joan's findings using crosstabulation procedures as presented in this chapter.

Interpreting and Drawing Conclusions

What had Joan learned from testing her directional hypothesis using crosstabulation? From her general knowledge of hypothesis testing, she knew that $p < .005$ was pretty impressive. It meant to her that the differences between the observed and expected frequencies were large. She also knew that if she rejected the null hypothesis based on her analysis, she would be wrong less than 5 times out of 1000. She was able to reject the null hypothesis and conclude that there was a statistically significant relationship between the two variables. Consequently, she had statistical support for her directional hypothesis.

Joan also knew that crosstabulation analysis entails looking not only at the issue of statistical significance but at the question of whether the relationship between the two variables was in the hypothesized direction. Like some other statistical tests that we will discuss, crosstabulation disregards the predicted direction of the hypothesis. Since crosstabulation analysis is concerned primarily with the *differences* between the observed and expected frequencies for all the cells, it will respond the same to relatively large or small observed frequencies for each cell regardless of what was predicted. We must remember that a difference is only a difference, whether it suggests smaller numbers than predicted or

Table 9.11
Readmission to Hospital by Discharge Status

Discharge Status	Readmission? Yes	No	Totals
Boarding Home	25	123	148
Relatives	71	179	250
Totals	96	302	398

$\chi^2 = 7.2$, $df = 1$, $p < .005$ (using Yates Correction Factor)

larger ones. A large difference between the observed and expected frequencies in a cell (*in either direction*) contributes a great deal to increasing a chi-square's value, which in turn increases the likelihood that the null hypothesis will be rejected. Either by looking for the cells where relatively large observed frequencies occur or by examining percentages, we must determine if the association is in the predicted direction.

Using Table 9.11, Joan was able to determine that roughly 17 percent (25 of 148) of patients discharged to boarding homes had been readmitted to the hospital, compared with 28 percent (71 of 250) of those discharged to relatives. These two percentages, 17 and 28, were consistent with the direction of her hypothesis; patients discharged to boarding homes were less likely to be readmitted than patients discharged to relatives.

Before Joan drew any conclusions about the "meaning" of the statistical significance between the two variables, she knew that she must acknowledge the effects of the research methodology she used in interpreting her findings. She had used a standardized and structured data collection instrument. However, the validity and reliability of the data in the patient records might be a problem, as well as other factors relating to bias. Because of the lack of an experimental design, the list of other variables that might have affected readmission soon became long. They included patient diagnosis, length of first hospitalization, availability of aftercare services, patients' use of medication, and myriad other factors that she had no reason to believe were equally represented in the two groups (boarding home/relatives) of patients. The possible confounding effects of the interaction of several of these variables on readmission was even more mind-boggling for Joan to consider.

So what did her findings really tell her about the hypothesis? The goal of crosstabulation procedures is to acquire evidence for or against the existence of a relationship between two variables; cause–effect knowledge was not a possibility from the beginning, based partly on the absence of an experimental design and partly on the limits of the crosstabulation analysis itself. What Joan learned was that, for whatever reasons, patients discharged to boarding homes from her particular hospital were not as likely to be readmitted as those discharged to relatives.

Joan did not limit her crosstabulation analysis just to the relationship between the independent and dependent variables. She also gathered data on patient diagnosis and length of first hospitalization. She could examine the relationship between these other variables and the dependent variable as well, using more complex crosstabulation analyses or other, more appropriate statistical tests. The patient records might have yielded insights into additional variables that went into the decision as to whether to live with relatives or to live in boarding homes; these data could be used to temper the results of her analysis and to shed more light on the statistical findings.

Relating the Findings to Practice

Given all the limitations that tempered the interpretation of Joan's findings, it might seem that, on the surface, her findings are virtually worthless. An association is a relatively weak relationship by definition; the likelihood of the existence of many other variables that might affect the dependent variable would seem to discount the social work practice utility of her research findings even further. Yet, despite a less than perfect research design and the use of the relatively low-powered crosstabulation analysis, several possibly valuable practice implications emerge.

The contributions of Joan's findings to our professional body of knowledge are limited but, nevertheless, present. Conditions relating to admission, treatment discharge, and readmission at Joan's hospital may differ somewhat from those in other, similar settings, but, on the whole, there would probably be more similarities than differences. We may be able to generalize her findings beyond her particular hospital. One of the major benefits of identifying a relationship between two variables is that it can improve our ability to predict the future. Knowing even tentatively that patients discharged to boarding homes are less likely to be readmitted than those patients discharged to relatives could be a valuable insight for social workers doing discharge planning with their clients in other in-patient state hospitals.

A few implications could be of immediate use to Joan based on her findings in Table 9.11. She began to ask herself the following questions.

1. Should I try to find boarding home placements for more of my clients?
2. Should I endeavor as a professional social worker to work toward the creation of more boarding home facilities?
3. Should I consider patients who choose to return to relatives as "at risk" for readmission?
4. Should I endeavor to provide additional sources of support for patients going to live with relatives in order to reduce the likelihood of their being readmitted?

These applications of the research findings are still only questions. None of them indicate that social work practitioners should be prepared to make drastic modifications in their service delivery methods without careful consideration and, what is more important, evidence of further research findings.

Note that the four questions also reflect quite different levels of commitment to a belief in the research findings. Question 4 would entail an activity that goes little beyond what is just good social work practice for a discharge planner. It is, however, reflective of the setting of modified practice priorities (greater time allocated to patients discharged to relatives) based on Joan's findings. Question 2 would require a greater commitment of effort and practice resources on the part of the social worker and the community; it would probably not occur unless Joan was convinced of the validity of her findings and their generalizability beyond her small sample.

Many other practice implications might be drawn from the data presented in Table 9.11. Some may reflect very humble and tentative shifts in social work practice that may be designed to improve services.

Caution is advised when interpreting all research findings. This is because radical changes in the delivery of social work services may negatively affect the lives of our clients. Practice applications derived from crosstabulation findings can be risky. Crosstabulations are sometimes best used to tentatively identify associations between variables and to formulate critical questions that can subsequently be answered through more high-powered statistical analysis.

MACRO PRACTICE EXAMPLE

Impetus for the Study

Jim is a social worker employed by a legislative committee. He is attempting to assist in the passage of an increased state sales tax. The proposed tax increase will provide additional revenues for public schools. As part of his job, he recently began gathering general personal data on state legislators in order to gain insight as to why they might vote for or against the proposed tax bill.

After he had examined some available data and hearsay on about 30 legislators, it seemed to him that legislators who favored the bill tended to have children who currently attended public schools; those legislators who were on record as not supporting the bill tended not to have children currently in public schools.

Jim wondered whether he could find statistical support for a relationship between the dependent variable (support/nonsupport for the bill) and the independent variable (use of public schools/no use of public schools).

The Hypothesis to Be Tested

After discussion with committee members and a review of the literature available on legislators' voting patterns on various tax issues, Jim concluded that he could justify formulation of a directional hypothesis.

Legislators who currently have children attending public schools will more likely support a bill that will increase taxes to generate revenue for public schools than will legislators who do not have children currently attending public schools.

Overview of Methodology

Jim continued to gather data on the state's legislators but made a special effort to learn about and systematically record data on his dependent and independent variables. He identified 160 legislators who had publicly stated support for or opposition to the tax bill. Of these, he obtained sufficient current biographical data on 125 (78 percent) of them and was able to conclude with reasonable certainty whether or not they were currently sending their children to public schools.

Findings

Table 9.12 presents Jim's findings using crosstabulation procedures as presented in this chapter.

Table 9.12
Legislators' Support for Tax Bill by Whether They Use Public Schools

Use Public Schools?	Support for Bill? Yes	No	Totals
Yes	39	36	75
No	21	29	50
Totals	60	65	125

$\chi^2 = 1.2$, $df = 1$, $p > .10$ (using Yates Correction Factor)

Interpreting and Drawing Conclusions

Jim was somewhat dismayed at the results of his crosstabulation analysis. Yet he was grateful that he had not trusted his subjective hunches before he prematurely spoke to the legislative committee. Based on his analysis, he would have had a fairly high likelihood of committing a Type I error if he had rejected the null hypothesis and claimed the existence of a relationship between the dependent and independent variables.

With one degree of freedom and a directional hypothesis, he knew his chi-square value should have been at least 2.71 (Table 9.6) to reject the null hypothesis at the standard .05 level of statistical significance. He now had reason to believe that the legislators' use or nonuse of public schools for their children was probably not associated with their voting preference on the tax bill.

Other variables may have reflected a stronger degree of association with the dependent variable—the legislators' voting record on *all* tax bills, their perceptions of the fairness of a sales tax versus other souces of revenue, marriage to a spouse who was teaching in the public school system, and so on. But Jim could be reasonably certain that, at least in his state, there was no reason to conclude that legislators' support for or opposition to the tax bill was related to whether they had children currently in the public school system.

Relating the Findings to Practice

The lack of statistical support for Jim's directional hypothesis in no way negated the value of Jim's research study. His small-scale study, while limited and singularly focused, was extremely useful. He avoided making an erroneous conclusion, based on inadequate evidence, that might have resulted in an inappropriate lobbying strategy. Portraying the motivation of legislators who opposed the bill as "self-serving" would have been ill-advised, to say the least. Jim wondered whether it would be productive to undertake further statistical analyses using the legislators' other demographic characteristics as independent variables. He could now spend his time more efficiently by pursuing other avenues to gain insight into the legislators' positions on the proposed tax.

Frequently, lack of statistical support for a hypothesis can be a valuable time saver. Most research studies generate additional research questions. In fact, research studies usually create more potential research questions than they answer. However, the fact that we can ask a series of relevant questions is a good indication that our research findings have contributed to an improvement in the social service delivery system.

SUMMARY

This chapter has provided a comprehensive discussion of crosstabulation analysis. We have explained its popularity and emphasized why it is valuable when appropriately used but misleading when misused. At this point, you should have a sound general understanding of how this statistical test works, how findings can be interpreted, and how they might be applied in social work practice. What you have mastered about chi-square will help you as you read through Chapter 10. What you don't yet totally understand may become clearer as we discuss the same principles in regard to another statistical test—Pearson's *r*.

STUDY QUESTIONS

1. Why is the frequent use of chi-square in social work research both good and bad?
2. How is the chi-square test particularly well suited to social work research?
3. What do the numbers in each of the cells in a crosstabulation table mean?
4. What is lost when chi-square is used with data that are, for example, interval-level and normally distributed?
5. Can chi-square tell us whether one variable causes variations in the second variable? Explain.
6. What are expected frequencies, and how are they used in chi-square testing?
7. How do degrees of freedom determine whether a chi-square value of a given size (for instance, 10.00) will be considered statistically significant?
8. What are the minimum expected frequency requirements for use of chi-square?
9. What is the two-step process for determining if chi-square has demonstrated support for a directional hypothesis?
10. How can chi-square be used to examine the relationship between two variables while controlling for the effect of a third variable?

FURTHER READING

Adams, G. R., & Schvaneveldt, J. D. (1985). *Understanding research methods* (Ch. 17). New York: Longman.

Craft, J. L. (1985). *Statistics and data analysis for social workers* (Ch. 6). Itasca, IL: F. E. Peacock.

MacEachron, A. E. (1982). *Basic statistics in the human services: An applied approach* (Ch. 11). Baltimore: University Park Press.
Reid, W. J., & Smith, A. D. (1981). *Research in social work* (Ch. 10). New York: Columbia University Press.
Schuerman, J. R. (1981). Bivariate analysis: Crosstabulation. In R. M. Grinnell, Jr. (Ed.), *Social work research and evaluation* (pp. 461–480). Itasca, IL: F. E. Peacock.
Schuerman, J. R. (1983). *Research and evaluation in the human services* (Ch. 12). New York: Free Press.

10

CORRELATION

Chapter 9 presented a way to analyze the relationship between two nominal-level variables by using crosstabulation. This chapter explains how to analyze the relationship between two interval- or ratio-level variables through procedures termed *correlational analyses*. Much of the format of the early portion of this chapter has been adapted and modified from the work of Kolevzon (1981).

RELATIONSHIPS

An example of a relationship between two interval-level variables can be seen in a hypothetical distribution of variables of clients' motivation for treatment and clients' level of functioning. Table 10.1 summarizes data for a sample of ten clients; for every value of the interval-level x variable (client motivational level) there is a corresponding, or paired, value of the y interval-level variable (client functioning level). A relationship between these two variables is evident because, without exception, higher motivational levels are associated with higher levels of functioning, and vice versa. Floyd, for example, scored lowest on both his motivational level (1) and his functioning level (2). Jane scored second lowest on both levels (scores of 2 and 3 respectively), and Lynne scored highest on both (scores of 10 and 11 respectively).

This relationship also can be depicted by means of a scattergram such as that illustrated by Figure 10.1. The horizontal axis represents the clients' individual scores, or values, of their motivational levels for treatment (x), while the vertical axis represents individual scores of their functioning levels (y). Each dot represents a case and that client's scores for measurements of the two variables. In our scattergram, there are ten dots representing the ten clients' scores on the two variables. The dots, if connected, would form a straight line, indicating that the two variables are perfectly correlated. Such perfection is rarely seen in social work

Table 10.1
Scores for Ten Clients on Motivational and Functioning Levels

Client's Name	Motivational Level (x)	Functioning Level (y)
Floyd	1	2
Jane	2	3
Robert	3	4
Sue	4	5
Herb	5	6
Bill	6	7
Margareta	7	8
Ann	8	9
Dorothy	9	10
Lynne	10	11

Source: Adapted and modified from Kolevzon, M. S. (1981). Bivariate analysis: Correlation. In R. M. Grinnell, Jr. (Ed.), *Social work research and evaluation* (p. 483). Itasca, IL: F. E. Peacock.

research. It is used here to illustrate the concept of correlation in its most vivid form, prior to our discussion of the kind of correlations that we would more commonly see.

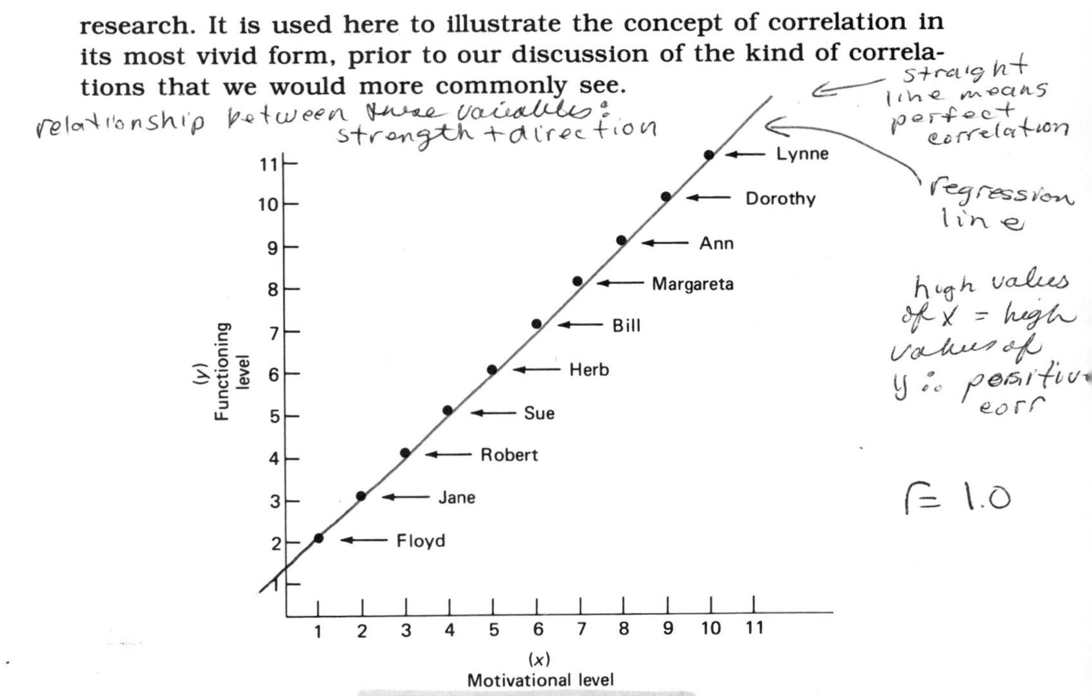

Figure 10.1 Perfect Positive Relationship Between Two Variables: Client Motivational Level and Client Functioning Level (from Table 10.1) (Adapted and modified from Kolevzon, M. S. (1981). Bivariate analysis: Correlation. In R. M. Grinnell, Jr. (Ed.), *Social work research and evaluation* [p. 484]. Itasca, IL: F. E. Peacock.)

Strength and Direction

Figure 10.1 demonstrates two important dimensions of the relationship between the variables: strength and direction. With regard to strength, the overall relationship between the two variables could not be stronger, as all of the clients' scores fall along a straight line. The line passing through all the dots (representing clients) on the scattergram is termed a *regression line*. In those very rare instances where there is a perfect relationship, we can predict with complete accuracy (100 percent of the time) the corresponding value of y if we have a specified value of x, and vice versa. In those more common cases where the strength of the relationship is less than perfect, the regression line becomes less distinct, and our ability to predict values of one variable from values of the other is subject to error.

In regard to the second dimension of a correlation, direction, the relationship between clients' motivational and functioning levels as displayed in Figure 10.1 can also be described as positive. High values of x are associated with high values of y, and vice versa. In a negative relationship (Figure 10.2), high values of one

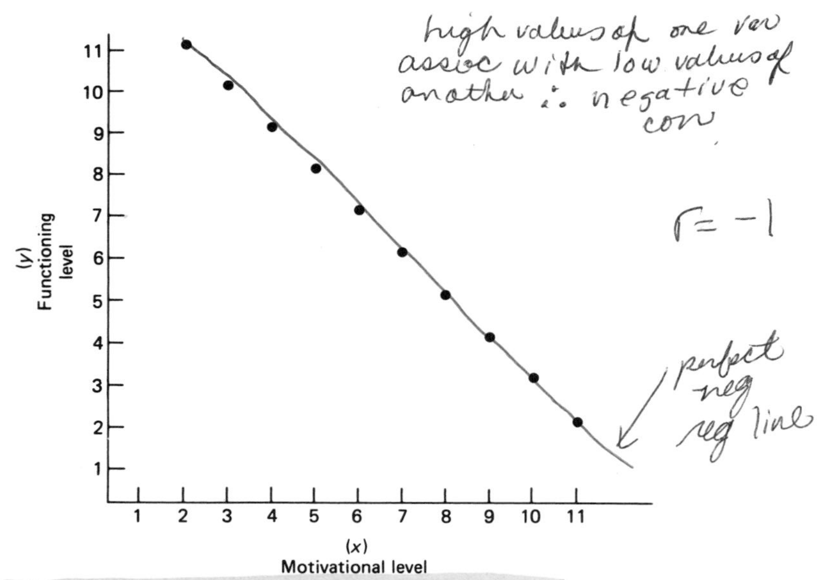

Figure 10.2 Perfect Negative Relationship Between Two Variables: Client Motivational Level and Client Functioning Level (Adapted and modified from Kolevzon, M. S. (1981). Bivariate analysis: Correlation. In R. M. Grinnell, Jr. (Ed.), *Social work research and evaluation* [p. 485]. Itasca, IL: F. E. Peacock.)

variable are associated with low values of the second variable, and vice versa. Like perfect positive correlations, perfect negative correlations are very rare in social work research; they appear primarily in disciplines such as the physical sciences.

In social work research, some relationships may have no discernible direction as well as no strength—that is, there is no relationship at all between the two variables. This, you will recall, is what the null hypothesis would contend. But most relationships between interval- or ratio-level variables reflect some degree of correlation, ranging from barely discernible to nearly perfect, or what might be described as *nonperfect correlations*.

Figure 10.3 is another scattergram illustrating a relationship between the variables of motivational and functioning levels that is still positive but not perfect like that illustrated in Figure 10.1. It shows that two clients scored a 1 on client motivational level, but one of them (Sue) scored a 2 on client functioning level and the other (Robert) scored a 4. The regression line is not nearly as distinct as in Figure 10.1; no straight line could possibly pass directly through all of the dots. It is therefore impossible to predict with 100 percent accuracy a functioning level score of a given cli-

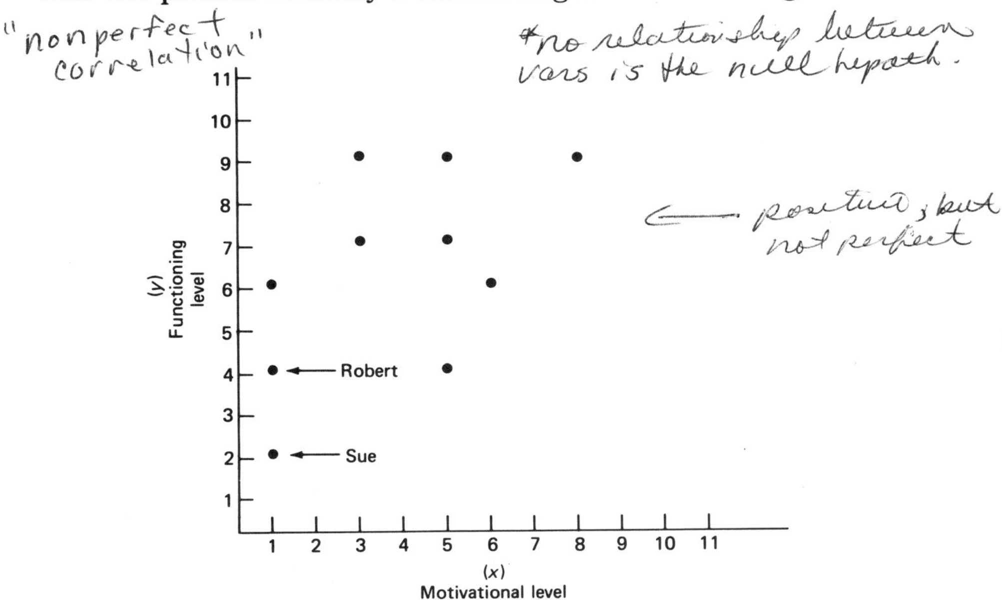

Figure 10.3 Nonperfect Positive Relationship Between Two Variables: Client Motivational Level and Client Functioning Level (Adapted and modified from Kolevzon, M. S. (1981). Bivariate analysis: Correlation. In R.M. Grinnell, Jr. (Ed.), *Social work research and evaluation* [p. 486]. Itasca, IL: F. E. Peacock.)

ent on the basis of a measurement of the client's motivational level. Similarly, Figure 10.4 provides an example of a negative relationship that is less than perfect. Figure 10.5 displays an example in which there is no perceivable relationship between the two variables.

THE LOGIC OF CORRELATIONS

Figures 10.1 through 10.5 are standard scattergrams. They are awkward and time-consuming ways of presenting the paired values of a large number of cases. A far more efficient way of displaying a relationship between interval- or ratio-level variables is by the use of a statistic called a *correlation coefficient*. It provides a numerical indicator of both the strength and the direction of a relationship. As Figure 10.6 shows, correlation coefficients range along a continuum, from −1.0 (perfect negative) at one extreme to 1.0 (perfect positive) at the other extreme, with 0.0 (no correlation) at the midpoint. A correlation coefficient cannot be greater than 1.0 or less than −1.0.

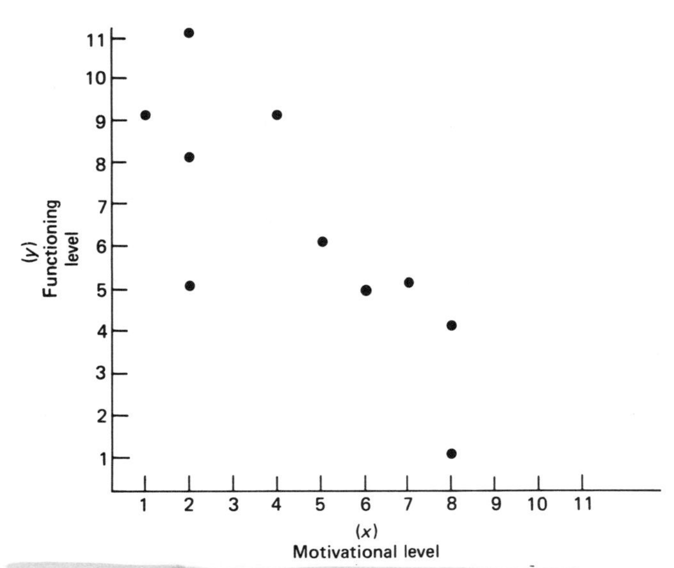

Figure 10.4 Nonperfect Negative Relationship Between Two Variables: Client Motivational Level and Client Functioning Level (Adapted and modified from Kolevzon, M. S. (1981). Bivariate analysis: Correlation. In R. M. Grinnell, Jr. (Ed.), *Social work research and evaluation* [p. 487]. Itasca, IL: F. E. Peacock.)

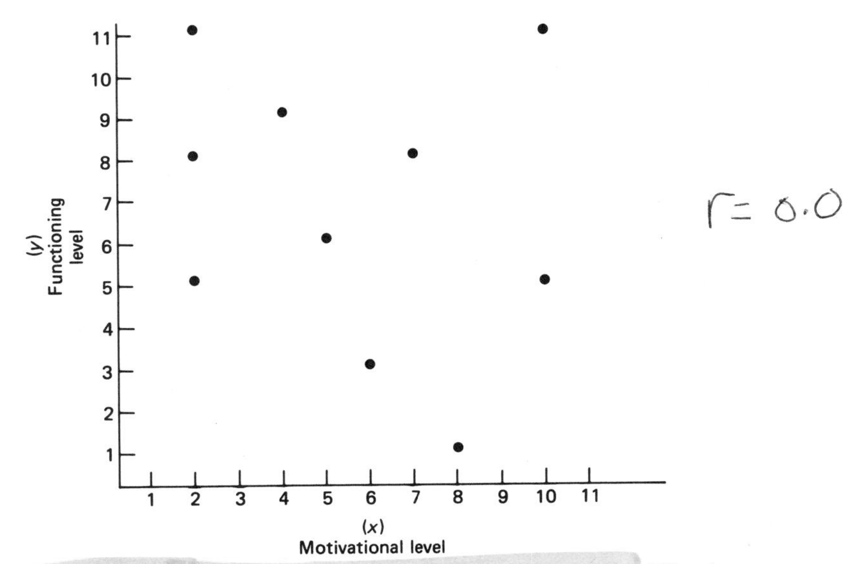

Figure 10.5 No Relationship Between Two Variables: Client Motivational Level and Client Functioning Level (Adapted and modified from Kolevzon, M. S. (1981). Bivariate analysis: Correlation. In R. M. Grinnell, Jr. (Ed.), *Social work research and evaluation* [p. 488]. Itasca, IL: F. E. Peacock.)

The closer the numerical value of the correlation coefficient is to either extreme (1.0 or −1.0), the stronger the relationship between the two variables. For example, a coefficient of .92 is closer to a perfect correlation than coefficients of either −.60 or .60 and, therefore, suggests a stronger correlation than either of the other two. The closer the coefficient is to the middle of the continuum, the weaker the relationship between the two variables. A correlation coefficient that is close to 0.0 suggests that, very likely, there is no relationship at all.

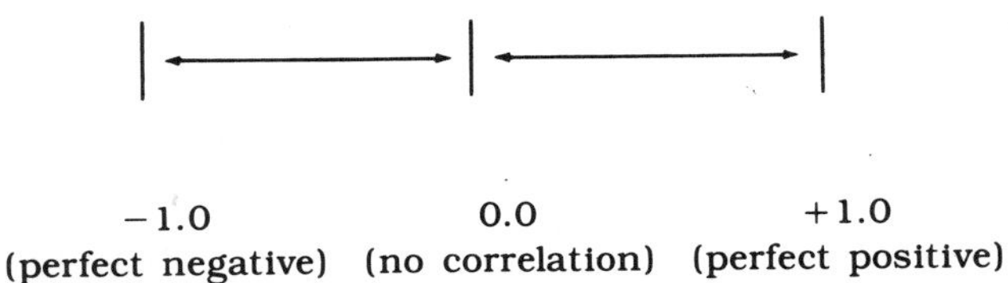

Figure 10.6 Correlation Coefficient Continuum (Adapted and modified from Kolevzon, M. S. (1981). Bivariate analysis: Correlation. In R. M. Grinnell, Jr. (Ed.), *Social work research and evaluation* [p. 484]. Itasca, IL: F. E. Peacock.)

The plus or minus sign indicates the direction of the relationship. For example, the correlation between a social worker's skill level and years of professional social work experience might be .85. The absence of the minus sign indicates a positive relationship. The correlation between skill level and level of apathy regarding one's work could be −.75, indicating a fairly strong negative relationship. That is, persons who are most apathetic and uninvolved in their work are likely to be less skillful, and vice versa.

A variety of correlational analyses can be utilized. A frequently employed procedure, and one that we will use to illustrate the correlation coefficient throughout this chapter, is *Pearson's product moment correlation* (Pearson's *r*), referred to as simply *r* in the discussion that follows.

Understanding the *r* Statistic

Using *r*, we attempt to determine statistically what a scattergram would visually display—that is, to what degree the dots representing scores on two variables for each case would tend to form a straight line. If the *r* value is high—if it approaches 1.0 or −1.0—the points would appear to "hug" the regression line; a low *r* value (approaching 0.0) would reflect a scattering of dots that diverge greatly from the regression line.

To understand how the *r* formula actually arrives at a meaningful indicator of the correlation between variables, it is helpful to remember that *r* is best seen as an expression of our ability to predict a value of one variable from our knowledge of a value of the other variable. In no way is causation implied. If a high *r* value results from statistical analysis, the finding can help us predict the value of one variable if we know the value of the other, but *r* cannot tell us why the variables tend to covary. Any argument that one variable causes the variation in the other must be based on other factors.

In the *r* formula (on page 144) it should be noted that the numerator of the formula is derived from the pairs of values (one for each variable) for each case. It results in a number that summarizes the degree to which the two variables vary together. Expressed another way, it tells us to what degree certain values of one variable tend to be found with certain values of the other variable.

The denominator of the formula introduces the total amount of variation in the data; it is the product of the standard deviations of the two variables. In this way, it puts the information in the numerator in perspective. The *r* value that results from the total formula is the proportion of all the variation that is represented by the covariation in the numerator of the formula. In a perfect correlation (r = 1.0 or −1.0) 100 percent of the total variation in the two variables will be explained by the covariation in the numerator. Conversely, in those rare instances in which there is absolutely no correlation (r = 0.0) between variables, none of the total variation will be explained by the covariation summarized in the numerator. Knowing the value for one variable for a case in which r = 0.0 will be of no help in predicting the value for the second variable for that case.

The r statistic that results from the formula tells us a great deal more. If we square the r value, the new figure will be the proportion of the variation in one variable that can be "explained" by its relationship to the other variable. Remember that *explanation*, as we are using the term here, falls short of *causality*. It refers only to our ability to predict the values of one variable if we know the values of the other. For example, an r value of .80 relating number of treatment interviews to scores on a self-concept inventory would mean that 64 percent (.80 × .80 = .64) of the variation in self-concept scores might be explained by the number of treatment interviews. The other 36 percent of variation in self-concept scores (1.00 − .64) remains unaccounted for. Our ability to predict clients' self-concept scores if we know the number of interviews they have had would be quite good, but certainly not perfect. Only an r of +1.0 or −1.0 (a perfect correlation) would allow for a 100 percent accurate prediction ($1.0^2 = 1.0$).

The r statistic is an indication of the strength and direction of any pattern of an association that exists between values of one variable and values of another variable. As we emphasized in our discussion of chi-square, a common misuse of a test frequently occurs when we attempt to go beyond its primary focus (prediction in the case of r) and attempt to attribute more to it (implications about causation) than it is capable of generating. The example and step-by-step application of the formula that follows will underline the fact that r (like other statistical tests) is really just a mathematical manipulation of numbers that can provide only a partial answer to our research questions. The balance of the answers must come from logic, theory, intuition, practice experience, or some other less "mechanical" process.

Computing the *r* Statistic

Table 10.3 provides a model for preparing data for calculating r using the data presented in Table 10.2. Table 10.3 shows that Floyd obtained a motivational score (x) of 5, which is recorded in column *a*, and a functioning score (y) of 10, recorded in column *b*. In column *c*, the square of his x score is recorded (5 × 5 = 25), and in column *d* the square of his y score is recorded (10 × 10 =

100). Column e contains the product of Floyd's x and y scores ($5 \times 10 = 50$). At the bottom of each column is the summation of the values for all cases. These summed values are then substituted into the formula below.

$$r = \frac{e - \frac{(a)(b)}{N}}{\sqrt{\left[c - \left(\frac{a^2}{N}\right)\right]\left[d - \left(\frac{b^2}{N}\right)\right]}}$$

Where

r = Correlation coefficient
a = Sum of values of x
b = Sum of values of y
c = Sum of values of x^2
d = Sum of values of y^2
e = Sum of products of x and y
N = Number of cases

Substituting values for letters, we get

r = Correlation coefficient
a = 175
b = 300
c = 4875
d = 11,000
e = 6750
N = 10

Substituting values into the formula, we get

$$r = \frac{6750 - \frac{(175)(300)}{10}}{\sqrt{\left[4875 - \left(\frac{175^2}{10}\right)\right]\left[11{,}000 - \left(\frac{300^2}{10}\right)\right]}}$$

$$= \frac{6750 - 5250}{\sqrt{(4875 - 3062.5)(11{,}000 - 9000)}}$$

$$= \frac{1500}{\sqrt{(1812.5)(2000)}}$$

$$= \frac{1500}{1903.94}$$

$$= .78784$$

$$= .79 \text{ (Correlation coefficient)}$$

Table 10.2
Scores for Ten Clients on Motivational and Functioning Levels

Client's Name	Motivational Level (x)	Functioning Level (y)
Floyd	5	10
Jane	15	20
Robert	25	30
Sue	35	40
Herb	45	50
Bill	0	10
Margareta	5	20
Ann	10	30
Dorothy	15	40
Lynne	20	50

Source: Adapted and modified from Kolevzon, M. S. (1981). Bivariate analysis: Correlation. In R. M. Grinnell, Jr. (Ed.), *Social work research and evaluation* (p. 489). Itasca, IL: F. E. Peacock.

Relating r to Chance

How large an r do we need in order to conclude that we can safely reject the null hypothesis and be able to claim statistical support for the position that two variables may be related? As is true with other bivariate relationships, the correlation coefficient is judged to be sufficiently strong if it reaches or surpasses our predeter-

Table 10.3
Format for the Calculation of Pearson's r (from Table 10.2)

	Variable				
	(*a*)	(*b*)	(*c*)	(*d*)	(*e*)
Client's Name	Motivational Level (x)	Functioning Level (y)	x^2	y^2	xy
Floyd	5	10	25	100	50
Jane	15	20	225	400	300
Robert	25	30	625	900	750
Sue	35	40	1225	1600	1400
Herb	45	50	2025	2500	2250
Bill	0	10	0	100	0
Margareta	5	20	25	400	100
Ann	10	30	100	900	300
Dorothy	15	40	225	1600	600
Lynne	20	50	400	2500	1000
Totals	175	300	4875	11,000	6750

Source: Adapted and modified from Kolevzon, M. S. (1981). Bivariate analysis: Correlation. In R. M. Grinnell, Jr. (Ed.), *Social work research and evaluation* (p. 491). Itasca, IL: F. E. Peacock.

mined level of statistical significance. Unless previously stated and justified, the .05 confidence level is used as the reference point for determining whether we can reject the null hypothesis.

The table of critical values of *r* (Table 10.4) illustrates the point at which statistical significance is achieved for differing correlation coefficient strengths, depending on the size of the sample. As the table shows, with a sample of 11 individuals, a correlation coefficient of .602 is required with nondirectional hypothesis to reach statistical significance at the .05 level (.735 at the .01 level) and thereby permit rejection of the null hypothesis. With a sample size of 400 cases, however, rejection of the null hypothesis is possible with a much weaker correlation coefficient (.098 at the .05 level and .128 at the .01 level). This is an important point to remember.

As with crosstabulation analyses, the likelihood of demonstrating statistical significance with *r* is directly related to sample size. It is more likely that chance, in the form of sampling error, will cause two variables to appear to be related with a small sample than with a larger one. With larger samples, an apparent relationship, even one that on the surface appears quite weak, is far less likely to be the work of chance. A table such as Table 10.4 incorporates this factor when it takes sample size into consideration in providing significance level.

Meaningfulness of the Correlation Coefficient

In interpreting the strength of a correlation coefficient, we must also take into consideration the way in which a correlational analysis is to be used. Even when a statistically significant correlation coefficient is obtained, the *r* itself is not necessarily meaningful and may not represent a substantive finding. For example, researchers who construct measurement instruments are concerned with validity and reliability. Yet the traditional cutoff point for accepting an instrument as reliable is often a coefficient above .85, whereas the cutoff point for accepting the same instrument's validity is frequently .40 or even lower. From a different perspective, identifying no association ($r = .00$) between two variables that are believed to be related may represent the most important finding of a study.

In interpreting a correlation coefficient, it is also important not to treat it as if it were equivalent to interval- or ratio-level data or to make statements that in any way give this impression. For example, a correlation coefficient of .80 is *not* twice as strong as .40. In fact, the .80 describes an association four times as strong ($.80^2 = .64$; $.40^2 = .16$; $.64 \div .16 = 4$) in its ability to account for the

Table 10.4
Critical Values of r

	Level of Significance for a One-Tailed Test				
	.025	.005		.025	.005
	Level of Significance for a Two-Tailed Test				
n	.05	.01	n	.05	.01
3	.997	.999	38	.320	.413
4	.950	.990	39	.316	.408
5	.878	.959	40	.312	.403
6	.811	.917	41	.308	.398
7	.754	.874	42	.304	.393
8	.707	.834	43	.301	.389
9	.666	.798	44	.297	.384
10	.632	.765	45	.294	.380
11	.602	.735	46	.291	.376
12	.576	.708	47	.288	.372
13	.553	.684	48	.284	.368
14	.532	.661	49	.281	.364
15	.514	.641	50	.279	.361
16	.497	.623	55	.266	.345
17	.482	.606	60	.254	.330
18	.468	.590	65	.244	.317
19	.456	.575	70	.235	.306
20	.444	.561	75	.227	.296
21	.433	.549	80	.220	.286
22	.423	.537	85	.213	.278
23	.413	.526	90	.207	.270
24	.404	.515	95	.202	.263
25	.396	.505	100	.195	.256
26	.388	.496	125	.170	.230
27	.381	.487	150	.159	.210
28	.374	.478	175	.148	.194
29	.367	.470	200	.138	.181
30	.361	.463	300	.113	.148
31	.355	.456	400	.098	.128
32	.349	.449	500	.088	.115
33	.344	.442	600	.080	.105
34	.339	.436	700	.074	.097
35	.334	.430	800	.070	.091
36	.329	.424	900	.065	.086
37	.325	.418	1000	.062	.081

Source: Wert, J. E., Neidt, C. O., & Ahmann, S. J. (1954). *Educational and psychological research*. New York: Appleton-Century-Crofts.

amount of variance in one variable from the variation in the other. It should also be remembered that in a correlation coefficient as strong as .80, there will be few exceptions to the pattern of relationships between values of one variable and values of the second variable—that is, virtually all high values of the first variable will be found in cases with high values of the second variable, and vice versa. A weaker correlation coefficient (such as .40) will have a much higher percentage of cases that are opposite to the overall direction of the association.

Presentations of Correlations

The actual presentation of a correlation coefficient in a research report is simple. After calculating the Pearson's r according to the format given in Table 10.3 and the equation and finding the probability level associated with the obtained r based on our sample size from Table 10.4, we determine if we can reject the null hypothesis. With the information derived we then can present our finding in a sentence. For example

> *The correlation between the independent and dependent variables for the 20 clients was* $r = -.57$, $p < .01$, *which indicates the presence of a statistically significant negative correlation between the two variables.*

CORRELATIONS WITH THREE OR MORE VARIABLES

Bivariate relationships frequently need further explication. For example, we are unlikely to be able to predict with complete accuracy how long a client will remain in treatment based solely on data on the severity of the client's presenting problem, the client's motivation for treatment, or any other single variable. Both a systems perspective and other theories of multiple causation argue that many variables work together to affect human behavior. The accuracy of prediction can be improved by expanding the pool of available data to include more than two variables at one time in the analysis. Decisions regarding the direction that this expansion takes, and the additional sources and types of data needed to improve our explanative and predictive abilities, frequently represent the critical next step along the data analysis continuum. We will not provide description of tests to examine correlations among three or more variables in this text (a well-known one is called partial r). For our discussion, it will suffice to say that we should be aware of their existence and what they can offer that a bivariate analysis using r cannot.

MICRO PRACTICE EXAMPLE

Impetus for the Study

Bill is a social worker in a family service agency. He leads several treatment groups consisting of adolescent girls. He recently became aware of the wide variation in verbal participation among the group members. While virtually all the girls would respond when spoken to, a few never made any unsolicited comments. He felt that these girls had low desire to get involved with the group. Over a period of several weeks, Bill made it a point to ask several of the nonverbal girls why they rarely volunteered with a comment. Of the seven girls he asked, five replied with essentially the same answer: each was an only child in her family and had been taught by her parents that it was not her role to initiate communication. Bill then asked three of the most verbal girls, who tended to dominate group discussions, how many brothers and/or sisters they had. Their responses were six, seven, and nine.

Based on his limited inquiries, Bill began to speculate on a possible relationship between a dependent variable, unsolicited comments in group treatment, and an independent variable, number of siblings in the family.

The Hypothesis to Be Tested

Bill conducted a limited literature review. He learned what he could about such phenomena as social traits of only children, communication patterns among siblings, and variations in verbal participation in adolescent groups. Most of the literature seemed to lead him to the conclusion that adolescents with more siblings would be more likely to volunteer comments than those with fewer siblings. This assumption was based upon the experience in communication they gained in growing up among siblings. However, other literature seemed to suggest just the opposite. It contended that only children who had primarily adults to communicate with would be more likely to have acquired verbal skills and be less intimidated by adults. The literature left Bill undecided. There appeared to be a certain theme, running through the various sources, that suggested that the dependent and independent variables might logically be related. But in which direction? Bill had the additional insight gained from his own (admittedly unscientific) observations. This served to "tip the balance." Finally, he designed a small-scale research study that would test a directional hypothesis:

> *Among female adolescents in a treatment group setting, there is a positive association between the number of their unsolicited comments and their number of siblings.*

Overview of Methodology

It was already common agency procedure to videotape group treatment sessions for use in staff supervision. Thus Bill had no problem with access to data that he could use to test his hypothesis. He readily received permission from the agency administrator to use the videotapes from all seven of his groups for use in his research study.

Bill operationally defined a case as being an adolescent girl who attended at least 75 percent of her group sessions during a four-month period. Having identified 35 girls who met this criterion, he reviewed all videotapes of the sessions with a colleague who was interested in his study. Bill and his friend developed an operational definition for the variable "unsolicited comment." Next, they recorded the number of these comments that each girl made during each group session. An unsolicited comment was judged to have been made only if both Bill and his colleague felt that it met the definition.

Bill and his colleague totaled the number of unsolicited comments for each of the girls (cases) and then divided by the number of sessions that the adolescent attended. This number provided them with the average number of unsolicited comments per session for each case (dependent variable). The agency's records provided a means for the easy recording of the independent variable, number of siblings, for each case. Bill compiled measurements for each of the two variables into a table such as Table 10.2.

Findings

Bill used Pearson's r to determine if he had any reason to claim support for his hypothesis. Using the formula for r, he learned that the correlation between the number of unsolicited comments per session and the number of siblings was .340. Thinking back to the general guidelines that relate to the strength of a correlation, he was somewhat disappointed, but he also remembered that with larger sample sizes (35 is relatively large for r), he may not need a very high correlation to have statistical significance. When he looked at a table for r that controls for sample size (Table

10.4), he saw that the likelihood of making a Type I error in rejecting the null hypothesis with a correlation of .340 and a sample of 35 was less than .025. (Note that .340 falls to the right of .334 but is smaller than .430.)

Interpreting and Drawing Conclusions

Bill knew that the .05 significance level is generally accepted as support for a relationship between two variables. He also knew that this meant that if he were to claim a relationship between the dependent and independent variables, he would be on statistically safe ground. However, as with crosstabulation, a second step to interpretation is required before support for his hypothesis could be claimed. Was the association in the *direction* which he had hypothesized it would be—that is, a positive association? He recalled that a positive association between two variables (Figures 10.1 and 10.3) means that high values of one variable tend to be found among cases that have high values of the other variable, and vice versa. This meant that, in his data set, girls who had high values for the variable "number of unsolicited comments" should have had high values for the variable "number of siblings," and vice versa. The data looked the way Bill had hypothesized that they would. He concluded that he had support for the hypothesis in the direction predicted.

Bill was realistic about his findings. He knew that there could be explanations for his statistically significant finding other than that a true relationship between variables exists. His research design had been of the mini-study variety. He had, for example, relied on a convenience sample and used only his own cases. Many potential biasing effects and other variables that might have affected his findings could have been present. These may have been related to such factors as (1) some bias created within the sample as a result of case loss, (2) Bill's possible inability to be a good facilitator with certain girls who were not used to being in group situations, and (3) the possible distortion of actual events by the limits of videotaping equipment used. In addition, the .340 correlation between variables was really not *that strong* in an absolute sense. His lack of total confidence in his findings and their magnitude told Bill that he was certainly not ready to publish an article from his study to communicate its findings to others.

Relating the Findings to Practice

Bill's findings, even qualified as they were, were certainly not without value. He summarized them in a weekly staff meeting for other social workers to consider. His colleagues provided a critique of his research methods, and identified possible biases and the presence of other variables that, if methodologically controlled, would make the design of subsequent research studies even better. All agreed that some replication of his study was certainly indicated.

Bill and a few other social workers decided to make some adjustments to their practice methods based on the assumption that the correlation that he had tentatively identified was a real one. They perceived little risk to clients in implementing some changes based on the results of his findings, and they agreed to evaluate the changes six months later. They decided to take the following steps.

1. They would use the variable number of siblings (available from the intake form) to create more homogeneous groups among new clients. They felt that by placing what might be the most verbally assertive members (with more siblings) in groups together, they could prohibit them from intimidating other group members who were less assertive. They also hoped that the more assertive clients would be less likely to dominate and monopolize discussion among persons most like themselves. In turn, some of those who the social workers believed to be less assertive (fewer siblings) would become more active and assertive in groups with persons more like themselves.
2. In other groups, new members from families with many siblings would be viewed as at risk to try to dominate discussions. Likewise, new members with no or few siblings would be viewed as at risk to be reticent to volunteer comments. This perception would affect the way in which the social workers would approach their role as facilitator with the more homogeneous groups.
3. In all groups, leaders would facilitate discussion around such areas as attitudes toward the presence or absence of siblings, parental attitudes toward children's assertiveness, and so on.

As in the examples using crosstabulation, the contribution to social work's overall body of knowledge offered by Bill's research study must be regarded as limited. The actual amount of knowledge acquired was small and tentative. However, on another level, Bill accomplished a great deal that might benefit himself, his colleagues, and clients. He laid the groundwork for further research studies that would use more sophisticated designs.

In addition, the social work staff started to think about doing research. They had gained experience in the application of research findings. They might now attempt to utilize future research studies published in professional journals. Perhaps, without even knowing it, Bill had also moved the staff closer to legitimizing research as an important component of their social work practice. More effective treatment groups might or might not be formed as a direct result of Bill's research. But, somewhere in the future, his small-scale research study might have positive effects on social work delivery of services to clients in his agency.

MACRO PRACTICE EXAMPLE

Impetus for the Study

Tanya is an administrator in a county public welfare agency. She recently became aware of a high recording error rate among financial assistance workers within her agency. When she was hired in her current position, the error rate for eligibility determinations among new AFDC applicants was among the highest in the state. She assumed that the problem was related, at least in part, to inadequately trained workers. She gained the appropriate approval and quickly took steps to increase the eligibility worker training requirement for all staff members who had been employed by the agency for less than six months. She also required that all senior workers who were not full-time supervisors perform a much greater percentage of eligibility determinations. One year after she implemented these decisions, the error rate had doubled.

Tanya was concerned about the newest error rate figures. She wondered how her efforts to address a problem could possibly have made it worse. How could increased training of newer workers, combined with use of more experienced personnel, have resulted in a dramatic *increase* in erroneous eligibility determinations? In discussing this paradox with a staff member, she got a hint of what may have gone wrong.

The staff member made the casual observation that there had been a series of major changes in federal AFDC eligibility requirements over the past few years. Tanya wondered whether the direct practice experience of senior people, derived under older standards, hadn't actually been more of a liability than an asset when they were asked to perform frontline duties. She speculated that, since no senior workers had received additional formal training when the changes occurred, they may have made a large number of errors because they lacked knowledge of current standards. Those "old-timers," who had worked under several sets of standards, might be among those most confused about standards and, therefore, most likely to make errors.

Tanya did not wish to make another decision that might not help the problem—or might even make it worse. If she were to recommend any future changes, she could not rely on a logical hunch. She intended to have data to back up her recommendations.

The Hypothesis to Be Tested

If experience was really positively correlated with error rate among senior workers, then, Tanya thought, she should be able to demonstrate this relationship using data already available in the agency's management information system. Since she was more interested in explaining differences in error rate among workers than differences in experience among workers, the former variable was identified as dependent and the latter variable as independent. She felt that her brief literature review and conversations with colleagues allowed her to formulate a directional hypothesis:

> *Among senior AFDC eligibility determination workers, there is a strong and statistically significant positive correlation between years of work experience in the agency and error rate.*

Overview of Methodology

Like Bill in the previous example, Tanya kept her research study simple. Since she needed a quick answer, she limited her study to an examination of the relationship between only the dependent and independent variables. With the assistance of the agency's data processing manager, she calculated a Pearson's r to assess the correlation between the variable for all 40 senior workers currently doing eligibility determinations. She used the number of identified errors per 100 cases (last 100) for her measurement of the dependent variable.

Findings

The correlation coefficient between error rate and years of experience was $-.215$. Tanya checked a table of critical values similar to Table 10.4 to see if chance might have been the explanation for this correlation. The table told her that she would need a minimum r value of .264 to achieve statistical significance at the .05 level with a sample of 40 and a directional (one-tailed) hypothesis. She had not demonstrated support for her hypothesis at the .05

level. What's more, the fact that the correlation coefficient carried a minus sign indicated that the trend was in the direction *opposite* to that which she predicted she would find.

Interpreting and Drawing Conclusions

Tanya had hoped to find support for her belief that, among senior workers, those with more experience made more errors and those with less experience made fewer errors. She planned to use these findings to recommend to supervisors that the most senior workers should no longer be used for eligibility determinations, or that they attend the training sessions usually attended by new workers. Her findings were a disappointment to her. The slight negative correlation actually suggested that the most senior workers may have made fewer mistakes than those with less experience. The county error rate would have been even higher if senior level workers had not been used!

Relating the Findings to Practice

Tanya knew enough about research to understand that the lack of statistical support for her hypothesis did not mean that no new knowledge had been generated. Her research study had shifted her focus away from past work experience of senior workers as a factor in the recent rise in error rate. She recalled that, in her haste to reduce error rate, she had originally introduced two variables to the situation: senior personnel were required to perform more eligibility determinations *and* newer staff were given expanded training for their role. Perhaps the problem had been made worse by the introduction of the training. She knew, after all, that an increase in training was not necessarily a guarantee that the training left workers better prepared for their work. What's more, the fact that senior workers with experience under obsolete regulations and no exposure to the new training did somewhat better overall than new workers exposed to training led her to question whether the training was achieving its objectives. Based on the analysis of her data, Tanya decided on the following procedures.

1. She would design and implement an evaluative study of the current training for new eligibility workers.
2. She would continue to use senior workers for increased responsibility for eligibility determinations and would encourage them to assist newer workers in learning their jobs.

3. She would report her research findings to her superiors, informing them of her approaches to the problem (1 and 2 above), to make them aware of her concern about the high error rate and her attempts to correct it.

Tanya's contribution to knowledge using correlation analyses was useful *despite* the fact that her hypothesis was not statistically supported. Because she used Pearson's *r* correctly and in an appropriate situation, her findings had credibility. They allowed her to approach decision making more knowledgeably in a practice setting and provided guidance for the selection and design of other needed research studies.

SUMMARY

This chapter has presented correlation analyses as a means of determining and expressing the strength and direction of an association (the extent of covariance) between two interval- or ratio-level variables. We have noted the effect that sample size has on statistical significance and the way this effect mathematically explains why a correlation coefficient may be statistically significant while actually quite weak. Correlation is one of many areas in which the ethical researcher must take special care not to deliberately or unintentionally misrepresent the research findings.

Like all statistical tests, Pearson's *r* does not control for possible bias or the effect of other variables. Ideally, these factors will have already been controlled through careful attention to the design of the research study before data collection and data analysis begin.

STUDY QUESTIONS

1. What would be the shape of a scattergram portraying a perfect negative correlation?
2. Which correlation coefficient suggests a stronger relationship between two variables, .74 or −.86?
3. Which correlation coefficient suggests *no* relationship between two interval-level variables?
4. How does sample size affect whether a correlation coefficient will be considered to be statistically significant?
5. How could a very low correlation, such as .10, be a valuable contribution to practice knowledge?
6. Why is it *not* correct to state that a correlation coefficient of .84 suggests a relationship twice as strong as a correlation coefficient of .42?

7. Why do bivariate analyses such as *r* frequently not provide a total explanation of a relationship between two variables?
8. Can a bivariate correlation analysis alone tell us which variable causes the variation in the second variable? Explain.
9. When can a correlation coefficient be used to provide a 100 percent accurate prediction of the values of one variable from the values of the other variable?
10. What is the usual format for presentation of findings from correlation analysis?

FURTHER READING

Adams, G. R., & Schvaneveldt, J. D. (1985). *Understanding research methods* (Ch. 17). White Plains, NY: Longman.

Craft, J. L. (1985). *Statistics and data analysis for social workers* (Ch. 7). Itasca, IL: F. E. Peacock.

Kolevzon, M. S. (1981). Bivariate analysis: Correlation. In R. M. Grinnell, Jr. (Ed.), *Social work research and evaluation* (pp. 481–499). Itasca, IL: F. E. Peacock.

MacEachron, A. E. (1982). *Basic statistics in the human services: An applied approach* (Ch. 11). Baltimore: University Park Press.

Reid, W. J., & Smith, A. D. (1981). *Research in social work* (Ch. 10). New York: Columbia University Press.

Schuerman, J. R. (1983). *Research and evaluation in the human services* (Ch. 12). New York: Free Press.

11

COMPARISONS OF AVERAGES

Chapter 9 presented a popular test (chi-square) that is frequently used to analyze a relationship between two nominal-level variables. In Chapter 10 we discussed a test (Pearson's *r*) designed to examine a relationship between two interval- or ratio-level variables. In this chapter, we will examine one of several tests that is appropriate when one variable, usually the dependent variable, is at least interval-level and the other, usually the independent variable, is regarded as nominal-level.

THE POPULARITY OF *t*

There are actually several different kinds of *t* tests designed for different data analysis requirements. We will look at only one of these, Student's *t*, which is both very popular and especially useful for the social work researcher.

What makes Student's *t* (referred to as simply *t* in the discussion that follows) so useful? One of social work's greatest needs is for research studies that can evaluate the effectiveness of different approaches to intervention. We need to know whether one intervention method is really better than another for obtaining some desired outcome. The *t* test is ideally suited for use in situations in which we have a two-category independent variable (Intervention A/Intervention B) that is at the nominal level, whereas the dependent variable (the behavior, attitude, value, or whatever) that we hope to affect is at least interval-level.

Frequently, we have reasonably precise measurements of the dependent variable. Examples might include variables such as self-esteem, attitudes toward welfare recipients, marital satisfaction, social functioning level, or other client characteristics. Thanks to the work of researchers who have refined instruments for their measurement over a period of many years, these variables now can be treated statistically as interval-level. Other frequently used dependent variables, such as number of appointments missed, number of stated oppositions to a social welfare program, or number of violent behaviors directed toward a spouse, are interval- or ratio-level by their very nature. If we can justify one variable as being interval- or ratio-level and the other is only nominal-level, *t* may be the statistical test of choice.

Another reason why social work researchers often use the *t* test is the relatively small sample size that is required. Large samples are not common in social work research, particularly in clinical situations. The *t* test is appropriate for research studies using a small number of cases (for instance, a total of only 20 or 30 cases). In addition, the two groups do not have to contain an equal number of cases. Even in the most carefully designed research studies on treatment effectiveness, people drop out before the study is completed. This results in a situation in which there are more cases in one group than in the other. The discrepancy between the two group sizes is automatically controlled for by the *t* formula.

THE LOGIC OF *t*

The *t* test, like the other statistical tests, is used to help determine whether an apparent relationship between two variables is a true relationship that exists within the population, or is the work of chance. With *t*, this determination is accomplished by a comparison of means. The sample is divided into two groups (subsamples) based on the value of each case for its two-category, nominal-level variable (for example, Intervention A/Intervention B). Interval- and ratio-level variable mean scores for the two groups are then compared using the formula for *t*.

Just on the basis of probability, the means of the two subsamples are likely to be different; *t* is an analysis of the amount of that difference. If the difference is mathematically shown to be small, so small that chance is a likely explanation for it, the null hypothesis cannot be rejected. We could conclude that, very likely, the difference between the means of the two groups is a function of chance and not reflective of a real difference that exists within the population. But if our *t* analysis indicates that the difference is large enough that it is unlikely to be the work of chance, we may be able to reject the null hypothesis and conclude that the difference observed in the sample is indeed reflective of a real dif-

ference in the population. Chance, in the form of sampling error, will have been effectively discounted as the explanation for the apparent relationship between the two variables.

Especially if a sample is small, even a fairly large difference between two means can usually be ascribed to chance. But there comes a point where the difference between two means is sufficiently large that chance alone is unlikely to have produced it. When is this point reached? The *t* test tells us. It determines the statistical likelihood of making a Type I error if we were to reject the null hypothesis and conclude that the difference between the two means is related to the presence of different values of the second (nominal-level) variable.

We will now return to an example we used in Chapter 2. This time we will use it to illustrate the logic of the *t* test. You may recall that we mentioned a hypothetical study guide that was developed to help social workers prepare for the state merit exam. To evaluate the effectiveness of such a study guide, we might randomly select 15 of the 30 social workers who plan to take the exam and provide them with a copy of it. We would give them specific directions to spend part of their study time each night using the guide as instructed.

The 15 social workers who used the guide would be regarded as the experimental group; the remaining 15 who did not use it would be regarded as the control group. After the 30 social workers all took the state merit exam, their results would be compared. We would not directly compare the scores of everyone who used the study guide with the scores of everyone who did not. Instead, we would compare the mean exam score of the 15 social workers in the experimental group with the mean exam score of the 15 social workers in the control group.

In comparing the mean scores for the two groups, we would need to ask certain questions. Is the difference in the mean scores of the two groups enough to allow us to reject the null hypothesis, which would say that there is no relationship between using/not using the study guide and social workers' scores on the exam? How confident can we be that the difference wasn't due to sampling error (probability)? To put it another way, is the difference between the means of the two groups likely to be reflective of a real association between the two variables?

With the *t* test we would compare the two mean scores, using a mathematical formula designed to tell us whether the difference between the mean scores of the two groups is large enough that it is very unlikely to be the work of chance. It could suggest whether the null hypothesis should be rejected and whether there is any statistical basis for believing that the study guide can really improve state merit examination scores. Of course, even if it can be demonstrated that a statistically significant relationship between the two variables exists, we would still need to decide whether the relationship is a *substantive* one—that is, does a difference on the examination justify the purchase price of the study guide?

COMPUTING AND INTERPRETING *t* VALUES

Because of the current computer capacity of university, social agencies, and even many homes, it may never be necessary to determine a t value without computer assistance. This is fortunate, as the formula is complex and would involve a considerable amount of time if worked through by hand. For readers who find it easier to understand how a formula is applied by seeing it in a step-by-step format, we have included Figure 11.1.

You will note that the t test involves much more than a simple comparison of two groups' means. Actually, it compares the between-group variation of scores with the variation within groups. The complexity of t analysis (along with the fact that all raw scores are used in its computation) explains why it is such a powerful test for examining an apparent relationship between two variables.

The probability level of a t value is determined as in Step 7 of Figure 11.1. In the sample format, the t value is 1.90 (Step 5), and the degrees of freedom is 8 (Step 6). The question is, "What is the likelihood of committing a Type I error with a t value of 1.90, given 8 degrees of freedom?" To answer this question, we need to consult a probability table of t values such as Table 11.1.

The t value in the sample format in Figure 11.1 (1.90) is nonsignificant (at the .05 level) for a two-tailed test, but it is statistically significant at the .05 level for a one-tailed test. As Table 11.1 indicates, if the t value had been between 2.306 and 2.895 (with 8 *df*), the p level would have been significant at the .05 level for a two-tailed hypothesis and at the .025 level for a one-tailed hypothesis.

PRESENTATION OF *t*

It is often useful to present the raw scores of cases in both groups (if the sample is not too large) so that readers can make their own comparisons. If we choose not to report raw scores, we should at least report the mean of each group. Remember that the actual difference in means assists the reader in determining whether a statistically significant relationship is really a substantive finding. Other findings related to t that are customarily reported include

Figure 11.1 Format for Calculating a *t* Value for Two Groups

STEP 1. Lay out raw data.

Group A		*Group B*	
Client's Name	*Score*	*Client's Name*	*Score*
Peter	5	Gary	0
Janice	15	Carol	5
Alice	25	Martha	10
Robert	35	Jeff	15
Rosalie	45	James	20

STEP 2. Compute summary statistics from Step 1.

Where
Na = Number of people in Group A
Nb = Number of people in Group B
Xa = Sum of raw scores in Group A
Xb = Sum of raw scores in Group B
Sa = Sum of squares of raw scores in Group A
Sb = Sum of squares of raw scores in Group B
N = Total number of cases ($Na + Nb$)

Substituting values for letters, we get

Na = 5 (Calculated by counting)
Nb = 5 (Calculated by counting)
$Xa = 5 + 15 + 25 + 35 + 45$
= 125 (Sum of raw scores in Group A)
$Xb = 0 + 5 + 10 + 15 + 20$
= 50 (Sum of raw scores in Group B)
$Sa = 5^2 + 15^2 + 25^2 + 35^2 + 45^2$
$= 25 + 225 + 625 + 1225 + 2025$
= 4125 (Sum of squares of raw scores in Group A)
$Sb = 0^2 + 5^2 + 10^2 + 15^2 + 20^2$
$= 0 + 25 + 100 + 225 + 400$
= 750 (Sum of squares of raw scores in Group B)
$N = 5 + 5$
= 10 (Total number of cases)

Source: Adapted and Modified from Gorsuch, R. L. (1981). Bivariate analysis: Analysis of variance. In R. M. Grinnell, Jr. (Ed.), *Social work research and evaluation* (pp.505–508). Itasca, IL: F. E. Peacock.

the *t* value for each comparative analysis, the respective degrees of freedom (*df*), and the *p* value associated with each analysis. If several *t* tests are performed, a single table with all the reported results is helpful. If only a few *t* tests are calculated, the findings are frequently reported in the body of the text rather than in a table.

As in all statistical studies, we report those analyses that did not support rejection of the null hypothesis as well as those that

Figure 11.1 (continued)

STEP 3. Compute means for both groups.

Set out formulas.

Group A

$$Ma = \frac{Xa}{Na}$$

Group B

$$Mb = \frac{Xb}{Nb}$$

Where:

Ma = Mean of Group A

Mb = Mean of Group B

Substituting values for letters, we get

Group A

$$Ma = \frac{125}{5}$$
$$= 25 \text{ (Mean of Group A)}$$

Group B

$$Mb = \frac{50}{5}$$
$$= 10 \text{ (Mean of Group B)}$$

STEP 4. Compute sums of squared deviations for both groups.

Set out formulas.

Group A

$$SSa = Sa - \frac{Xa^2}{Na}$$

Group B

$$SSb = Sb - \frac{Xb^2}{Nb}$$

Where:

SSa = Sum of squared deviations for Group A

SSb = Sum of squared deviations for Group B

Substituting values for letters, we get

Group A

$$SSa = 4125 - \frac{125^2}{5}$$
$$= 4125 - \frac{15{,}625}{5}$$
$$= 4125 - 3125$$
$$= 1000 \text{ (Sum of squared deviations for Group A)}$$

Group B

$$SSb = 750 - \frac{50^2}{5}$$
$$= 750 - \frac{2500}{5}$$
$$= 750 - 500$$
$$= 250 \text{ (Sum of squared deviations for Group B)}$$

---

did. In the former cases, merely stating that the variables were not found to reflect a statistically significant relationship will probably suffice. In situations in which the null hypothesis is the central research hypothesis (that is, we are trying to disprove a relationship commonly believed to be true), statistical support or nonsupport for rejecting the null hypothesis should, of course, be reported.

Figure 11.1 (continued)

STEP 5. **Compute t value.**

Set out formula.

$$t = \frac{Ma - Mb}{\sqrt{\left(\frac{SSa + SSb}{Na + Nb - 2}\right)\left(\frac{Na + Nb}{(Na)(Nb)}\right)}}$$

Where $t = t$ value

Substituting values for letters, we get

$$t = \frac{25 - 10}{\sqrt{\left(\frac{1000 + 250}{5 + 5 - 2}\right)\left(\frac{5 + 5}{(5)(5)}\right)}}$$

$$= \frac{15}{\sqrt{\left(\frac{1250}{8}\right)\left(\frac{10}{25}\right)}}$$

$$= \frac{15}{\sqrt{(156.25)(.4)}}$$

$$= \frac{15}{\sqrt{62.5}}$$

$$= \frac{15}{7.9057}$$

$= 1.8974$

$= 1.90$ (t value)

STEP 6. **Compute degrees of freedom.**

Set out formula.

$$df = N - 2$$

Where df = Degrees of freedom

Substituting values for letters, we get

$$df = 10 - 2$$
$$= 8 \text{ (Degrees of freedom)}$$

STEP 7. Determine probability level of t value.

a. Use calculated t value (Step 5) and degrees of freedom (Step 6).
b. Use Table 11.1, "Critical Values of t."
c. Find proper row under the far-left-hand column labeled "df."
d. Compare calculated t value against tabled values for either one- or two-tailed test.

Table 11.1 Critical Values of t

	Level of Significance for a One-Tailed Test					
	.10	.05	.025	.01	.005	.0005
	Level of Significance for a Two-Tailed Test					
df	.20	.10	.05	.02	.01	.001
1	3.078	6.314	12.706	31.821	63.657	636.619
2	1.886	2.920	4.303	6.965	9.925	31.598
3	1.638	2.353	3.182	4.541	5.841	12.941
4	1.533	2.132	2.776	3.747	4.604	8.610
5	1.476	2.015	2.571	3.365	4.032	6.859
6	1.440	1.943	2.447	3.143	3.707	5.959
7	1.415	1.895	2.365	2.998	3.499	5.405
8	1.397	1.860	2.306	2.896	3.355	5.041
9	1.383	1.833	2.262	2.821	3.250	4.781
10	1.372	1.812	2.228	2.764	3.169	4.587
11	1.363	1.796	2.201	2.718	3.106	4.437
12	1.356	1.782	2.179	2.681	3.055	4.318
13	1.350	1.771	2.160	2.650	3.012	4.221
14	1.345	1.761	2.145	2.624	2.977	4.140
15	1.341	1.753	2.131	2.602	2.947	4.073
16	1.337	1.746	2.120	2.583	2.921	4.015
17	1.333	1.740	2.110	2.567	2.898	3.965
18	1.330	1.734	2.101	2.552	2.878	3.922
19	1.328	1.729	2.093	2.539	2.861	3.883
20	1.325	1.725	2.086	2.528	2.845	3.850
21	1.323	1.721	2.080	2.518	2.831	3.819
22	1.321	1.717	2.074	2.508	2.819	3.792
23	1.319	1.714	2.069	2.500	2.807	3.767
24	1.318	1.711	2.064	2.492	2.797	3.745
25	1.316	1.708	2.060	2.485	2.787	3.725
26	1.315	1.706	2.056	2.479	2.779	3.707
27	1.314	1.703	2.052	2.473	2.771	3.690
28	1.313	1.701	2.048	2.467	2.763	3.674
29	1.311	1.699	2.045	2.462	2.756	3.659
30	1.310	1.697	2.042	2.457	2.750	3.646
40	1.303	1.684	2.021	2.423	2.704	3.551
60	1.296	1.671	2.000	2.390	2.660	3.460
120	1.289	1.658	1.980	2.358	2.617	3.373
∞	1.282	1.645	1.960	2.326	2.576	3.291

The obtained value of t is significant if it is greater than or equal to the value listed in the table.

Source: Richard P. Runyon and Audrey Haber, *Fundamentals of Behavioral Statistics*, 2nd ed. (Reading, MA: Addison-Wesley Publishing Co., 1974). Taken from Table III of Ronald A. Fisher and Frank Yates, *Statistical Tables for Biological, Agricultural and Medical Research*, published by Longman Group, Ltd., London (previously published by Oliver and Boyd, Ltd., Edinburgh), and by permission of the authors and publishers.

WHEN NOT TO USE *t*

As with the chi-square test, the popularity of the *t* test among social workers sometimes can lead to its misuse. In our natural haste to use a statistic that is familiar to us, easily understood, and relatively unintimidating to the readers of research reports, we may sometimes use *t* tests in situations in which they are inappropriate and in which other, more appropriate tests could be used. Two misuses of the *t* are (1) when we ignore the shape of the distribution of the interval-level variable in the population and (2) when we use the shotgun approach to data analyses.

Shape of the Distribution

The fact that the independent variable is at the nominal level and the dependent variable is at the interval level does not provide sufficient justification for use of *t* to determine the presence of a relationship between the two variables. The *t* test is described as parametric, which means that it is designed for use only when the interval-level variable is considered to be normally distributed within the population. If a frequency distribution for values of the variable within the population would be noticeably skewed, another test, such as one of those presented in Chapter 12, should be used in place of *t*. The credibility of the research findings is seriously jeopardized if *t* is used with interval- or ratio-level data that do not reflect the normal curve.

The Shotgun Approach

A second common misuse involves calculating a series of *t* tests with a single dependent variable and many *possibly* related independent variables. In some particularly glaring examples of this error, researchers have calculated *t* tests using hundreds of different possible independent variables (with little basis for a relationship in the literature), only to announce proudly that they have found a statistically significant relationship between one of the independent variables and the dependent variable.

Probability theory would suggest that such findings are likely to reflect a Type I error and that the apparent relationship would be related to chance and nothing more. The phenomenon is little more than "data-dredging," a variation on the principle that "with an infinite number of monkeys and an infinite number of typewriters, a monkey will write a Pulitzer Prize–winning novel." It is only logical, given the laws of probability, that the dependent variable would appear to have a statistically significant association with *some* independent variable if enough relationships are tested. In situations where there is *reason* to believe that many different independent variables may relate to the dependent variable, we should use other statistical tests, specifically designed for such situations.

MICRO PRACTICE EXAMPLE

Impetus for the Study

Frank is a social worker in a large family service center. He was taught in his agency orientation that the best format for marital counseling is to see both partners (husband and wife) together. Five years ago, he treated 20 couples, all of whom could only be seen individually (husband or wife) because of their work schedules. He was surprised to note that, although they were never seen as a couple after their initial interviews, all 20 couples seemed to make excellent progress in solving their marital problems.

Over the intervening years, Frank saw more and more couples on an individual basis. Since he believed he was having good client outcomes, he encouraged six of his colleagues also to counsel couples with marital difficulties by seeing them separately rather than together. The other social workers were also surprised with their clients' excellent progress. Frank was not ready to conclude that the individual counseling format was really preferable to couple counseling. He decided to conduct a small-scale research study to see if he could find quantitative support for his hunch that couples seen individually make better progress toward solving marital problems than couples seen together.

The Hypothesis to Be Tested

As Frank began to search the social work literature, he found considerable support for the position that marital satisfaction is best enhanced when couples are treated in counseling *together*, not individually. But as he ventured into the literature from other fields such as psychology and pastoral counseling, Frank found a fair amount of support for the belief that marital satisfaction may be more likely to result from individual counseling. A reason sometimes given is that clients tend to discuss areas of dissatisfaction more readily and candidly when the spouse is not present. Frank concluded that the literature was conflicting. However, he felt that his own observations and those of his colleagues were sufficient to tilt the balance enough to justify a directional hypothesis.

Among couples receiving marital counseling, those seen individually will reflect a higher level of marital satisfaction than those seen together.

Overview of Methodology

Frank designed a small-scale research study to test his hypothesis. He received permission from the agency director to randomly assign new clients who requested marital counseling during a three-month period to either individual or couple counseling. In a research sense, the clients were randomly assigned to one of two subject groups. All six social workers who had previously used the individual counseling format (and were experienced with it) participated as counselors in Frank's study. Beginning the next month every other couple seen at intake was assigned to one of the six social workers to be seen together for counseling 50 minutes per week; the remaining couples were assigned to be seen individually for 25 minutes each per week. Those who could not agree to this arrangement were also treated but were not included as subjects in the study.

The counseling method (individual or couples) was the independent variable. It was decided that the dependent variable, marital satisfaction, would be measured after ten consecutive weeks of counseling. A marital satisfaction scale was chosen to measure marital satisfaction. The scale was assumed to produce interval-level data.

Fourteen couples were seen in individual counseling sessions, and fourteen were seen as couples. All clients completed the marital satisfaction scale. Frank compared the mean score of the scale for the clients who were seen individually (experimental group) with the mean score of the scale for the clients who were seen as couples (control group). The variable "marital satisfaction" as measured by the scale has been found to be normally distributed, so Frank felt justified in using the t test for his statistical analysis. He was attempting to determine whether the difference between the mean scores (for the two groups) was sufficiently large to allow him to reject the null hypothesis. He hoped to be able to conclude that a real relationship between the two variables (not chance or sampling error) was the likely explanation for the differences observed in the sample.

Findings

The value of t for Frank's data was 1.312. From a table of critical values of t (Table 11.1), he learned that he would have needed a minimum t value of 1.706 to be able to reject the null hypothesis (using a statistical significance of .05, a sample of 28, and 26 degrees of freedom, and having a directional hypothesis).

Interpreting and Drawing Conclusions

Frank noted that if he were to reject the null hypothesis based on the analysis of his data, he would have slightly more than a 1 in 10 (10 percent) chance of committing a Type I error. He clearly lacked statistical support for his hypothesis. His initial disappointment was made even worse when he looked at the mean scores of the two groups. The clients who had participated in individual counseling scored somewhat worse, on the average, than did those seen together. Frank looked at his findings more objectively. It was then that he realized that his lack of demonstrated support for a relationship between counseling method and marital satisfaction might reflect a useful finding in and of itself. His inability to reject the null hypothesis could be interpreted to mean that it makes little difference which counseling method is used!

Frank also wondered how he could have been mistaken. The quantitative findings from his study were inconsistent with his previous impressions. He wondered whether he and the other social workers had perhaps *perceived* their individual counseling clients as doing better because they had overreacted to their surprise that these clients did about as well as those seen in couple counseling. Of course, he also wondered whether his hypothesis might still be correct. Perhaps the true relationship between the dependent and independent variables had been hidden by biased measurements or the influence of other variables (for instance, the social workers' greater experience with couple counseling). As he thought about it, he concluded that additional studies employing tighter research designs were indicated.

Relating the Findings to Practice

In the interim, before further research studies could be conducted, Frank wondered what practical use he could make of his findings. During the next agency staff meeting he was given time to present his study results. He was able to draw implications for social work practice within the agency. As frequently happens in social work research, his study generated more questions than answers. However, these questions served to focus the staff's attention on potentially productive areas of inquiry. Based on his findings, Frank and other staff members began to ask the following questions.

1. Since type of counseling (individual or couple) *may* have little or no effect in enhancing marital satisfaction, should attempts continue to be made to encourage clients to enter couple counseling if they seem resistive or if it represents a scheduling difficulty for them?
2. Should involvement of both partners in counseling continue sometimes to be a prerequisite to counseling, or should this policy be changed?
3. Should funds be allocated for a staff development program to enhance the social workers' use of individual counseling in treatment of marital problems?
4. Should the staff develop a single treatment model that combines individual and couple counseling, or should the professional staff be allowed freedom to select the counseling format that they prefer to use?

These questions (and others) ranged from issues that affected the individual social work practitioner to those that related to agency policies. The principal value of Frank's study was to call into question certain unchallenged practices within the agency and to encourage the staff either to justify or to discard them based upon further examination. Even if no changes resulted, the social workers would be practicing on a sounder theoretical base until subsequent research findings provided a more definitive answer to the questions.

MACRO PRACTICE EXAMPLE

Impetus for the Study

Nan is the chief of social services for a large state health agency. In her professional role, she oversees social work services offered in the 50 district health offices within the state. It was recently brought to her attention that the agency was having a serious problem with social worker staff turnover. A preliminary examination of agency data revealed that the problem was statewide and appeared to be normally distributed among the 50 district offices.

Nan spoke with the personnel officer who was responsible for conducting outprocessing interviews with employees leaving the agency. At first, he preferred not to suggest possible reasons why so many social workers were resigning. But after Nan assured him that she did not plan to ask him to identify workers who made complaints to him, he volunteered that the reasons given by caseworkers for leaving appeared to be amazingly similar. He recalled that "many" of them seemed totally frustrated with the lack of autonomy in decision making they were given. While they recognized that in some professional and administrative matters the final decision had to be made by the supervisor, they saw no reason why many other decisions could not be made by them and their fellow professionals through a democratic process.

Afterward, Nan thought about what had been said. While her first inclination had been to be annoyed with the district supervisors for their autocratic approach to decision making, she quickly remembered that she had to take much of the responsibility for their supervisory style. It was she who had come to rely on the use of staff authority when it seemed to work so well with persons in her secretarial pool. She had hired trainers from outside the agency and required that all district supervisors attend training in the use of staff authority. She had also commented regularly at supervisors' meetings how effective she thought the approach was. Apparently the supervisors were only responding to Nan's message that extensive use of staff authority is a sign of good supervision. By making their workers only advisory to them and unable to make decisions or implement them, they were really complying with Nan's implicit directive.

The Hypothesis to Be Tested

Nan knew that she needed an objective way to determine whether social workers' level of autonomy in decision making is related to staff turnover. She did not want to trust the impressions of the personnel officer without further evidence. She would not attempt to help all her supervisors to become more democratic in delegating decision making until she could be reasonably certain that there was some relationship between the two variables. She decided to conduct a small research study to test the hypothesis:

The rate of staff turnover will be lower in democratic decision-making environments than in autocratic ones.

Overview of Methodology

Nan knew that recent management literature stressed the use of quality circles as a promising way to solve some administrative problems by arriving at decisions via the group process. (The approach is characteristic of "Theory Z" management methods that have been viewed as successful in Japan for many years.) Because Nan had been considering the use of quality circles anyway, she saw this as a good time to try them. Quality circles seemed to her to be a good operationalization of a more democratic approach to decision making in the district offices.

Nan randomly selected ten districts to serve as her experimental group. She then provided release time to the ten district supervisors to attend an out-of-state workshop on the use of quality circles. She told the supervisors that she expected them to implement quality circles in their supervision and she asked for a report on their methods of implementation to insure that this had been done. They were asked to not share their experiences with other supervisors.

At the same time, Nan randomly selected ten other districts to constitute her control group. Their ten district supervisors were given no additional training and no new instructions as to how they should handle decision making within their work groups.

After one year, Nan computed the average rate of turnover for districts in the experimental group and for those in the control group. She had two categories of the nominal-level, independent variable, decision-making environment (democratic and autocratic). Her dependent variable, turnover rate, was ratio-level. The situation seemed to be well-suited to the use of t to test whether there might be statistical support for her directional hypothesis.

Findings

The t value for Nan's data was 1.992. She concluded that there were 18 degrees of freedom ($10 + 10 = 20 - 2 = 18$). Using a table of critical values of t (see Table 11.1), she noted that, for the row corresponding to 18 degrees of freedom, her t value fell between 1.734 and 2.100. She moved to the left (1.734) and observed that it was in the column headed by .05 for one-tailed tests and .10 for two-tailed tests. The p corresponding to her data was, therefore, less than .05.

Interpreting and Drawing Conclusions

From her knowledge of statistics Nan knew that she had found support for a statistically significant relationship between the dependent and independent variables. She knew that, if she were to reject the null hypothesis, she would have less than a 5 percent chance of committing a Type I error (on the basis of statistical probability alone). She also was pleased to see that the relationship was in the direction predicted; the mean turnover rate for district offices in the experimental group was lower than the mean turnover rate for district offices in the control group.

Because her study had been very limited in scope, Nan was reluctant to view her findings as an unequivocal endorsement of quality circles or other more democratic methods of problem solving/decision making as a method of reducing social worker staff turnover. She recognized that it would be precipitous on her part to proceed to implement her findings as though she had uncovered a simple cause-effect relationship. The weak design of her study had certainly not eliminated either bias or other variables as possible explanations for the difference in staff turnover rate between the two groups of district offices. Certain methodological questions remained. For example, how much did the opportunity to go out-of-state for training positively affect the morale of the experimental group supervisors? Perhaps they came back in a better mood and more inclined to be considerate of their workers. If so, this may have been a better explanation than the implementation of quality circles for their lower staff turnover rate. Or did the workers view the supervisors in the experimental group as more considerate simply because they made an effort to try something new? If so, this might have been a major factor in reduced turnover rate.

Despite the fact that Nan's findings would have to be viewed as tentative, she was still able to use them both to understand the problem of staff turnover and to begin to address it through her actions. She started by asking herself several questions in light of her findings.

1. How can I adjust my supervisory style with district supervisors so that I do not unintentionally communicate to them that I expect extensive use of staff authority relationships in their supervision of social workers?
2. How can I help district supervisors to identify decisions that are appropriate for use of the democratic process and to make them feel more comfortable in using that process?
3. How can I help district supervisors to identify decisions that are inappropriate for the democratic process (for example, personnel matters) and to continue to use staff authority and other less democratic approaches without harming the morale of workers?
4. What use of the democratic process, besides quality circles, would help social workers feel that they have more input into decisions if they possess the necessary expertise?
5. Would it be advisable to send all district supervisors to quality circle training?
6. What future research studies can be designed to provide additional support for my conclusion that democratic decision making is associated with lower staff turnover rates?

After thinking about these and other questions that emerged from her study, Nan discussed her ideas for implementing her findings with friends who are social work administrators in other large state agencies. She then settled on a plan of action.

At the next meeting of all supervisors, Nan shared the findings of her research study. She reiterated her support for the use of staff authority in certain situations but also stated her belief that social workers at all levels are professionals and need to be involved in decision making. She emphasized that she believed that overreliance on autocratic supervisory approaches can hurt morale and, even more important, does not take advantage of the expertise of supervisees in addressing problems. She supported these contentions with her actions by asking one of the former experimental group members to use part of the next supervisors' meeting to teach all the supervisors (including herself) the basic principles of quality circles. In the meeting, the other nine supervisors who had used them were asked to share their experiences.

Nan was convinced that the sharing of certain decision making by district supervisors with their staff was indicated. In another meeting, she emphasized this belief to the supervisors. But, consistent with it, she allowed them individually to decide whether they preferred to receive training in quality circles in order to implement that technique in their districts or to develop their own plan (with her approval) for introducing ways to increase democratic decision making among their staff.

Finally, Nan set aside time to develop a more comprehensive and rigorous analysis of the problem of staff turnover. The study would examine other factors (in addition to approaches to decision making) that the literature suggests are related in some way to staff morale and turnover. She hoped that, ultimately, the findings from a larger-scale study could be generalized to other social work settings and that a report of them would have potential for publication in a social work professional journal.

SUMMARY

This chapter has presented the use of a popular statistical test that compares the means of two samples, the t test. We have noted that it is particularly useful within social work research. The case examples have illustrated the point that while the t test is often used in major research efforts, it is also valuable for preliminary, limited efforts.

The micro and macro practice examples, viewed in concert with those in Chapters 9 and 10, also make another important point. The reader will note that those statistical findings that support hypotheses are of practical value at many different levels for the social work practitioner. But if a study is designed and implemented well and statistical testing is conducted correctly, findings that fail to support our research hypothesis are also of utility for practice. It is reassuring to know that conscientious researchers who use common sense in interpreting their findings cannot lose. They will have advanced the body of knowledge available to social work practice, even if they *never* achieve statistical support for a directional or nondirectional hypothesis.

STUDY QUESTIONS

1. What is the appropriate combination of levels of measurement of two variables for the use of t?
2. Why do sample size and subsample size comparability requirements of t frequently make it ideally suited for social work research?
3. If the null hypothesis were correct, would the mean value of a variable in one sample be very similar to or very different from the mean value for that variable in the other sample?
4. Would common sense tell us that sampling error is a more likely explanation of a difference of 5 years in the average age of students in two sections of a course if the sections each have 10 students or if they each have 25?
5. Why does the t formula suggest that the test should be used only with normal distributions?
6. What determines the degrees of freedom for t in a given data set?
7. What additional step is required in determining whether a t value that is statistically significant reflects support for a directional hypothesis?
8. What policy should the researcher employ regarding the reporting of statistical analysis using t that fails to provide statistical support for a hypothesis?
9. How might a t that is not statistically significant still reflect a finding that is useful for the practitioner?
10. How have researchers used many different t analyses employing a single dependent variable to produce misleading "findings"?

FURTHER READING

Gorsuch, R. L. (1981). Bivariate analysis: Analysis of variance. In R. M. Grinnell, Jr. (Ed.), *Social Work Research and Evaluation* (pp. 500–529). Itasca, IL: F. E. Peacock.

MacEachron, A. E. (1982). *Basic statistics in the human services: An applied approach* (Ch. 11). Baltimore: University Park Press.

Reid, W. J., & Smith, A. D. (1981). *Research in social work* (Ch. 10). New York: Columbia University Press.

Schuerman, J. R. (1983). *Research and evaluation in the human services* (Ch. 12). New York: Free Press.

12

ADDITIONAL STATISTICAL TESTS

You may recall from the preface that we promised you a chance to gain an appreciation of statistical procedures and their contributions to knowledge development for social work practice. By now, you should have acquired a general understanding of the characteristics that statistical tests share and, from Chapters 9 to 11, insights into some different ways in which statistics attempt to refute the researcher's old nemesis, chance.

The last three chapters have provided a detailed look at three tests that are extremely useful to the social work researcher. In fact, a major portion of all social work research uses chi-square, Pearson's r, and Student's t in its statistical analysis. Sometimes, as we have suggested earlier, these techniques are used whether they are appropriate or not, thereby weakening the credibility of the research study. In this chapter, we will briefly mention some other statistical tests that are seen fairly frequently in the social work literature. They are a representative (not comprehensive) list of alternatives to the three in Chapters 9, 10, and 11. Coverage of these tests will be necessarily superficial. In no way will readers learn all they will need to know in order to use them. There will be no formulas. In only one discussion (the first one) is there an example of how statistical findings are generally displayed; this is provided only for clarification of the description within the text. As in the rest of this book, we have attempted to keep our discussion "reader-friendly." The objective of the brief discussions that follow is to provide enough information for you to have some general insight into the way the tests work and the kind of social work research situations in which they might be used. The reader will need to consult any one of several standard references to make the final decision as to their appropriateness and to gain the additional familiarity required for their use (see "Advanced References for Further Reading").

CROSSTABULATION ALTERNATIVES

Every social worker's favorite, chi-square, is not appropriate for all statistical analysis involving nominal-level variables; for instance, sample size or independence of samples can cause the researcher to look for alternatives. We will briefly examine two that are commonly seen.

McNemar's Test

This test (also referred to as the *test for the significance of changes*) is designed for use with two "related samples." In fact, it is most commonly applied in research that employs a before-and-after design and two different measurements of a single variable using the same subjects, with the measurements occurring at two different times. It is frequently used in determining if a type of intervention may have had an effect—for instance, was the presence of an educational program associated with a change in attitude or behavior?

In social work practice, we often wonder whether an intervention is having any effect at all. Of course, we are most interested in causing change to occur in a desirable way. But because of the existence of so many other variables that can influence client behavior, we often cannot say with certainty just how influential the social work services might be in any changes that occur. The McNemar test provides at least a crude indication of whether the presence of a "treatment" seems to be associated with change.

An Example

A social worker, Carlos, requested time to address a meeting of a parents' group to present his position in favor of the hiring of four additional social workers for the district. He wondered whether the parents would be influenced by his arguments or do little more than listen politely. Or perhaps they wouldn't even listen at all; maybe they would be planning their weekend while he talked. Before Carlos even considered giving up subsequent evenings to speak to other parents' groups, he needed to know whether his first presentation was associated with a desirable change in parents' thinking.

A straw vote on the perceptions of parents regarding the hiring issue taken before Carlos's presentation and immediately after provided before-and-after measurements. The parents thus served as their own control group. Carlos took the two sets of measurements and placed them into a two-by-two contingency table (similar to the one we use with χ^2) with one variable (before measurements) on one side and the other (after measurements) on the other side. He then used the appropriate formula and checked the table to see whether there was statistical support for rejection of the null hypothesis.

The numbers Carlos placed in each of the four cells were the number of cases (frequencies) from among the 25 parents who reflected each of the four possible combinations of before-and-after measurements (see Table 12.1). If, for instance, before the presentation Mr. Brown favored the hiring of the social workers but changed his mind after hearing Carlos, he would be represented as one of the 13 cases in the lower right-hand cell (cell *d*). If Ms. Rodriguez had been opposed but was won over by Carlos's arguments, she would be represented as one of the 5 cases in the upper left-hand cell (cell *a*). McNemar's test looks at change. Cells *a* and *d* represent change; cells *b* and *c* reflect no change in position between the times before Carlos's presentation and immediately after it. The test is really not very interested in cases where no change occurred. Thus, the focus of analysis is on cells *a* and *d*. Chance (the null hypothesis) says that change would certainly occur with some cases even if Carlos had no effect, but, overall, the most likely phenomenon attributable to chance would involve change in one direction in about half of those cases in which change occurred, and about half the changes would be in the other direction.

Statistically, the McNemar test seeks to determine whether the null hypothesis can be rejected by demonstrating that the preponderance of change that occurred was in any one direction. Carlos was able to reject the null hypothesis. Unfortunately, the direction of the relationship indicated that his presentation may have been associated with more negative learning (parents' turning against the proposal), than positive learning (parents' being influenced to accept the proposal). Only seven parents failed to change their po-

Table 12.1
Tabular Presentation of Significance of Changes Analysis (McNemar's Test)

	After		
Before	Positive	Negative	Totals
Negative	5 (*a*)	4 (*b*)	9
Positive	3 (*c*)	13 (*d*)	16
Totals	8	17	25

$x^2 = 4.50$, $df = 1$, $p < .025$

sitions (cells *b* and *c*). But of the 18 who changed their positions (cells *a* and *d*), only 5 moved from negative to positive (cell *a*) while 13 (cell *d*) who had previously favored the proposal opposed it after the presentation. The demonstration of a statisticaly significant change was an endorsement of Carlos's change success but not the predicted change he had sought. Had he said something to "turn off" the parents, since so many of them seemed to have been negatively affected?

As can be seen, the McNemar test is quite limited. It has certain requirements as to sample size and distribution and is best applied when the situation involves nominal-level variables and when before-and-after requirements are possible. In these circumstances it is a useful test for the social work researcher.

Fisher's Exact Test

The Fisher's exact test, like chi-square, is used when two independent samples are available for the research study. The independent samples may have resulted from the random sampling of cases drawn from two identifiable groups (for instance, group or individual counseling).

The principal advantage of the Fisher's exact test over chi-square is that it can be employed when the sample size is too small to meet the criteria for using chi-square. It is also designed for analyzing data using only a two-by-two contingency table—that is, when there are *only* two values of each of the two variables under study or when three or more categories of a variable can logically be collapsed into a two-by-two table.

An Example

Joyce is a social work supervisor in a child protection agency. During a recent week, 27 cases of alleged sexual abuse were investigated by her workers. Twenty of the cases were closed for lack of evidence. Eighteen of these were investigated by male workers. She became concerned—were the male workers too quick to close cases? Could there be an association between the sex of the worker and the decision to close or not close suspected sexual abuse cases?

Joyce placed her data into a contingency table exactly like Table 12.1 and used the Fisher's exact test. The data analysis confirmed Joyce's suspicions. She was able to document a statistically significant association between sex of worker and whether cases remained open or closed. The male supervisors (based on one month's data) *were* apparently more likely to close cases than were the female workers. The phenomenon merited further investigation.

Fisher's exact test is ideally suited to research needs such as the one Joyce experienced. Because it is limited to a two-by-two table and is best used with small samples, its application is sometimes limited to the drawing of tentative conclusions that can later be verified with larger samples or more complex designs.

ALTERNATIVES THAT REQUIRE ORDINAL-LEVEL MEASUREMENT

In Chapters 10 and 11, we discussed two tests (Pearson's *r* and Student's *t*) that, while commonly used for hypothesis testing and other analyses, have some rigorous requirements. Pearson's *r* is designed to determine the degree of correlation between the interval-level measures of one variable and the interval-level measures of a second variable. While the *t* test requires that only one of the two variables be at the interval level, the test is parametric—that is, the interval-level variable should be normally distributed within the population. If the dependent variable can yield a precise interval-level measurement or if a refined scale is available for measurement and (in the case of *t*) a normal distribution exists, these may be the tests of choice. But what if the dependent variable is not normally distributed within the population or defies precise measurement? Perhaps the scale is relatively new and we do not yet feel comfortable in declaring that the intervals of measurement are equal in size. Or the dependent variable may be of a nature that "always, sometimes, or never," "improvement, no change, or decline," or some other comparable rank ordering of values is all we can hope to achieve. Fortunately, there are some good alternative tests that the social work researcher can consider for use with ordinal-level data. We will mention four of these and give a brief example of how each one might appropriately be used.

Mann-Whitney *U*

The Mann-Whitney *U* is especially useful in research studies involving two small independent samples. It is frequently used in small experiments or in ex post facto, quasi-experimental situations to determine whether a "treatment" given to the experimental group but not to the control group appears to result in a difference in regard to some dependent variable that can be rank-ordered (ordinal). The groups need not be identical in size. It is effective with very small samples (under eight) or larger ones, but we must be careful to use the appropriate table of critical values for the size of the sample used.

The test is easily computed by hand or pocket calculator, especially if our sample is small. It is based on the assumption that a good indicator of difference between the two groups is the number of cases in one group that fall below each respective score of the other group when all scores are rank-ordered. The logical premise underlying it is that a clustering of the higher scores drawn from one group and the lower scores drawn from the other group probably suggests that, on the whole, the two groups are different in regard to the dependent variable. *U* is a mathematical way of determining whether this pattern is sufficiently strong to reject the null hypothesis.

An Example

Scott is a social worker employed by a large corporation. During July he had 17 referrals of workers identified as having an "attitude problem" on their job. He asked each of their supervisors to name another worker at the same level whom they would describe as having a very good attitude who might join him when the problem worker was being counseled. Seven of the supervisors complied with his request; the other ten did not.

Scott saw all 17, the seven with a coworker and the others alone for five sessions. After the fifth interview, he asked their respective supervisors to complete a ten-item, five-point job attitude scale that had recently been developed in the personnel department for supervisors to evaluate workers. He then rank-ordered the scores of the 17 and used the Mann-Whitney *U* to test for group independence. He was optimistic that the "experimental" counseling approach involving a coworker would be found to be superior to the one-on-one approach used in the control group because three of the top four attitude scores were achieved by experimental group members.

In fact, *U* did not allow Scott to reject the null hypothesis. Two of the lowest scores also came from experimental group members. Even if *U* had achieved statistical significance, alternative explanations to a true relationship (lack of random assignment to groups, the effect of other variables, and so forth) could not have been ruled out because of the lack of rigor of Scott's research design. Scott decided to tighten up the design and to pursue his inquiry further by using larger samples, and by including a pretest.

The Mann-Whitney *U* is often used as a preliminary method of examining relationships between variables without investing great amounts of effort in research design and implementation. Because it requires only ordinal-level data, it is appropriate for situations in which the development of a new data collection instrument precludes any claim by the researcher that there is adequate measurement precision to generate interval- or ratio-level data. Its small sample-size requirements also lend themselves well to preliminary analysis of possible relationships.

U should not be viewed as a crude indicator of relationship or merely a tool of early evaluation, however. It is the *only* test that has been applied in some very rigorous and useful research studies. In certain situations—as with every test we have mentioned and will mention—it is the best and most appropriate approach to analysis. It is one of the more commonly used tests in social work research and, usually, for the correct reasons.

The Median Test

Another useful test for situations that cannot yield interval-level measurement and/or a normal distribution is the median test. Like *t*, it employs a comparison of a measurement of central tendency, but unlike *t*, only ordinal measurement of one variable is required. It is also similar to *t* in that it is designed to assess the likelihood that two subsamples (sometimes an experimental group and a control group) are sufficiently different from each other in regard to the dependent variable to warrant rejection of the null hypothesis.

Essentially, the "workings" of the median test are relatively simple. Scores are rank-ordered, and the median for all scores is established. Then the number of scores above and below the median (those at the median are dropped or added to one group or the other) are tabulated for both groups, and the frequencies are placed into a two-by-two contingency table. When the total number of cases (both groups) is between 20 and 40, Fisher's exact test is generally used to determine the likelihood of committing a Type I error if the null hypothesis were to be rejected. With larger samples, use of chi-square may be justified.

The median test is based on the assumption that, if the two groups are not really different or reflect differences largely attributable to chance, each will have approximately the same percent (sample sizes need not be equal) of cases above and below the median. A clustering above the median by one group and below by the other may indicate a real difference in the variable, depending on the strength of this pattern.

An Example

Lou Ann is a social worker employed in a genetic counseling center. She observed that only about half of those older pregnant women (over 35) who were referred for amniocentesis (a test to determine if the fetus has any of several genetic problems) followed through with the referral. In her rather unscientific observation, she noticed what she thought might be a factor related to this phenomenon. It seemed to her that women who did not follow through on the referral tended to have several children already; those who did, seemed to have fewer children.

The variable "number of children" is at the ratio level. But Lou Ann knew that the variable is not normally distributed. She decided to use the median test. She grouped the data into four cells of a contingency table based on where each case fell in regard to the dependent variable, completed/uncompleted referral, and the independent variable, number of children (above or below the median). The criteria for size of expected frequencies for chi-square were met, so she completed her analysis using the appropriate formula. Her initial impressions were confirmed by her use of the median test. She speculated on her findings, wondering whether the possible birth of a child with, for instance, Down's syndrome, was of less concern in larger families because of additional child-care help available from older siblings. She decided to pursue the possible explanation in subsequent research studies.

The example is a little unusual for use of the median test in that it was the independent variable that was treated as ordinal. (It was really ratio-level but badly skewed.) More typically, it is the dependent variable that is ordinal, while the independent variable (for example, type of treatment) is at the nominal level. The test is a good one when either combination of measurement precision is present.

The median test, unlike some of the others in this chapter, is presented here because it is potentially useful to the social work researcher, not because it is commonly used in social work research. All too frequently, we have observed that the criteria for *t* cannot be met and have turned quickly to chi-square. In many instances, the median test is a preferable alternative. It treats the measurement of the interval- or ratio-level variable as ordinal, thereby using more available precision of measurement than does chi-square, which treats all variables as if they are only nominal-level. To use chi-square in such situations is to run the risk of throwing away available precision of measurement and to increase the risk of an error in drawing conclusions from the research.

The Kolmogorov-Smirnov Two-Sample Test

This test (hereafter referred to as K-S) has some similarities with the median test. But it compares more than just central tendency data, focusing also on dispersion, skewness, and other characteristics of the distribution of values of an ordinal-level variable within two samples. (A variation, the K-S one-sample test, works similarly, except that it compares a sample with another theoretical distribution of the variable.)

The K-S is based on the assumption that if two samples are randomly drawn from the same population and the null hypothesis is correct, variations in the ordinal-level variable and the distribution of values of the variable should be very similar. If differences between the two samples are considerable, they are probably not just random deviations that probability would cause to occur; a true difference might exist. The test is a way of determining if the differences in the distribution of the values of the variable are large enough to rule out chance and to justify rejection of the null hypothesis.

The K-S analyzes the data by comparing the cumulative frequencies for intervals in the ordinal-level variable (for instance, how many cases were rated "slightly improved" for the control group vs. the experimental group). Actually, the formula focuses on the point (interval) at which the cumulative frequency difference between the two groups was the largest.

An Example

Roland is a county director in a public assistance agency. Several of his black workers had complained that white workers were displaying excessively suspicious and punitive attitudes toward AFDC clients. They stated that they believed that clients were not being trusted and were assumed to be "cheaters."

No good single measurement of suspicious and punitive attitudes was available, but Roland concluded that "number of referrals for fraud investigation" was an adequate, if less than precise, indicator of quantity of the variable. Although an exact count of referrals was possible, when used as a measurement of attitudes (the *real* dependent variable), ordinal-level data were all that could be claimed. He requested his secretary to compile a count of fraud referrals for each worker during the previous three months. He then assembled a cumulative frequency distribution for black workers and for white workers, using 8 intervals of number of referrals for each. The decision to use 8 intervals (referrals ranged from 9 to 32) was made in an effort to "conserve" the precision of measurement available (using 3 intervals would throw away too much data) while not "cutting too thin" by claiming that, for example, a difference of only one referral was a valid indicator of a real difference in attitude. The decision relied primarily on common sense and research ethics.

Having identified the interval at which the cumulative frequency distributions were most different from each other, Roland applied the K-S formula. He learned that, in fact, there was little real difference between black and white workers for the measurement of the variable, at least not enough to rule out chance and to reject the null hypothesis. While he did not totally discount the complaints of his workers (a better measurement *might* have revealed an attitudinal difference), he did feel that he lacked sufficient evidence to confront his workers about what some perceived as a problem. He chose instead to reinforce what he believed to be appropriate attitudes toward AFDC clients in future staff meetings.

The K-S two-sample test is useful in looking at the relationship between an ordinal-level variable and a nominal-level variable when just a comparison of central tendency may be insufficient. By examining the whole distribution of values of the ordinal-level variable, we get a more complete picture of the similarity of two samples. Still another test, the Wald-Wolfowitz Runs test (which will not be discussed here), goes even further in that it identifies differences that the K-S does not detect.

The Wilcoxon Matched-Pairs Signed-Rank Test (Wilcoxon Sign)

Social work researchers often find themselves with measurements that are a little more precise than ordinal-level but not precise enough to qualify as interval-level. This is frequently the case with newly developed scales for measurements of attitudes, perceptions, or beliefs. Sometimes the amorphous nature of what we are measuring prevents us from claiming that the value labels we assign reflect precise intervals—that is, equal difference in quantity of a variable. The Wilcoxon Sign test is useful in those situations where, for instance, we know that a score of 70 is reflective of more of a variable than a score of 60 *and* where we know that this difference is greater than the difference between 62 and 60. If this latter determination can be made, we would be throwing away available measurement precision if we were to look at only the direction (more, less, or the same) of difference between pairs of matched cases who constitute two groups. Another test, the sign test, is appropriate when only this less precise determination can be made.

The Wilcoxon Sign test is based on the assumption that, if a treatment makes no difference, there will be essentially no difference in regard to the dependent variable among the cases in one group and their counterparts in the other group (the null hypothesis). The ideal situation would require the use of identical cases (identical twins?) in every respect. But, for practical purposes, cases that are paired based on a pretest measurement of the dependent variable and/or one or more of the most likely intervening variables are usually sufficient. Once pairs are identified, one member is randomly assigned to one group; the second goes to the other group. The test examines the amount of difference between each pair after treatment as well as the direction of difference. In the process, the differences between pairs are themselves rank-ordered. If the preponderance of differences suggest higher scores for one group *and* the greatest differences are also among those cases, the Wilcoxon Sign test is likely to suggest a statistically significant difference in the groups, and the null hypothesis can be rejected. The stronger the pattern in this direction, the more likely the null hypothesis can be safely rejected, and vice versa.

An Example

Denise is a social work counselor in a student health center. From years of observation, she wondered whether college students having social adjustment problems benefited more from counseling by untrained student volunteers or from counseling by trained professional staff. Using standard intake screening measurements over a one-month period, she identified a group of prospective clients who were all diagnosed as having "moderate social adjustment problems." Before assignment for counseling, she identified 15 matched pairs (matched on such key variables as sex, grade point average, and the like) and randomly assigned one member of each pair to be seen by a student volunteer; the other was seen by a social worker. After six one-hour counseling sessions, all clients were administered a scale that measured social adjustment. The instrument, which Denise considered as an indicator of college students' social adjustment, was deemed to be capable of generating the "ordinal-plus" data required for use of the Wilcoxon Sign test. Data were compared for each pair, and direction and amount of difference were noted. The differences were rank-ordered.

Denise was relieved to learn that the members of the pairs seen by the social workers scored much better on the scale than did those seen by student volunteers. The Wilcoxon Sign test allowed her to feel comfortable in rejecting the null hypothesis: the direction of the differences let her conclude that it was the clients seen by social workers who scored higher on the scale. She was, of course, not ready to discount student volunteers as effective counselors based on this single bit of evidence, but she wondered whether they might be used more effectively in work with students having other problems. She also decided to replicate her mini-study, using another measurement of social adjustment to see if consistent findings would be obtained.

The Wilcoxon Sign test is clearly limited to situations in which it is possible to identify matched pairs. When the pairs are available, however, it is a relatively powerful test that is well suited to situations where measurement of a variable is precise enough that treating it as "only ordinal" might mean not taking advantage of the strength of measurement available.

SUMMARY

In this chapter we have mentioned some of the other tests that are seen fairly frequently in the social work literature. They are tests that are useful alternatives to those discussed in Chapters 9, 10, and 11. With the exception of t, this book has looked at only one kind of test, nonparametric measures that do not assume normal distributions. The reader should know that another whole group of tests, the parametric, is available when data distributions justify their use.

We should also note that this book has focused on an understanding of the common elements of statistical testing and, in the process of attempting to achieve this objective, we have primarily used tests and examples designed for examining the simplest of relationships, the relationship between only two variables. The many tests that explore more complex relationships were rarely mentioned. In fact, one of the most common misuses of statistics occurs when a series of univariate analyses are applied when multivariate testing is appropriate. Such an error can easily lead to erroneous conclusions. Our explanation for this omission is that we have concentrated on building a basic understanding that will serve readers well when and if they decide to pursue the topic further. We have chosen to sacrifice comprehensiveness for simplicity to accomplish our goal of providing a "reader-friendly" introduction to statistics.

STUDY QUESTIONS

1. Why would McNemar's test be especially well suited for social workers who wish to evaluate the impact of a group experience on a stereotype about minorities?
2. In what situations can Fisher's exact test be used when chi-square should not?
3. What conditions for use of the Mann-Whitney *U* make it particularly well suited for the individual practitioner who wishes to evaluate the effectiveness of a new treatment method?
4. Why is the median test preferable to chi-square if interval- or ratio-level data do not meet the necessary criteria for use of *t*?
5. Why is the Kolmogorov-Smirnov test a more comprehensive comparison of ordinal-level or skewed interval data drawn from two groups than the median test?
6. What specialized type of sampling is required for the Wilcoxon Sign test?
7. What are some of the situations that suggest the need for tests like those described in this chapter rather than those explained in Chapters 9, 10, and 11?
8. What limitations do all the tests in this chapter and those in Chapters 9, 10, and 11 have in common?
9. In what ways do all the tests work in a similar manner?
10. Discuss the possible disadvantages of using statistical tests that are less well known.

FURTHER READING

MacEachron, A. E. (1982). *Basic statistics in the human services: An applied approach* (Ch. 12). Baltimore: University Park Press.

Reid, W. J., & Smith, A. D. (1981). *Research in social work* (Ch. 10). New York: Columbia University Press.

GLOSSARY OF FORMULAS: SELECTED LIST

$$\text{Mean} = \frac{\text{Sum of all values in a distribution}}{\text{Total number of values in the distribution}}$$

(See Chapter 4)

Range = Maximum value − minimum value + 1 (See Chapter 5)

Interquartile range = 75th percentile − 25th percentile

(See Chapter 5)

$$\text{Semi-interquartile range} = \frac{\text{75th percentile} - \text{25th percentile}}{2}$$

(See Chapter 5)

Deviation score for value = value − mean (See Chapter 5)

$$\text{Mean deviation} = \frac{\text{Sum of deviation values (ignoring} - \text{or} + \text{signs)}}{\text{Number of values in the distribution}}$$

(See Chapter 5)

$$\text{Median} = LRL + \left[\frac{\frac{1}{2}N - Cfb}{fw}\right] \times i$$

Where LRL = lower real limit of interval containing median
N = number of scores
Cfb = cumulative frequency *below* interval containing median or below LRL
fw = frequency within interval containing median
i = width or size of interval containing median

Standard deviation

$$s = \sqrt{\frac{\Sigma(X - \overline{X})^2}{N}}$$

(See Chapter 6)

$$z \text{ score} = \frac{\text{Raw score} - \text{mean}}{\text{Standard deviation}}$$

(See Chapter 6)

Expected frequency (chi-square)

$$E = \frac{(R)\ (C)}{N}$$

(See Chapter 9)

Chi-square

$$\chi^2 = \Sigma \frac{(O - E)^2}{E}$$

(See Chapter 9)

Degrees of freedom (chi-square)

$$df = (r - 1)\ (c - 1)$$

(See Chapter 9)

Pearson's Product Moment Correlation

$$r = \frac{e - \dfrac{(a)(b)}{N}}{\sqrt{\left[c - \left(\dfrac{a^2}{N} \right) \right] \left[d - \left(\dfrac{b^2}{N} \right) \right]}}$$

(See Chapter 10)

Student's t

$$t = \frac{\overline{X}_1 - \overline{X}_2}{\sqrt{\dfrac{\Sigma X_1^2 - (\Sigma X_1)^2/n_1 + \Sigma X_2^2 - (\Sigma X_2)^2/n_2}{n_1 + n_2 - 2} \left[\dfrac{1}{n_1} + \dfrac{1}{n_2} \right]}}$$

Where $\overline{X}_1$ = mean of the first group
$\overline{X}_2$ = mean of the second group
ΣX_1^2 = sum of the squared values of the first group
ΣX_2^2 = sum of the squared values of the second group
$(\Sigma X_1)^2$ = sum of the squared values in the first group
$(\Sigma X_2)^2$ = sum of hhe squared values in the second group
n_1 = number of values in the first group
n_2 = number of values in the second group

(See Chapter 11)

GLOSSARY

Absolute frequency The actual number of times that a value of a variable is observed to occur within a given group of data.

Absolute zero The zero value assigned to a ratio-level variable that indicates the point at which there is no measurable quantity of the variable.

Arbitrary zero A point on an interval-level scale selected to be assigned the value zero for the variable. It does not suggest the absence of any quantity of the variable.

Array A numerical ordering of cases based on the relative quantity of a variable that each possesses—that is, highest to lowest or lowest to highest values.

Association The degree to which certain values of one variable tend to be found with certain values of another variable.

Bar graph A pictorial representation of a frequency distribution of a nominal-level variable in which the lengths of bars correspond to the frequencies for different values of the variable. The bars do not touch.

Bias A systematic source of distortion in sampling, measurement, or data processing that tends to occur in a single direction.

Bimodal The characteristic of a frequency polygon that suggests that it has two distinct "peaks" reflecting equal or nearly equal frequencies.

Cause–effect relationship A relationship between variables in which variations of one variable are believed to result in variations of the other variable.

Central tendency An expression of what is a typical or characteristic value for a variable among cases studied.

Chance Also referred to as luck, probability, or the law of averages. It is often used in research as a synonym for sampling error. It may cause variables to appear to be related within a sample when, in fact, they are not.

Conceptualization The process of selecting the most meaningful variables to study in order to attempt to answer a research question.

Correlation coefficient An indicator of both the strength and direction of an association between two interval- or ratio-level variables. It is either positive or negative, and ranges from +1.0 to −1.0.

Covariance The degree to which certain values of one variable tend to be found with certain values of a second variable. It is often expressed as a correlation coefficient.

Crosstabulation table Also known as a chi-square table or contingency table. It contains cells that reflect the number of cases that posses a given combination of one value (for one variable) and another value (for another variable). Multiple contingency tables may include frequencies relating to the values for more than two variables.

Data All observations made in a research study (singular = datum).

Degrees of freedom A number, based on sample size and/or other factors, that is applied in helping to determine the probability level when using a statistical test. Different tests have different formulas for degrees of freedom.

Dependent variable (criterion variable) The variable whose variation a researcher is most interested in explaining.

Descriptive statistics Statistics that summarize the principal characteristics of data in such a way as to make them more usable or comprehensible. No inferences are made about cases not studied.

Directional hypothesis A hypothesis that (1) states that two variables will be found to be related and (2) predicts the direction of their relationship; also called one-tailed.

Dispersion The distribution of values around a measure of central tendency.

Distribution All observations in a study.

Expected frequencies The theoretical frequencies for each cell in a crosstabulation that are most likely to occur on the basis of chance if the variables are not related (the null hypothesis).

Frequency distribution A distribution in which categories are established and the number of cases in each is counted and presented in some systematic way.

Frequency polygon A graph representing a frequency distribution in which lines connect the midpoints of frequencies for each interval.

Histogram A pictorial representation of a frequency distribution of ordinal-, interval-, or ratio-level data in which the height of the bars is proportional to the number of cases that possess a given value for the variable. The bars do not have spaces between them.

Hypothesis A statement of a presumed relationship between variables; also, a tentative answer to a research question.

Independent variable The variable that the researcher believes may explain all or some of the variation of the dependent variable.

Inferential statistics Statistics that suggest the researcher's ability to generalize or infer properties of a population from data obtained relative to a sample.

Interquartile range The difference between the 75th percentile and 25th percentile points of a frequency distribution that is in the form of an array.

Interval scale A measurement scale that meets all criteria for an ordinal scale but also indicates the exact distances between values. Value labels represent a precise measurement of the quantity of the variable.

Level of measurement The amount of precision (nominal, ordinal, interval, or ratio) assumed to be present in the measurement of a variable.

Line diagram A pictorial representation of a frequency distribution of a nominal-level variable in which the lengths of the lines correspond to the frequencies for different values of a variable.

Mean (arithmetic) The sum of the scores in a distribution of an interval- or ratio-level variable divided by the total number of cases.

Mean deviation The sum of the deviations between each score and the mean divided by the number of scores.

Median The midpoint in a distribution of case values of a variable that have been positioned to form an array. It precisely divides the array into two equal parts.

Mode The most frequently occurring value in a distribution.

Negatively skewed The characteristic of a frequency polygon that suggests that it possesses a few very low values that make the distribution asymmetrical.

Nominal scale Classification of categories of a variable that reflects difference in only quality or kind.

Nondirectional hypothesis A hypothesis that states that two variables are related but does not predict the direction of the relationship; also called two-tailed.

Nonparametric tests Tests that do not make any assumptions about the nature or shape of the distribution of a variable.

Normal distribution A symmetrical, bell-shaped frequency polygon in which the mean, median, and mode occur at the same point; also called bell-shaped curve or normal curve.

Null hypothesis The form of a hypothesis that states that there is no relationship between two variables.

Observed frequencies The frequencies in a crosstabulation that are compiled from the values observed for cases in a research study.

Operationalization The process of selecting the specific devices to be used to measure variables in a research study.

Ordinal scale A measurement scale that possesses all the qualities of the nominal scale plus the quality of being able to rank-order the categories with respect to the quantity of the variable they possess.

$p < .05$ The conventional level for declaring adequate statistical evidence to support rejection of the null hypothesis. It suggests that if the researcher were to reject the null hypothesis, there would be less than a 1 in 20 mathematical chance of committing a Type I error.

Parametric test A statistical measure designed for use with a variable that is normally distributed within the population.

Percentile The position occupied by a case that indicates the percent of scores that fall above or below that position.

Pie chart A pictorial representation of a frequency distribution in the form of a circle or a pie.

Population The entire group of cases from which a sample is drawn.

Positively skewed The characteristic of a frequency polygon that suggests that it possesses a few very high values that make the distribution asymmetrical.

Power of a test The strength or capacity of a test to detect a true relationship between variables.

Probability The proportion of times, in the long run, we would expect to obtain a given result. It ranges from zero (never) to 1 (certainty).

Proportion The number of cases in a data set divided by the total number of cases.

Quartile One-fourth of the total rank-ordered distribution of values. The 1st quartile includes the lowest 25 percent of all values.

Range The span between and including the highest and lowest scores in a frequency distribution of an interval- or ratio-level variable.

Rank-order To arrange the values of a variable in sequence according to the quantitative difference reflected in the values; to form an array.

Ratio scale A measurement scale that meets all criteria for an interval scale but also possesses an absolute or nonarbitrary zero point, where zero quantity of the variable exists.

Raw score The unsorted and unanalyzed value or score for a case studied.

Regression line The line formed by connecting the pattern of dots on a scattergram. It reflects both the strength and the direction of a correlation between variables.

Replication Repetition of a research study in order to confirm or refute its findings.

Sample Cases selected for study from among all those in the population.

Sampling error The degree to which the characteristics of cases in a sample are likely to differ from the characteristics of the population from which the sample was drawn.

Scattergram A pictorial representation of data in which each case is represented by a dot and the position of each dot is determined by the case's values for each of two variables.

Semi-interquartile range One-half the difference between the 75th percentile and the 25th percentile points in a frequency distribution that is in the form of an array.

Significance level The probability of making a Type I error (rejecting a correct null hypothesis).

Skewness The characteristic of a frequency distribution to have a disproportionate number of extreme values at one end or the other. The distribution is not considered to be normally distributed.

Specifying variable A third variable that, when controlled, provides additional clarification regarding the relationship between the dependent and the independent variables.

Standard deviation A commonly used measure of dispersion computed with interval- or ratio-level data. It is the square root of the mean of all of the squared deviations from the mean—that is, the square root of the variance.

Statistical significance The mathematical support for a statement of a relationship between variables. It indicates that chance has been effectively ruled out as the explanation for the apparent relationship.

Substantive finding A research finding that is more than just a statistically significant relationship between variables; it is also judged to be of importance.

Suppressor variable (obscuring variable) A variable that tends to have the effect of making the dependent and independent variables appear to be less related than they really are.

Type I error Rejection of the null hypothesis when it is, in fact, correct.

Type II error Failure to reject the null hypothesis when it is, in fact, false.

Unity The term used to suggest that all scores or values for a normally distributed variable will fall within the normal distribution for that variable; more commonly referred to as "one."

Value The name or number assigned to the property or category of a variable for a given case.

Variable A characteristic of all cases in the population that varies in amount or kind among cases.

Variability A description of the degree to which values of a variable differ from each other within a frequency distribution of the variable.

x-axis The horizontal axis used in the graphic presentation of data.

y-axis The vertical axis used in the graphic presentation of data.

z-score (standard score) A raw score converted to units of standard deviation.

ADVANCED REFERENCES FOR FURTHER READING

Achen, C. H. (1982). *Interpreting and using regression*. London: Sage.

Agresti, A., & Agresti, B. F. (1979). *Statistical methods for the social sciences*. San Francisco: Dellen.

Alexander, H. W. (1961). *Elements of mathematical statistics*. New York: Wiley.

Allen, M. J., & Wendy, M. Y. (1979). *Introduction to measurement theory*. Monterey, CA: Brooks/Cole.

Anastasi, A. (1937). *Differential psychology*. New York: Macmillan.

Anderson, R. L., & Bancroft, T. A. (1952). *Statistical theory in research*. New York: McGraw-Hill.

Anderson, T. W. (1958). *Introduction to multivariate statistical analysis*. New York: Wiley.

Attneave, F. (1959). *Applications of information theory to psychology*. New York: Holt, Rinehart & Winston.

Babbie, E. R. (1986). *The practice of social research* (4th ed.). Belmont, CA: Wadsworth.

Babbie, E. R. (1982). *Social research for consumers*. Belmont, CA: Wadsworth.

Bailey, K. D. (1982). *Methods of social research* (2nd ed.). New York: Free Press.

Bancroft, T. A. (1968). *Topics in intermediate statistical method*. Ames: Iowa State University Press.

Bannister, D., & Mair, J. M. (1968). *The evaluation of personal constructs*. London: Academic Press.

Beless, D. W. (1981). Univariate analysis. In R. M. Grinnell, Jr. (Ed.), *Social work research and evaluation* (pp. 445–460). Itasca, IL: F. E. Peacock.

Bennett, C. A., & Franklin, N. L. (1954). *Statistical analysis in chemistry and the chemical industry*. New York: Wiley.

Bennett, S., & Bowers, D. (1976). *An introduction to multivariate techniques for the social and behavioral sciences*. New York: Wiley.

Beyer, W. H. (1968). *Handbook of tables for probability and statistics* (2nd ed.). Cleveland: Chemical Rubber Company.

Birkhoff, G., & MacLane, S. (1953). *A survey of modern algebra*. New York: Macmillan.

Birnbaum, Z. W. (1962). *Introduction to probability and mathematical statistics*. New York: Harper & Row.

Bishop, Y. M., Fienberg, S. E., & Holland, P. W. (1975). *Discrete multivariate analysis: Theory and practice*. Cambridge, MA: MIT Press.

Blackwell, D., & Girshick, M. A. (1954). *The theory of games and statistical decisions*. New York: Wiley.

Bloom, B. S. (1964). *Stability and change in human characteristics*. New York: Wiley.

Bostwick, G. J., & Kyte, N. S. (1981). Measurement. In R. M. Grinnell, Jr. (Ed.), *Social work research and evaluation* (pp. 93–129). Itasca, IL: F. E. Peacock.

Bradley, J. V. (1968). *Distribution-free statistical tests*. Englewood Cliffs, NJ: Prentice-Hall.

Bronowski, J. (1978). *The common sense of science*. Cambridge, MA: Harvard University Press.

Brown, R. V., Kahr, A. S., & Peterson, C. (1974). *Decision analysis for the manager*. New York: Holt, Rinehart & Winston.

Bruning, J. L., & Kintz, B. L. (1977). *Computational handbook of statistics* (2nd ed.). Glenview, IL: Scott, Foresman.

Brunk, H. D. (1965). *An introduction to mathematical statistics* (2nd ed.). Waltham, MA: Ginn/Blaisdell.

Burington, R. S., & May, D. C. (1953). *Handbook of probability and statistics with tables*. New York: McGraw-Hill.

Campbell, D. T., & Stanley, J. C. (1966). *Experimental and quasi-experimental designs for research*. Skokie, IL: Rand McNally.

Carmines, E. G., & Zeller, R. A. (1979). *Reliability and validity assessment*. London: Sage.

Champion, D. J. (1970). *Basic statistics for social research*. Scranton, PA: Chandler.

Chernoff, H., & Moses, L. E. (1959). *Elementary decision theory*. New York: Wiley.

Cheshire, L., Saffir, M., & Thurstone, L. L. (1933). *Computing diagrams for the tetrachoric correlation coefficient*. Chicago: University of Chicago Bookstore.

Clelland, R. C., deCani, J. S., Brown, F. E., Bursk, J. P., & Murray, D. S. (1966). *Basic statistics with business applications*. New York: Wiley.

Clyde, D. J., Cramer, E. M., & Sherin, R. J. (1966). *Multivariate statistical programs*. Coral Gables, FL: University of Miami.

Cochran, W. G. (1963). *Sampling techniques* (2nd ed.). New York: Wiley.

Cochran, W. G., & Cox, G. (1957). *Experimental designs* (2nd ed.). New York: Wiley.

Cohen, J. (1977). *Statistical power analysis for the behavioral sciences* (rev. ed.). New York: Academic Press.

Cohen, J., & Cohen, P. (1975). *Applied multiple regression/correlation analysis for the behavioral sciences.* Hillsdale, NJ: Lawrence Erlbaum.

Coleman, J. S. (1966). *Equality of educational opportunity.* Washington: Government Printing Office.

Conover, W. J. (1971). *Practical nonparametric statistics.* New York: Wiley.

Cook, T. D., & Campbell, D. T. (1979). *Quasi-experimentation: Design analysis issues for field settings.* Chicago: Rand McNally.

Cooley, W. W., & Lohnes, P. R. (1971). *Multivariate data analysis.* New York: Wiley.

Coombs, C. H., Dawes, R. M., & Tversky, A. (1970). *Mathematical psychology: An elementary introduction.* Englewood Cliffs, NJ: Prentice-Hall.

Cox, D. R. (1958). *Planning experiments.* New York: Wiley.

Cramer, H. (1945). *Mathematical methods of statistics.* Princeton, NJ: Princeton University Press.

Cronbach, L. J. (1949). *Essentials of psychological testing.* New York: Harper.

David, F. N. (1938). *Tables of the correlation coefficient.* New York: Cambridge University Press.

de Finette, B. (1974). *Theory of probability: A critical introductory treatment* (vol. 1). London: Wiley.

DeLury, D. B. (1950). *Values and integrals of the orthogonal polynomials up to $n = 26$.* Toronto: Toronto University Press.

Dempster, A. P. (1969). *Elements of continuous multivariate analysis.* Reading, MA: Addison-Wesley.

Derman, C., Gleser, L. J., & Olkin, I. (1973). *A guide to probability theory and application.* New York: Holt, Rinehart & Winston.

Dixon, W. J., & Massey, F. J. (1969). *Introduction to statistical analysis* (3rd ed.). New York: McGraw-Hill.

Draper, N. R., & Smith, N. (1966). *Applied regression analysis.* New York: Wiley.

DuBois, P. H. (1965). *An introduction to psychological statistics.* New York: Harper & Row.

Duehn, W. D. (1981). The process of social work practice and research. In R. M. Grinnell, Jr. (Ed.), *Social work research and evaluation* (pp. 11–34). Itasca, IL: F. E. Peacock.

Dwyer, P. S. (1961). *Linear computations.* New York: Wiley.

Dyckman, T. R., Smidt, S., & McAdams, A. K. (1969). *Management decision making under uncertainty.* New York: Macmillan.

Edgington, E. S. (1969). *Statistical inference: The distribution-free approach.* New York: McGraw-Hill.

Edwards, A. L. (1964). *Expected values of discrete random variables and elementary statistics.* New York: Wiley.

Edwards, A. L. (1950). *Experimental design in psychological research.* New York: Holt, Rinehart & Winston.

Edwards, A. L. (1979). *Multiple regression and the analysis of variance and covariance.* San Francisco: Freeman.

Edwards, A. L. (1973). *Statistical methods* (3rd ed.). New York: Holt, Rinehart & Winston.

Edwards, W., & Newman, J. R. (1982). *Multiattribute evaluation.* London: Sage.

Eisenhart, C., Hastay, M. W., & Wallis, W. A. (1947). *Techniques of statistical analysis.* New York: McGraw-Hill.

Elashoff, J. D., & Snow, R. E. (1971). *Pygmalion reconsidered.* Worthington, OH: Jones.

Everitt, B. S. (1977). *The analysis of contingency tables.* London: Chapman & Hall.

Federer, W. T. (1955). *Experimental design: Theory and application.* New York: Macmillan.

Feller, W. (1957). *An introduction to probability theory and its applications* (2nd ed.). New York: Wiley.

Fellner, W. (1965). *Probability and profit.* Homewood, IL: Irwin.

Ferguson, G. A. (1965). *Nonparametric trend analysis.* Montreal: McGill University Press.

Ferguson, G. A. (1981). *Statistical analysis in psychology and education* (5th ed.). New York: McGraw-Hill.

Furguson, T. S. (1967). *Mathematical statistics: A decision-theoretic approach.* New York: Academic Press.

Fienberg, S. E. (1977). *The analysis of cross-classified categorical data.* Cambridge, MA: MIT Press.

Finn, J. D. (1974). *A general model for multivariate analysis.* New York: Holt, Rinehart & Winston.

Finn, J. D. (1972). *Multivariance: Univariate and multivariate analysis, covariance and regression.* Ann Arbor, MI: National Educational Resources.

Fishburn, P. C. (1964). *Decision and value theory.* New York: Wiley.

Fisher, R. A. (1951). *The design of experiments* (6th ed.). Edinburgh: Oliver & Boyd.

Fisher, R. A. (1936). *Statistical methods for research workers* (6th ed.). Edinburgh: Oliver & Boyd.

Fisher, R. A., & Yates, F. (1953). *Statistical tables for biological, agricultural and medical research* (4th ed.). Edinburgh: Oliver & Boyd.

Fisz, M. (1963). *Probability theory and mathematical statistics* (3rd ed.). New York: Wiley.

Fleiss, J. L. (1973). *Statistical methods for rates and proportions.* New York: Wiley.

Fransella, F., & Bannister, D. (1977). *A manual for repertory grid technique.* London: Academic Press.

Freund, J. E. (1971). *Mathematical statistics* (2nd ed.). Englewood Cliffs, NJ: Prentice-Hall.

Fryer, H. C. (1966). *Concepts and methods of experimental statistics.* Boston: Allyn & Bacon.

Gagne, R.M. (1970). *The conditions of learning* (2nd ed.). New York: Holt, Rinehart & Winston.

Garner, W. R. (1962). *Uncertainty and structure as psychological concepts.* New York: Wiley.

Gibbons, J. D. (1971). *Nonparametric statistical inference.* New York: McGraw-Hill.

Gilliland, A. R., & Clark, E. L. (1939). *Psychology of individual differences.* Englewood Cliffs, NJ: Prentice-Hall.

Glass, G. V., & Stanley, J. C. (1970). *Statistical methods in education and psychology.* Englewood Cliffs, NJ: Prentice-Hall.

Good, I. J. (1965). *The estimation of probabilities.* Cambridge, MA: MIT Press.

Goodenough, F. L. (1949). *Mental testing.* New York: Holt, Rinehart & Winston.

Goodman, L. A. (1978). *Analyzing qualitative categorical data.* Cambridge, MA: Abt Associates.

Gordon, M., & Schaumberger, N. (1978). *A first course in statistics.* New York: Macmillan.

Gorsuch, R. L. (1981). Bivariate analysis: Analysis of variance. In R. M. Grinnell, Jr. (Ed.), *Social work research and evaluation* (pp. 500–529). Itasca, IL: F. E. Peacock.

Gorsuch, R. L. (1974). *Factor analysis.* Philadelphia: Saunders.

Graybill, F. A. (1961). *An introduction to linear statistical models* (vol. 1). New York: McGraw-Hill.

Graybill, F. A. (1969). *Introduction to matrices with applications in statistics.* Belmont, CA: Wadsworth.

Green, P. E., & Carroll, J. D. (1976). *Mathematical tools for applied multivariate analysis.* New York: Academic Press.

Grinnell, R. M., Jr. (Ed.). (1985). *Social work research and evaluation* (2nd ed.). Itasca, IL: F. E. Peacock.

Guenther, W. C. (1964). *Analysis of variance.* Englewood Cliffs, NJ: Prentice-Hall.

Guenther, W. C. (1965). *Concepts of statistical inference.* New York: McGraw-Hill.

Guilford, J. P. (1967). *The nature of intelligence.* New York: McGraw-Hill.

Guilford, J. P. (1954). *Psychometric methods* (2nd ed.). New York: McGraw-Hill.

Guilford, J. P., & Fruchter, B. (1973). *Fundamental statistics in psychology and education.* New York: McGraw-Hill.

Gulliksen, H. (1950). *Theory of mental tests.* New York: Wiley.

Hadley, G. (1967). *Introduction to probability and statistical decision theory.* San Francisco: Holden-Day.

Hajek, J., & Sidak, Z. (1967). *Theory of rank tests.* New York: Academic Press.

Harber, A., & Runyon, R. P. (1973). *General statistics* (2nd ed.). Reading, MA: Addison-Wesley.

Harman, H. H. (1967). *Modern factor analysis.* Chicago: University of Chicago Press.

Harris, R. J. (1975). *A primer of multivariate statistics.* New York: Academic Press.

Hartwig, F., & Dearing, B. E. (1979). *Exploratory data analysis.* Beverly Hills, CA: Sage.

Hays, W. L. (1981). *Statistics* (3rd ed.). New York: Holt, Rinehart & Winston.

Hays, W. L. (1973). *Statistics for the social sciences* (2nd ed.). New York: Holt, Rinehart & Winston.

Hays, W. L. (1963). *Statistics for psychologists.* New York: Holt, Rinehart & Winston.

Hays, W. L., & Winkler, R. L. (1970). *Statistics: Probability, inference, and decision* (vols. 1 & 2). New York: Holt, Rinehart & Winston.

Hicks, C. R. (1963). *Fundamental concepts in the design of experiments.* New York: Holt, Rinehart & Winston.

Hodges, J. L., & Lehmann, E. L. (1970). *Basic concepts of probability and statistics* (2nd ed.). San Francisco: Holden-Day.

Hoel, P. G. (1971). *Elementary statistics* (3rd ed.). New York: Wiley.

Hoel, P. G. (1947). *Introduction to mathematical statistics.* New York: Wiley.

Hogg, R. V., & Craig, A. T. (1970). *Introduction to mathematical statistics* (3rd ed.). New York: Macmillan.

Hohn, F. E. (1964). *Elementary matrix algebra* (2nd ed.). New York: Macmillan.

Hollander, M., & Wolfe, D. A. (1973). *Nonparametric statistical methods.* New York: Wiley.

Horst, P. (1963). *Matrix algebra for social scientists.* New York: Holt, Rinehart & Winston.

Householder, A. S. (1964). *The theory of matrices in numerical analysis.* New York: Blaisdell.

Hout, M. (1983). *Mobility tables.* London: Sage.

Howell, D. C. (1982). *Statistical methods for psychology.* Boston: Duxbury Press.

Huck, S. W., & Sandler, H. M. (1979). *Rival hypotheses.* New York: Harper & Row.

Huckfeldt, R. R., Kohfeld, C. W., & Likens, T. W. (1982). *Dynamic modeling: An introduction.* London: Sage.

Huff, D. (1954). *How to lie with statistics.* New York: Norton.

Huitema, B. E. (1980). *The analysis of covariance and alternatives.* New York: Wiley.

Jeffreys, H. (1961). *Theory of probability.* Oxford, England: Clarendon Press.

Johnson, H. H., & Solso, R. L. (1978). *An introduction to experimental design in psychology: A case approach* (2nd ed.). New York: Harper & Row.

Johnson, M. K., & Liebert, R. M. (1977). *Statistics: Tool of the behavioral sciences.* Englewood Cliffs, NJ: Prentice-Hall.

Johnson, P. O. (1949). *Statistical methods in research.* Englewood Cliffs, NJ: Prentice-Hall.

Kalton, G. (1983). *Introduction to survey sampling.* London: Sage.

Kelley, T. L. (1923). *Statistical method.* New York: Macmillan.

Kelley, T. L., Madden, R., Gardner, E. F., & Rudman, H. C. (1965). *Stanford modern mathematics concepts tests.* New York: Harcourt.

Kemeny, J. G., Mirkil, H., Snell, J. L., & Thompson, G. L. (1959). *Finite mathematical structures.* Englewood Cliffs, NJ: Prentice-Hall.

Kempthorne, O. (1952). *The design and analysis of experiments.* New York: Wiley.

Kendall, M. G. (1955). *Rank correlation methods* (2nd ed.). London: Griffin.

Kendall, M. G., & Stuart A. (1973). *The advanced theory of statistics* (3rd ed.). London: Griffin.

Keppel, G. (1982). *Design and analysis: A researcher's handbook* (2nd ed.). Englewood Cliffs, NJ: Prentice-Hall.

Keppel, G., & Saufley, W. H. (1980). *Introduction to design and analysis: A student's handbook.* San Francisco: Freeman.

Kerlinger, F. N. (1973). *Foundations of behavioral research* (2nd ed.). New York: Holt, Rinehart, & Winston.

Kerlinger, F. N., & Pedhazur, E. J. (1973). *Multiple regression in behavioral research.* New York: Holt, Rinehart & Winston.

Kershner, R. B., & Wilcox, L. R. (1950). *The anatomy of mathematics.* New York: Ronald.

Kim, J. O., & Mueller, C. W. (1978). *Factor analysis: Statistical methods and practical issues.* London: Sage.

Kirk, R. E. (1968). *Experimental design: Procedures for the behavioral sciences.* Belmont, CA: Brooks/Cole.

Kish, L. (1965). *Survey sampling.* New York: Wiley.

Klecka, W. R. (1980). *Discriminant analysis.* London: Sage.

Knoke, D., & Burke, P. J. (1980). *Log linear-models.* London: Sage.

Knoke, D., & Kuklinski, J. H. (1982). *Network analysis.* London: Sage.

Kolevzon, M. S. (1981). Bivariate analysis: Correlation. In R. M. Grinnell, Jr. (Ed.), *Social work research and evaluation* (pp. 481–499). Itasca, IL: F. E. Peacock.

Kurtz, T. E. (1963). *Basic statistics.* Englewood Cliffs, NJ: Prentice-Hall.

Kyburg, H. E., & Smokler, H. E. (1964). *Studies in subjective probability.* New York: Wiley.

Lawley, D. N., & Maxwell, A. E. (1963). *Factor analysis as a statistical method.* London: Butterworth.

Lehmann, E. L. (1975). *Nonparametrics: Statistical methods based on ranks.* San Francisco: Holden-Day.

Lehmann, E. L. (1959). *Testing statistical hypotheses.* New York: Wiley.

Leonard, W. H., & Clark, A. G. (1939). *Field plot techniques.* Minneapolis: Burgess.

Lewis, D. (1960). *Quantitative methods in psychology.* New York: McGraw-Hill.

Lewis-Beck, M. S. (1980). *Applied regression: An introduction.* London: Sage.

Li, C. C. (1964). *Introduction to experimental statistics.* New York: McGraw-Hill.

Liebetrau, A. M. (1983). *Measures of association.* London: Sage.

Lindgren, B. W. (1960). *Statistical theory.* New York: Macmillan.

Lindgren, B. W., & Berry, D. A. (1981). *Elementary statistics.* New York: Macmillan.

Lindgren, B. W., & McElrath, G. W. (1969). *Introduction to probability and statistics* (3rd ed.). New York: Macmillan.
Lindley, D. V. (1965). *Introduction to probability and statistics from a bayesian viewpoint* (2 vols.). New York: Cambridge University Press.
Lindman, H. R. (1974). *Analysis of variance in complex designs*. San Francisco: Freeman.
Lindquist, E. R. (1953). *Design and analysis of experiments in psychology and education*. Boston: Houghton Mifflin.
Lindquist, E. R. (1940). *Statistical analysis in educational research*. Boston: Houghton Mifflin.
Lippman, S. A. (1971). *Elements of probability and statistics*. New York: Holt, Rinehart & Winston.
Lodge, M. (1981). *Magnitude scaling: Quantitative measurement of opinions*. London: Sage.
Long, J. S. (1983). *Confirmatory factor analysis: A preface to LISREL*. London: Sage.
Long, J. S. (1983). *Covariance structure models: An introduction to LISREL*. London: Sage.
Lord, F. M., & Novick, M. R. (1968). *Statistical theories of mental test scores*. Reading, MA: Addison-Wesley.
Lorge, I., Thorndike, R., & Hagen, E. P. (1966). *Technical manual Lorge-Thorndike multi-level intelligence tests*. Boston: Houghton Mifflin.
Lovejoy, E. P. (1975). *Statistics for math haters*. New York: Harper & Row.
Luce, R. D., & Raiffa, H. (1957). *Games and decisions*. New York: Wiley.
Magnusson, D. (1967). *Test theory*. Reading, MA: Addison-Wesley.
Marascuilo, L. A., & McSweeney, M. (1977). *Nonparametric and distribution-free methods for the social sciences*. Monterey, CA: Brooks/Cole.
Mather, K. (1947). *Statistical analysis in biology* (2nd ed.). New York: Interscience.
Matheson, D. W., Bruce, R. L., & Beauchamp, K. L. (1974). *Introduction to experimental psychology* (2nd ed.). New York: Holt, Rinehart & Winston.
Maxwell, A. E. (1961). *Analysing qualitative data*. London: Methuen.
McDowall, D., McCleary, R., Meidinger, E. E., & Hay, R. A. (1980). *Interrupted time series analysis*. London: Sage.
McIver, J. P., & Carmines, E. G. (1981). *Unidimensional scaling*. London: Sage.
McNemar, Q. (1962). *Psychological statistics* (3rd ed.). New York: Wiley.
Miller, I., & Freund, J. E. (1965). *Probability and statistics for engineers*. Englewood Cliffs, NJ: Prentice-Hall.
Miller, R. G. (1966). *Simultaneous statistical inference*. New York: McGraw-Hill.
Minium, E. W. (1978). *Statistical reasoning in psychology and education* (2nd ed.). New York: Wiley.
Mode, E. B. (1966). *Elements of probability and statistics*. Englewood Cliffs, NJ: Prentice-Hall.
Mood, A. (1950). *Introduction to the theory of statistics*. New York: McGraw-Hill.

Morrison, D. F. (1967). *Multivariate statistical methods.* New York: McGraw-Hill.

Moses, L. E., & Oakford, R. V. (1963). *Tables of random permutations.* Stanford, CA: Stanford University Press.

Mosteller, F., & Tukey, J. (1977). *Data analysis and regression.* Reading, MA: Addison-Wesley.

Mosteller, F., Rourke, R. E., & Thomas, G. B. (1961). *Probability with statistical applications.* Reading, MA: Addison-Wesley.

Mulaik, S. A. (1972). *The foundations of factor analysis.* New York: McGraw-Hill.

Myers, J. E. (1979). *Fundamentals of experimental design* (3rd ed.). Boston: Allyn & Bacon.

Neale, J. M., & Liebert, R. M. (1980). *Science and behavior* (2nd ed.). Englewood Cliffs, NJ: Prentice-Hall.

Neter, J., & Wasserman, W. (1974). *Applied linear statistical models.* Homewood, IL: Irwin.

Newmark, J. (1983). *Statistics and probability in modern life* (3rd ed.). Philadelphia: Saunders.

Noble, B. (1969). *Applied linear algebra.* Englewood Cliffs, NJ: Prentice-Hall.

Novick, M. R., & Jackson, P. H. (1974). *Statistical methods of educational and psychological research.* New York: McGraw-Hill.

Nunnally, J. C. (1975). *Introduction to statistics for psychology and education.* New York: McGraw-Hill.

O'Nell, W. M. (1963). *A guide to elementary statistics in psychology.* Sydney, New South Wales, Australia: University Co-operative Bookshop.

Osterlind, S. J. (1983). *Test item bias.* London: Sage.

Overall, J. E., & Keltt, C. J. (1972). *Applied multivariate analysis.* New York: McGraw-Hill.

Owen, D. B. (1962). *Handbook of statistical tables.* Reading, MA: Addison-Wesley.

Pagano, R. R. (1981). *Understanding statistics in the behavioral sciences.* St. Paul, MN: West.

Parzen, E. (1960). *Modern probability theory and its applications.* New York: Wiley.

Pearson, E. S., & Hartley, H. O. (1967). *Biometrika tables for statisticians* (vol. 1, 3rd ed.). New York: Cambridge University Press.

Peng, K. C. (1967). *The design and analysis of scientific experiments.* Reading, MA: Addison-Wesley.

Peters, C. C., & Van Voorhis, W. R. (1940). *Statistical procedures and their mathematical bases.* New York: McGraw-Hill.

Pfeiffer, K., & Olson, J. N. (1981). *Basic statistics for the behavioral sciences.* New York: Holt, Rinehart & Winston.

Phillips, L. D. (1974). *Bayesian statistics for social scientists.* New York: Crowell.

Pillai, K. (1960). *Statistical tables for tests of multivariate hypotheses.* Manila: University of the Philippines.

Pratt, J. W., Raiffa, H., & Schlaifer, R. (1965). *Introduction to statistical decision theory.* New York: McGraw-Hill.

Press, S. J. (1972). *Applied multivariate analysis.* New York: Holt, Rinehart & Winston.

Raiffa, H. (1968). *Decision analysis.* Reading, MA: Addison-Wesley.

Raiffa, H., & Schlaifer, R. (1961). *Applied statistical decision theory.* Cambridge, MA: Harvard University Press.

Rand Corporation. (1955). *A million random digits with 100,000 normal deviates.* New York: Free Press.

Rao, C. R. (1952). *Advanced statistical methods in biometric research.* New York: Wiley.

Rao, C. R. (1965). *Linear statistical inference and its applications.* New York: Wiley.

Reagan, L. M., Ott, E. R., & Sigley, D. T. (1948). *College algebra* (rev. ed.). New York: Holt, Rinehart & Winston.

Rosenberg, M. (1968). *The logic of survey analysis.* New York: Basic Books.

Rosenthal, R., & Jacobson, L. (1968). *Pygmalion in the classroom.* New York: Holt, Rinehart & Winston.

Royer, M. L. (1981). Expressing concepts and results in numeric form. In R. M. Grinnell, Jr. (Ed.), *Social work research and evaluation* (pp. 431–444). Itasca, IL: F. E. Peacock.

Sasaki, K. (1968). *Statistics for modern business decision making.* Belmont, CA: Wadsworth.

Savage, I. R. (1962). *Bibliography of nonparametric statistics.* Cambridge, MA: Harvard University Press.

Savage, L. J. (1954). *The foundations of statistics.* New York: Wiley.

Scheffe, H. (1969). *Analysis of variance.* New York: Wiley.

Schlaifer, R. (1969). *Analysis of decisions under uncertainty.* New York: McGraw-Hill.

Schlaifer, R. (1961). *Introduction to statistics for business decisions.* New York: McGraw-Hill.

Schlaifer, R. (1959). *Probability and statistics for business decisions.* New York: McGraw-Hill.

Schuerman, J. R. (1981). Bivariate analysis: Crosstabulation. In R. M. Grinnell, Jr. (Ed.), *Social work research and evaluation* (pp. 461–480). Itasca, IL: F. E. Peacock.

Schuerman, J. R. (1983). *Research and evaluation in the human services.* New York: Free Press.

Searle, S. R. (1966). *Matrix algebra for the biological sciences.* New York: Wiley.

Shaffer, L. F. (1936). *The psychology of adjustment.* Boston: Mifflin.

Siegel, S. (1956). *Nonparametric statistics for the behavioral sciences.* New York: McGraw Hill.

Simon, J. L. (1969). *Basic research methods in social science: The art of empirical investigation.* New York: Simon & Schuster.

Slonim, M. J. (1960). *Sampling.* New York: Simon & Schuster.

Snedecor, G. W. (1946). *Statistical methods* (4th ed.). Ames, IA: State College Press.

Snedecor, G. W. (1956). *Statistical methods applied to experiments in agriculture and biology* (5th ed.). Ames: Iowa State University Press.

Spector, P. E. (1981). *Research designs.* London: Sage.

Spurr, W. A., & Bonini, C. P. (1967). *Statistical analysis for business decisions.* Homewood, IL: Irwin.

Stevens, S. S. (1951). *Handbook of experimental psychology.* New York: Wiley.

Sullivan, J. L., & Feldman, S. (1979). *Multiple indicators: An introduction.* London: Sage.

Tatsuoka, M. M. (1971). *Multivariate analysis: Techniques for educational and psychological research.* New York: Wiley.

Thompson, W. A. (1969). *Applied probability.* New York: Holt, Rinehart & Winston.

Thomson, G. H. (1950). *The factorial analysis of human ability* (5th ed.). London: University of London Press.

Thorndike, R. L. (1978). *Correlational procedures for research.* New York: Gardner.

Thorndike, R. L. (Ed.). (1971). *Educational measurement* (2nd ed.). Washington, DC: American Council on Education.

Thorndike, R. L., & Hagen, E. (1969). *Measurement and evaluation in psychology and education* (3rd ed.). New York: Wiley.

Thrall, R., Coombs, C., & Davis, R. (1959). *Decision processes.* New York: Wiley.

Thurstone, L. L. (1947). *Multiple factor analysis.* Chicago: University of Chicago Press.

Thurstone, L. L. (1935). *The reliability and validity of tests.* Ann Arbor, MI: Edwards.

Timm, N. H. (1975). *Multivariate analysis with applications in education and psychology.* Belmont, CA: Brooks/Cole.

Tippett, L. (1941). *The methods of statistics* (3rd ed.). London: Williams & Norgate.

Torgerson, W. (1958). *Theory and methods of scaling.* New York: Wiley.

Tripodi, T. (1983). *Evaluative research for social workers.* Englewood Cliffs, NJ: Prentice-Hall.

Tripodi, T. (1981). The logic of research design. In R. M. Grinnell, Jr. (Ed.), *Social work research and evaluation* (pp. 198–225). Itasca, IL: F. E. Peacock.

Tripodi, T. (1974). *Uses and abuses of social research in social work.* New York: Columbia University Press.

Tripodi, T., Fellin, P. A., & Meyer, H. J. (1983). *The assessment of social research: Guidelines for the use of research in social work and social service* (2nd ed.). Itasca, IL: F. E. Peacock.

Tukey, J. W. (1977). *Exploratory data analysis.* Reading, MA: Addison-Wesley.

Ullman, N. R. (1972). *Statistics: An applied approach.* Lexington, MA: Xerox College Publishing.

Underwood, B. J. (1957). *Psychological research.* Englewood Cliffs, NJ: Prentice-Hall.

Underwood, B. J., & Shaughnessy, J. J. (1975). *Experimentation in psychology.* New York: Wiley.

Von Neumann, J., & Morgenstern, O. (1944). *Theory of games and economic behavior.* Princeton, NJ: Princeton University Press.
Wald, A. (1950). *Statistical decision functions.* New York: Wiley.
Walker, H. M. (1943). *Elementary statistical methods.* New York: Holt, Rinehart & Winston.
Walker, H. M. (1951). *Mathematics essential for elementary statistics* (rev. ed.). New York: Holt, Rinehart & Winston.
Walker, H., & Lev, J. (1953). *Statistical inference.* New York: Holt, Rinehart & Winston.
Wall, F. J. (1968). *The generalized variance ratio of U-statistics.* Albuquerque: Dikewood.
Wallis, W. A., & Roberts, H. V. (1957). *Statistics: A new approach.* New York: Free Press.
Walpole, R. E. (1974). *Introduction to statistics* (2nd ed.). New York: Macmillan.
Walpole, R. E., & Myers, R. H. (1972). *Probability and statistics for engineers and scientists.* New York: Macmillan.
Walsh, J. E. (1962). *A handbook of nonparametric statistics* (2 vols.). New York: Van Nostrand.
Webb, E. J., Campbell, D. T., Schwartz, R. D., & Sechrest, L. (1966). *Unobtrusive measures: Nonreactive research in the social sciences.* Chicago: Rand McNally.
Weinberg, G. H., & Schumaker, J. A. (1974). *Statistics: An intuitive approach* (3rd ed.). Monterey, CA: Brooks/Cole.
Weiss, R. S. (1968). *Statistics in social research: An introduction.* New York: Wiley.
Western, D. W., & Haag, V. H. (1959). *An introduction to mathematics.* New York: Holt, Rinehart & Winston.
Wilkinson, J. H. (1965). *The algebraic eigenvalue problem.* New York: Oxford University Press.
Wilks, S. S. (1962). *Mathematical statistics.* New York: Wiley.
Wine, R. L. (1964). *Statistics for scientists and engineers.* Englewood Cliffs, NJ: Prentice-Hall.
Winer, B. J. (1971). *Statistical principles in experimental design* (2nd ed.). New York: McGraw-Hill.
Wonnacott, T. H., & Wonnacott, R. J. (1972). *Introductory statistics* (2nd ed.). New York: Wiley.
Wood, G. (1974). *Fundamentals of psychological research.* Boston: Little, Brown.
Young, R. K., & Veldman, D. J. (1981). *Introductory statistics for the behavioral sciences* (4th ed.). New York: Holt, Rinehart & Winston.

INDEX